CAMILLO SITTE AND THE BIRTH OF MODERN CITY PLANNING

This is a companion volume to No. 2 in this series
CITY PLANNING ACCORDING TO ARTISTIC PRINCIPLES
by Camillo Sitte.

CAMILLO SITTE AND THE BIRTH OF MODERN CITY PLANNING

by George R. Collins
and Christiane Crasemann Collins

Columbia University Studies in Art History and Archaeology

Number 3

Random House / New York

First published 1965 by Phaidon Press Ltd, London,
and by Random House, Inc., New York.

Library of Congress Catalog Card Number 64–15893

MANUFACTURED IN GREAT BRITAIN

CONTENTS

ILLUSTRATIONS

SOURCES OF ILLUSTRATIONS

(For abbreviations, see the Bibliography)

Sitte, Bibl. 9: Figs. 3–29; Plates XV–a, XV–b, XVI.
Der Architekt, 1895, Bibl. 74: Plates V, VI, VII.
Der Städtebau, 1904, Bibl. 88, 90: Plates II, III–a, III–b, IV.
Der Städtebau, 1910, Bibl. 311: Plate XIII.
Town Planning Review, 1910–11, Bibl. 172: Plate X.
Maertens, Bibl. 353: Fig. 1.
Wien am Anfang des XX Jahrhunderts, Bibl. 472: Plate XI.
Borlui: Plate XIV.
Harvard University Library: Plate XII.
Francis G. Mayer and Hermann Brammer: Plate I and portrait on p. 7.
New York Public Library: Plate VIII.
Old photographs: Plates IX, XII.

We are indebted to the following for permission to quote from their publications: Architectural Book Publishing Co., Bibl. 326; Paul and Percival Goodman, Bibl. 182; Reinhold Publishing Corp., Bibl. 21.

PREFATORY NOTE

THE purpose of this book, as a companion volume to our new translation of Camillo Sitte's *Der Städtebau*,* is to re-open a chapter in the development of modern city planning that has been for years neglected—that of the architectural, city-building tradition.

Sitte and his book occupied a pivotal position in this particular phase of the nascent city-planning profession, and it is to a study of their impact that the present volume is almost exclusively dedicated. We make no pretence at surveying the whole development of modern city building—even from the point of view of civic art, which was Sitte's primary concern. We have intentionally restricted ourselves to those empirical, architectural aspects that motivated Sitte, and we have strayed as little as possible from his own career, his writings, and the ripples they set in motion within the professions of architecture and planning.

In fact, in our effort to explain the sources and the repercussions of his book *Der Städtebau*, we have stressed the German contributions to modern city planning to an almost embarrassing exclusion of all others. If only to temper this one-sidedness somewhat, we touch briefly, toward the end of our discussion, on some phases of the modern movement in which the Germans played only a marginal or relatively insignificant role. In short, our book is basically a commentary on Sitte's text and career, and as such it represents part of a survey of the ideas and theories of modern city planning, in which we are engaged and of which we have already published portions (Bibl. 453 and 456).

As part of the critical apparatus which is provided in the present volume for the study of Sitte and his times, the reader will find following the notes to this book a series of Critical

* Camillo Sitte, *City Planning according to Artistic Principles* (trans. by G. R. and C. C. Collins), New York, Random House, 1965. It is referred to here as '*Sitte*', and the present volume is called '*Collins*' in cases where a cross reference might lead to confusion. 'Bibl.' denotes the bibliographical listing at the end of this volume.

Notes to Sitte's own text as we have translated it. Also included is a bibliography of Sitte's writings and related aspects of the German city-planning movement.

For assistance with our task we express our appreciation again to those whom we have mentioned in the preface to our translation of Sitte, in particular Katherine McNamara, Adolf K. Placzek, and John N. Waddell. Also to Marina Krassensky and Sabine Gildemeister Cournoyer, who helped us with research in the Library of Congress and at Amherst.

Without the Viennese materials made available by the generosity of Professor Eduard Sekler of Harvard University, Dr. Josef Schwarzl and Dr. Franz Sturm of Vienna, we would have been unable to carry on. Others who have helped us with Viennese matters include Maria Sitte, Marily von Zeileisen, Francis G. Mayer, Felix Nemečič, Dr. Franz Glück, and the Austrian Cultural Institute of New York. Further invaluable aid from abroad was rendered by P. J. Crasemann of Santiago de Chile, Carl Alfred Godeffroy of Hamburg, and Emilio Canosa of Madrid. Among those who have sent us essential data are Arthur Holden, Dr. Félix Martí-Ibáñez, Elbert Peets, and Robert S. Weinberg; of our associates at Columbia we are particularly grateful to Alice Fischer, and Etta Arntzen, Dr. Henry Wells, Professors Edith Porada and Evelyn Harrison. For assistance in preparation of the plans and illustrations in both volumes we are indebted to Jaime Ardiles-Arce, Lisa E. Basch, and Edwin J. Daniel.

The reader is advised that to save space we have referred to most books that appear in our Bibliography simply by their serial number; many titles of periodicals have been abbreviated in accordance with a code that is explained at the beginning of the Bibliography.

G.R.C./C.C.C.

INTRODUCTION

In May of 1889 there appeared in Vienna a small volume of essays entitled *Der Städtebau nach seinen künstlerischen Grundsätzen*: 'City Planning according to Artistic Principles.' In it the author, Camillo Sitte, analyzed the civic and artistic character of old European towns that had survived in relatively unspoiled state from the pre-industrial age. He abstracted from the apparently casual—in fact even jumbled—layout of their squares, streets, buildings, and monuments a series of clear principles by which he proceeded to judge the accomplishments of city planners in his own day. The indictment was clear and almost irrefutable. He pointed out the absurd and clichéd nature of many precepts being followed in the modernizing of old towns and in the laying out of new sections of cities. He then went on to make a number of practical suggestions as to how city planning could be restored to an artistic basis. This he did mainly with reference to Vienna, in particular its new Ringstrasse development, and he stated that his ultimate aim was to secure convenient and effective spots for the placement of public statues and monuments—an ideal of civic beauty and betterment in his day.

Whether Sitte actually affected city planning for better or for worse is still today frequently disputed. But that his impact on the profession was instantaneous and profound has never been questioned. The little book by this Viennese artist and critic exerted an influence far out of proportion to its own size and to the position of its author among architects.

Ever since the city planning profession established itself in the course of the last century, it has received many of its most potent ideas from individuals who were either external to it or not deeply involved in its practice; pivotal theories and 'discoveries' in modern city planning have tended to come from collateral professions and disciplines or even from rank amateurs. Sitte's *Städtebau* is no exception. The sudden effect of this book seems to have been anticipated by nobody, least of all by the publisher. Professional journals did not take much notice of its appearance, but sales proved so extraordinary that a new edition was necessary immediately, and others followed, including translations into at least five foreign languages.

Sitte himself suggested a decade later in the Preface to his third edition that the popularity of his ideas could be explained by the fact that the time was ripe for the expression of such a point of view: 'Only when everyone is already feeling and thinking more or less along the same line, and it therefore depends only on one person finally expressing the matter clearly, are such happy results possible.' He was either too modest or too close to the events of his day to realize the actual truth of the matter—that in the literature on the building of cities there are three milestones, three handy practical-aesthetic architectural writings, the first by the Roman Vitruvius, the second by the Florentine Alberti, and the third by Camillo Sitte. Right or wrong as he may have been in his facts and his conclusions, Sitte played a unique role in defining for us the spirit and the architectural essence of urban life.

Just how the cello-playing principal of an applied-arts school who had never been involved with a major building project and had apparently never associated with the company of planners could shake the planning profession to its roots and cause every city dweller to view his architectural surroundings from a new point of view is a bit of a mystery. It is our purpose to throw such light as we can on this problem.

Ultimately, his book is best understood in terms of its own argumentative text—the alarmed outcry of a cultured and sensitive citizen about the disturbing urban developments of his day. For this reason we have published our translation of his writings on city planning as an integral whole unencumbered by notes, in the companion volume to this one.

It is always helpful to situate a piece of writing in its own historical context. After all, during the fourteen short years between the composing of his book and his death in 1903, Sitte's name became a factor to conjure with in the realm of city planning, and since that time there have been few writings on the subject that do not bear consciously or unconsciously the impress of his thought. It would seem, therefore, that a general commentary on Sitte, his career, and his work is called for in order to provide as broad as possible a perspective for the users of his text. With this in mind we include in the present volume, along with a section of critical notes to the translation of his book, a description of Sitte's life and environment, an account of the character of the city-planning profession in his day and of his effect on it, an analytical summary of his ideas, some evidence of the manner in which his book and his subsequent planning activities were received by the public of that time, and, finally, some suggestions as to the significance of Sitte for our own generation.

For students who may want to carry further our preliminary effort to chronicle the rise of modern city planning in Germany, we offer what we believe to be the first organized bibliography of materials for such a study, at the end of this volume.

1

CAMILLO SITTE'S BACKGROUND, LIFE, AND INTERESTS

THE life of Camillo Sitte was one of an intense intellectual and artistic activity that encompassed a wide range of interests.[1] His relatively early death, coming at a time when he was completing historical projects that had been his lifelong ambition, is thought to have been brought on by habits of feverish research and mental concentration, which had in his last years caused him to neglect his physical well-being.

He was born on April 17, 1843, in the Landstrasse District (III) of Vienna. His father, Franz Sitte (1818–1879), was an artist and architect, born in northern (German) Bohemia but partly trained in Vienna, where he spent the greater portion of his career. Some details of the father's professional life are of interest for their bearing on the subsequent development of Camillo, an only child.[2]

Franz Sitte, the youngest of 19 children, was from a tender age exposed to artistic influence, in part through his relationships with a nearby family of painters named Führich, with whom Franz was later to collaborate in various Viennese architectural projects. He was apprenticed to a local architect, and moved on to Vienna about 1838, where he studied two years in the Academy under the Swiss classicist Peter von Nobile. Franz finally rebelled against the repressive atmosphere at the Academy, left, and earned enough as a draftsman and foreman to make his way to Munich, the mecca of German and Austrian artists at that time.

Shortly after his return to Vienna in 1842 he married Theresia Schabes, also from the provinces; their son Camillo was born the following year. Although apparently successfully occupied at all times (his son's childhood is described as peaceful and happy), Franz's most important single commission came as a result of a rather curious revolutionary incident that is always cited in accounts of the Sitte family and provides an interesting insight into the professional ambient in mid-nineteenth-century Vienna.

In the late 1840's an important new suburban church, that of Altlerchenfeld (District VII), was being started in an Italian Renaissance style by the Court architect Paul Eduard Sprenger. The younger architects of Vienna rebelled against the dictatorship of both the style and the man. They invited from Munich to address them a youthful Swiss architect, Johann Georg Müller, whose unusual talent was already known from his design for the completion of Florence Cathedral and other works in the new medievalizing manner.[3] Müller and his friends were seeking an ecclesiastical style that was not pagan or otherwise imitative of the classical and which would at the same time express the pan-Germanic spirit. There was also abroad in Vienna—and Camillo's later teacher Eitelberger played a vital role in this—a strong opposition to the court-appointed architects and a pressure for the establishment of public architectural competitions. Müller's lecture on the Altlerchenfeld church, which was printed and distributed by the architects, led to such an outcry and atmosphere of rebellion (1848!) that a competition *was* held, as a result of which the commission was transferred to Müller and he was also appointed to teach at the Hochschule. He died tragically the next year, but not before naming as his successor Franz Sitte, whom he had apparently met in Munich and who had been assisting him with the plans. Franz was occupied for more than a decade with the task of carrying out Müller's building plans and completing the decoration of the church—keeping in close contact with many artists in his effort to make a totally-unified whole out of the building.

The importance of the Altlerchenfeld church lies not only in its change from a Renaissance-type to a medieval-type *Rundbogenstil*, but even more in the fact that on this occasion the younger architects had broken the existing bureaucratic monopoly of important building commissions in Austria and had established the principle of civic projects being open to public competition. This was to have its repercussions a few years later in the competition for the Votive Church, won by Ferstel (another of Camillo's teachers), and then in the Ringstrasse competition. Nevertheless, memory was short, and Vienna's vast new building program soon produced another clique which in turn monopolized construction; half a century afterward a student of Müller's could complain that Müller and

Bas-relief portrait of Camillo Sitte[4]

Franz Sitte had been largely forgotten and the Altlerchenfeld church was popularly believed to have been finished by Van der Nüll and Siccardsburg who had been nominally in charge while the work was being carried out by Franz.[5]

Biographies of the Sitte family tend to emphasize the qualities of rebellious genius and artistic imagination of father and son, characteristics which find a parallel in the events just described. Camillo's book, a protest against the established order of things, is quite contentious in style. Franz, in turn, became considerably nettled, and appears to have broken with his son when, in 1875, Camillo gave up the free life of an artist to accept a state (i.e., bureaucratic) position in Salzburg. On the other hand, Camillo's even being an artist had been held against him by the mother of his future wife; the couple had to wait until after her death to become engaged. All these conflicting attitudes may have arisen out of the social differential that seems to have existed between the anointed few and the large fringe of independent artists in nineteenth-century Vienna. There are indications that the artistic family-circle of the Sittes occupied a somewhat marginal position vis-à-vis the Viennese cultural renaissance of the period.

Franz Sitte's other known projects, perhaps as a result of this, were also ecclesiastical in character and in patronage.[6] We are told that in most of them he collaborated closely with a group of artists and decorators and that the polychromatic effects of his work were outstanding. He was apparently assisted by Camillo in all his building construction and his competition designs between about 1860 and 1873.

It was thus in an atmosphere of crafts, beauty, and somewhat non-conformist creativity that Camillo was reared. Furthermore, key years of his youth—those of his secondary-school education—were spent with his family in the district of Josefstadt (VIII), residing in the Piaristen parish house which Franz had built, a short distance from a number of projects in which his father was engaged. (See Note 281.) His biographers always emphasize Camillo's close friendships with talented youths who attended the Piaristen Gymnasium with him or the adjacent Löwenburgisch School for the Court choir boys.

Many of them went on to the Hochschule and University together and became renowned artists, musicians, scholars, journalists, or jurists.

Upon finishing gymnasium in 1863 (the year his mother died), Camillo entered the atelier of the architect Heinrich von Ferstel (see Note 57) in the Technische Hochschule. At the University, where he was also in attendance from 1863–68, he pursued art-historical and archaeological studies under Rudolf Eitelberger, taking part, along with his friend, Albert Ilg, in work on the *Quellenschriften für Kunstgeschichte.*[7] He also studied the physiology of vision and of space perception, researches that led eventually to his manuals of drawing and perspective and his studies of Piero della Francesca.[8] He spent three semesters in the faculty of medicine, studying anatomy and the practice of dissection.

It is clear that his interests were not purely academic. He had learned to draw, to paint, and to design and render objects. With the encouragement of Eitelberger he made renderings of numerous works of art, many of which were kept by the Library of the K.K. Österreichisches Museum and some of which were published in corpuses of art objects of the time.[9] Immediately after finishing his university studies he continued his education through travel, taking two trips to Italy and several to Germany in order to study Renaissance art. Throughout the rest of his life he made repeated trips outside Austria, visiting at different times Germany, Italy, France, Greece, Asia Minor, Constantinople, and Egypt. He apparently taught art history at various private schools during this period.

In 1873 his career as an independent architect was launched when he took over from his father (who had been working on their monastery) the design of the church of the Mechitarists, in Neubau just off the Ringstrasse (Pl. I).[10] At this time he was courting Leopoldine Blume, sister of a schoolmate, the writer Ludwig Blume (Bibl. 117); Leopoldine was herself a member of a group of intellectual young Viennese ladies. In those years the Austrian government was, like others, in the process of reorganizing the teaching of trades and professions. On the recommendation of Eitelberger, Camillo was offered in 1875 the direction of the State School of Applied Arts in Salzburg, which he accepted over the strenuous objections of his father. In July of 1875 he and Leopoldine were married in the Mechitaristen church (an occasion he was to memorialize in the paintings which he did for the interior of the church in the 1890's), and they departed for Salzburg, where he was occupied until 1883.

Although he was later accused of being inimical to modern art, and in particular to the Austrian Sezession, Camillo was still in the 1870's a non-conformist, in the tradition of his family. His Mechitaristen church, little known and seldom illustrated, is novel in design, to say the least, and seems to be the first church building to resume an ordered Renaissance appearance after the fad for the medieval that had marked his father's generation. In Salzburg, with support from his influential friends in Vienna who had installed him there, he seems to have reorganized the school drastically.[11] He brought in new artists and scholars, including Josef Salb, with whom he was to publish a study of Renaissance letter design (Bibl. 108). In 1877 he founded a periodical, the *Salzburger Gewerbeblatt*, and for it he wrote a number of articles. He delivered lectures on several crafts, including bookbinding, leatherwork, porcelain, and ceramics, a number of which were eventually published.[12] In addition, from 1869 until the end of his life he contributed innumerable pieces of art criticism to newspapers, principally to the *Neues Wiener Tagblatt*, of which his schoolmate, Victor K. Schembera, was editor. During the Salzburg period he also became concerned with problems of the restoration of historical monuments, a subject on which he was to publish several learned articles.[13]

His travels continued. He was invited to serve as a juror at the Paris Exposition of 1878. He went to Italy in connection with his Piero della Francesca studies (Bibl. 105), and the winter of 1882–83 was also spent in that country. A high point of these years was his visit to Bayreuth at the invitation of his school friend Hans Richter, now concertmaster for Richard Wagner. Sitte had already written on Wagner, who was his idol for a number of reasons (Bibl. 101), and on this occasion he actually met the composer and seems to have been commissioned to design stage sets for 'Parsifal.'[14]

In 1883 Sitte was called to Vienna to organize the new State School of Applied Arts, whose building was going up on the Schwarzenbergstrasse at the edge of the old city. Here he not only established a vigorous center of teaching as in Salzburg, but he and his wife made their own home and atelier, which were in the school, a model of arts-and-crafts activities and intellectual and musical soirees—very similar to and perhaps in the image of William Morris' Red House. Furniture, rugs, and tapestries were made after their designs, its paintings were by their friends, and a great deal of handwork was carried out by Sitte and his associates or by his wife and her friends.

In addition to the direction of this school, a responsibility which he retained until the end, Sitte immersed himself in his studies, and a prodigious quantity of lectures, manuscripts, and articles flowed from his pen. A large part of his writings were at all times on subjects other than city planning, and hence they are only of secondary concern to us here (Bibliography C), but during this period his attention returned to architecture, the profession for which he had been trained, and we begin to see essays on the larger aspects of city building. It has been suggested that his interest in city planning derived from his teacher, Eitelberger, who had lectured and published in learned fashion on the subject many years before (Bibl. 290, 291). In any case, Sitte's immediate stimulus to write about it was certainly, as had been the case with Eitelberger, the current building activity on the Vienna Ringstrasse, a block away. His first major effort in this direction was, significantly enough, an exposition of the city-planning ideas of Gottfried Semper, an architect for whom he held a life-long admiration and whom he had apparently met personally through Wagner and Hans Richter.[15] We are in no way prepared, however, for the emergence of his book *Der Städtebau* four years later in 1889. The origins of the book seem to have lain in his innermost thoughts during his European travels rather than in any of his prior articles or lectures.

The appearance of the book and the remarkable enthusiasm it evoked at once transformed Sitte's life. He was catapulted far beyond the horizons of the somewhat parochial Viennese cultural milieu in which he had been immersed—out into the international coterie of town planners—and, for better or for worse, he soon became the darling of the architectural wing of the planning profession. His articles on city planning proliferated (see Bibliography B), and he was invited to lecture at important gatherings. He served as a juror on some of the many German city-planning competitions of the day and so became an acquaintance and colleague of the old guard of the planning profession like Baumeister and Stübben, and the mentor of many young aspirants.[16] We are told that he was invited to prepare plans for Adelaide, Melbourne, and Sydney in Australia and that he was invited to Hamburg and to San Francisco to advise about the placement of monuments. To no one's surprise, he received little encouragement from the City Planning Office of Vienna, which failed to take his advice on anything. Nevertheless, he was engaged during the few remaining years of his life in the layout of a number of small industrial cities in the Austrian provinces—sometimes a total city plan or a central civic center, but more often the layout of a new section or suburb. (Pls. II, III, V.)[17]

The character of his interest in city-planning problems broadened considerably. By 1891, in speaking on the future of Vienna he included a discussion of such extra-artistic matters as traffic and commercial development (Bibl. 57). In 1900 he wrote two articles for a Hamburg periodical about the myths and clichés associated with the use of vegetation in cities (Bibl. 79). Added as an appendix to the later editions of his book, this material increased appreciably the scope of the work. Shortly before his death he collaborated in the founding of the magazine *Der Städtebau* which was devoted, as its subtitle indicates (*Sitte*, App. II), to *all* factors involved in the building of cities. At the time of his death he was preparing 'Volume II' of his book, which was to deal with 'City planning according to scientific and social principles.'[18] One of his last articles, published posthumously in his own periodical, dealt with condemnation procedures (Bibl. 88).

Meanwhile in Vienna his circle of intellectual friends expanded, and he achieved a certain amount of aristocratic patronage. Although he never attained the eminence of teaching at the Hochschule—and he was, in fact, sensitive about this—he enjoyed numerous friendships at that level. He was invited to contribute to the inaugural issues of two important Viennese art periodicals which made their appearance at this time, *Der Architekt* (1895) and *Kunst und Kunsthandwerk* (1898). His Viennese atelier attracted many students, and in the midst of all these other activities, he managed to carry out a number of architectural commissions, tasks that for him meant direct control over all aspects of their execution—architecture, sculpture, painting, and any other decoration (Pls. III–a, VI, VII).[19] If the design of a villa which he published in *Der Architekt* for 1895 was typical of his style, however, we can understand why he did not see eye to eye with the new modernists of Vienna like Otto Wagner.

Sitte continued to drive himself in spite of the advice of his doctor and his friends. The summer of 1903 he spent in Berlin working on the new journal, instead of at a spa as had been recommended. On November 11, 1903, he suffered a cerebral stroke; on the 16th of November he died.

His funeral was held in St. Stephen's of Vienna near the chapel his father had designed, and a cenotaph bearing his likeness in bronze (identical to our p. 7) was erected by the municipality in the central cemetery. He was memorialized even more appropriately by the City of Vienna when it named a street after him, one of the streets issuing from a 'turbine plaza', a type of square which he had done so much to popularize.[20] During his life he had been honored twice by the Academie Française (1878, 1881), had received from the Vatican its Order of Gregory (1901), and from his own nation the Order of the Crown, third class (1898).

Sitte's wife survived him by more than two decades, maintaining their home as a center of artistic and musical gatherings much as it had been during his lifetime. They had two sons. Heinrich (1879–1953) became a professor of classical art history and an authority on J. S. Bach. Siegfried (1876–1945), a city planner, did much to carry on the tradition established by his father. He represented the 'Sitte school' at a number of planning exhibitions and congresses at the beginning of this century and largely supervised the re-editing of his father's book in its later editions. His own interests were, however, more in the line of housing and land reform, on which he published extensively.[21] That Siegfried eventually dedicated his career to these matters is interesting in the light of the fact that it was he who had been expected to complete and publish the book on these aspects of city planning left unfinished by his father. Why he did not do so is not clear. Perhaps the manuscript was in too fragmentary a condition; Camillo Sitte's style of writing and manner of thinking were highly personal and would have been difficult, if not impossible, to duplicate.

Any discussion of the life of Camillo Sitte as a city planner should mention another immense historical project with which he was concerned and which was interrupted by his untimely death. This is important to us because it makes clear that for Sitte the building of cities was simply one aspect of a greater totality of the arts (*Gesamtkunstwerk*) of which city building was only a part, albeit a totality of several arts in itself. His theories about an art of total design and a synthesis of the arts he probably owed in part to his father, but they at the same time explain his intense admiration for Richard Wagner. From an early age it had been his ambition to compose a veritable encyclopedia of art history, and the wide range of subjects that make up his published works must be understood as the building stones for this opus. We are told that this monumental publication was to examine the arts from philosophical, psychological, and physiological points of view and to go into their prehistoric origins. He had mapped out seven volumes: I, the development of the basic forms of Greek architecture and ornament; II, the roots of Etruscan and Roman architecture; III, a history of perspective; IV and V, matters of mythology and national psychologies; VI, physiological and psychological bases of a *Weltanschauung*; VII, the German work of art of the future. Some idea of the scope of this undertaking is indicated by the existence at his death of 300 boxes of notes for the project, the results of his voracious and widely-ranging research.

The emphasis in this plan on national psychology and on German art in particular was characteristic of Sitte. Although it is not especially apparent in his book on city building, we are told by all his biographers who knew him intimately that he was intensely Germanic or 'Teutonic' in outlook and felt that any true art must have a basis in the 'national impulse' of a people. Of French culture, for instance, he remarked that he could not understand it, did not want to understand it, and that anyway it counted for nothing. He once wrote to a friend that the basic philosophy of his life's work was that, especially in art, every serious subjective feeling, every higher spiritual aspiration must be and could only be *national.*[22]

Richard Wagner was for Sitte the hero of German art, and Sitte in turn patterned himself on Wagner's Germanic heroes, giving battle, like the Siegfried for whom he named his eldest son, to the ill-informed and evilly-motivated forces that repressed artistic creativity in his century. His most compelling ambition and most Wagnerian conception was a project reported by his closest friends after his death but about which they are rather vague because he had apparently confided very little to anyone about it. This was his vision of a national monument based upon the spirit and accomplishments of German art and culture. It was to take the form of a great tower on a deserted beach called, for some reason, his 'Holländer Turm.' This was to be an immense *Gesamtkunstwerk*, its many floors devoted to a presentation of Germanic creativity from the different aspects represented in his own enormous collection of research materials. The precise purpose of this monument is not entirely clear, but among the many comparisons that it brings to mind is the Outlook Tower that had been arranged in Edinburgh in the 1890's by Patrick Geddes to include on its several floors a sort of overview of the problems and accomplishments of city planning throughout the ages. Although they were both venerators of Darwin (Sitte kept Darwin's portrait beside Beethoven's and Wagner's and considered the 'struggle for survival' to be a Germanic concept), it is hard to imagine two city planners of the same generation who were more widely separated in interests than Sitte and Geddes at that time; it is doubtful that their tower images were in any way related. However, to appreciate these differences in point of view, it is important to look into the state of the city planning profession, especially in Germany and Austria, during the lifetime of these two 'founders' of the discipline.

2

THE STATE OF CITY PLANNING IN GERMANY AND AUSTRIA

It would be useful to review here some of the developments in the planning profession as they relate to Sitte's book. There are, of course, many possible angles from which to survey the evolution of modern city planning; we will restrict ourselves mainly to those aspects of its practice which aroused Sitte's concern and to those persons or incidents which may have contributed to his own ideas or may otherwise have stimulated his interest in the topic. This means, inevitably, a considerable emphasis on German theory and methods.[23] Although the repercussions of his writing were international in scope, Sitte's little book was originally directed toward the public and the problems of German-speaking lands—specifically Vienna, as he made clear on his original title page.

As far as the contemporary scene was concerned, one of Sitte's major criticisms was levelled against the 'technicians and specialists.' It would appear that what he was indicting was more a state of mind common among architects, engineers, and city-fathers than any specific profession as such. However, subsequent events, such as the critiques of Lichtwark,[24] suggest that the engineers were at the root of the evil in Germany—in that country they seem to have played a much more important role in the establishment of city planning than in the United States, where landscape architects tended to be the architects' collaborators in that mission. City-building offices in German cities seem to have been largely controlled by the engineering profession. Although the 'engineer vs. architect' confrontation has been dealt with in great detail in connection with the development of modern architecture, it has received much less attention in discussions of city planning.[25] In any case, the various excesses or lapses on the part of technicians that Sitte attacked were an outstanding characteristic of town planning at the time Sitte became involved with it.

Perhaps Sitte's most fundamental complaint was against the prevalence of plans made up by surveyors and representing only a surface-survey (*Grundriss*, *Stadtplan*, or *Stadtanlage*). He urged the use of a *Bebauungsplan* (he called it *Verbauungsplan*[26]), that is to say a city plan conceived in three dimensions, showing the elevation of buildings that are to be built on the sites. The *Bebauungsplan* eventually became the basis for stricter and more detailed building regulations, especially as regards zoning for height, as German planners became increasingly concerned with its use in the 1890's.[27]

Later commentators on Sitte (e.g. Brinckmann, Bibl. 267) make clear to us what had been going on in German city-building offices when they point out that his book put an end to the use of 'a-priori' plans which did not take into account accidents of the terrain and other special characteristics of the area in question. Sitte was particularly disdainful of 'geometers'—surveyors who laid out towns or parts of cities with a meaningless geometrical exactitude. It was not merely their indiscriminate use of the ruler (*Lineal*) or even their reliance on the grid (*rechteckige*) layout that upset him—these he accepted as inevitable in the accelerated growth of modern cities—but rather their stereotyped employment of compact and solid building-blocks (*Blockrastrum*) as the primary element of design instead of basing their plans on what he considered to be the fundamental spatial units of cities—public squares, streets, and private courts,—thereby opening, limbering up, and humanizing their arrangements. Their geometrical bias (hardly one of a Platonic idealism in the nineteenth century) had led planners everywhere to see some peculiar virtue in a square square, a straight street, a triangular open space, and a radial or star-shaped plaza, all of which Sitte scorned.

The triangular and star plazas developed, of course, out of another of Sitte's anathemas, the growing reliance on traffic considerations in laying out new towns and in regularizing old ones. Sitte wrote when vehicles—although still drawn by horses—were beginning to assume the dominant role in the arranging of streets and plazas that they have never lost. That modern specialist, the traffic engineer, had not yet put in his appearance, but the writings of Sitte's contemporaries,

Baumeister and Stübben, were renowned for their emphasis on such matters. Baumeister's book of 1876 on city expansion (Bibl. 252) is generally credited with orienting city-building around traffic problems, and Stübben's *Handbuch* evolved a veritable hierarchy of street-types, classified according to the importance of their arterial function: through-streets as opposed to local streets, diagonal streets which cut across existing networks, belt-roads that ring a city nucleus, etc. The traffic plaza, which Sitte ignores, became established as a major category of urban space. One of Sitte's basic criticisms of Mayreder's plan for the reorganization of the inner city of Vienna in the 1890's (cf. p. 44) was that the proposed street lay-out would lead traffic right through old squares like Am Hof and the Graben instead of circumventing them and leaving them in peace.[28] Over and again one reads in planning handbooks of the day that crooked streets are pretty, *but* straight streets are better for traffic; it was a period of obsession with traffic, and all obstacles to its flow were being removed. A major concern of the period was over the relative merits of introducing a central railroad station into the nucleus of the city or leaving the various terminals on the outskirts with the train yards; in either case new large access routes were being cut through the existent street pattern. The emphasis that Baumeister and Stübben gave to traffic and arterial problems explains to a large extent the satisfaction that they both expressed about the accomplishments of the French school of planning in Paris.[29] In his 1907 *Handbuch* Stübben stated bluntly, 'The traffic systems and direction of their flow form the basis of the plan of construction of cities,' (p. 312). This was in conformity with the charter statements of German planning, the 1874 and 1906 resolutions of the Berlin *Verein*, both of which had been prepared by Baumeister.

Another characteristic of German planners that had tended to put the profession at the mercy of the engineers was their extraordinary emphasis on sanitation or hygiene—what we would today call public health. With the increase in knowledge about the nature of contagious diseases and epidemics there developed that characteristically nineteenth-century branch of architecture: underground water and sewage systems. The portion of one of Baumeister's books which dealt with the latter subject went through several American editions (Bibl. 258). Sitte balked when the designing of these municipal plumbing systems began to effect adversely the free and organic character of above-ground planning. One authority has pointed out (Brix, Bibl. 177) that hygiene was such an important concern in the 1870's and 1880's in Germany that all other matters were pushed aside for the moment, explaining perhaps why Sitte's writings, coming at the end of that period, had far greater impact than Baumeister's book of 1876, which was much more professional in tone and had also made some aesthetic suggestions. The great pioneer in these matters of hygiene was Max Pettenkofer who made the science of public health a German one; Munich, under his direction, became a model of salubrity. His students and followers made masterly studies of European cities.[30] Within the planning movement itself, the most important group in Germany was the Association for the Preservation of Public Health which was founded in 1873 and met annually to consider urban sanitary conditions; on these occasions it published important directives.[31]

The English were also concerned with these questions of the public weal, but, characteristically, approached them from a somewhat different, much less centralized point of view. When Horsfall returned from Germany and published his report in 1904 on housing and planning conditions in that country, he observed that the situation there was complementary to that in England; in Germany the general environment was much more healthy for the worker, but the English worker was much better off as regards his own home, if he had one. The Germans were well aware of this as we know from the studies and reports that Hermann Muthesius had been commissioned to make on the English house. But one area in which the English were far in advance of the Germans with regard to the urban environment was in the character of their verdured squares and large park layouts in cities. The planted English squares that had developed in London since the seventeenth century had given rise to use of the word *Square* in German by Baumeister, Sitte, Stübben, and others to describe precisely that type of plaza.[32] German writers also sometimes used the word *Park* instead of *Anlage* to describe that other speciality of the English engineers which Lichtwark claimed to have laid a curse on German planning (cf. Note 310). What appears to have happened is that, impressed by the hygienic value and the marvelously clever drainage systems of English city parks, such as those designed by Paxton, German city fathers commissioned their engineers to do likewise.[33] These engineers not only adapted the British drainage techniques in their German city parks, but, untrained as they were in matters of architectural design, they also copied England's romantic surface effects. Thus the German engineers were not only responsible for the rigid geometry of straight streets and sewers that Sitte castigated in German planning, but also for some of the most artificially picturesque effects of the urban scene. Informality and a certain picturesqueness in planning also seem to have invaded German cities quite early under the influence of the first English garden suburbs. The Cottage Anlagen of Vienna's XVIII District, to which Sitte refers at several points, was an early (1872 on) and rather exceptional example. It was laid out by an architect (Sitte's teacher, Ferstel) in large, rather regular blocks that provided a common garden area in their interior. Its detached houses, insulated from each other and from the street by strips of greenery, anticipated by many years the enthusiasm with which Germany was to take up Ebenezer Howard's Garden City ideas. By the time the Garden City came to Germany, Europeans were also becoming aware of the exemplary park movement in the United States that was producing such extensive and interconnected greenery belts as those of Boston—laid out well within the city and not simply exploiting the site of abandoned fortifications as was the case in so many European cities. Up until this point German writers, including Sitte, had expressed nothing but contempt for planning procedures in the new world.[34]

The question of open spaces with greenery in the city and how they affect the human organism has seldom been handled with purely scientific detachment, but more often has been the subject of fads and misconceptions. Nineteenth-century Germany was no exception, and Sitte took great delight in exposing the mythical bases of some of the ideas that had governed such planning. His fullest treatment of this subject came in his article of 1900 on greenery in the city that was printed as an appendix in the posthumous editions of his book—our Appendix I. The question as to whether trees and shrubbery function as 'the lungs of the city' in an actual physical sense or merely metaphorically is still with us today. It is a subject charged with human emotions and instinctive associations.

Other preoccupations of the profession in Sitte's day were of a more legalistic character. For instance, zoning, a matter that drew little of Sitte's attention, was virtually an invention of the Germans. Promoted with fervor by Baumeister and others, it was, like the American anti-trust laws, a necessary device to maintain some sense of order and to protect the general public in a period of uncontrolled growth and unbridled land speculation—an unsophisticated necessity of the early days of city planning.

Another issue was that of the building frontage line or flushline (*Baufluchtlinie*) and the street line (*Strassenfluchtlinie*). These were of special importance in the widening of streets in old parts of towns and cities. The basic law governing these matters was that of Prussia of 1875 (printed in Stübben's *Handbuch*, Appendix), which was rather primitive according to 20th-century standards and apparently led to that indiscriminate reliance on straight lines in street planning of which Sitte disapproved so heartily. Sitte contended that the old irregular building lines and projecting elements have a certain charm in themselves and that uniform flushlines are not aesthetically preferable (cf. *Sitte*, pp. 84, 89, 107, 109). By 1907 Stübben had come around to Sitte's point of view, especially as regards those historic buildings which could only be preserved by varying the frontage lines (*Handbuch* 1907, added Chap. 8 of part II), and this was written into German laws of the day. Sitte was also delighted with Hamburg's new regulation about 'inner building lines,' designed to guarantee adequate space in the interior of solidly built blocks.[35]

A really crucial affair of that time which we find amusing today was whether streets should be straight or curved (and crooked): *krumme oder gerade Strassen.* For nearly everyone the individual street and the street network were primary elements of city planning, so this matter was one of overriding importance and gave rise to some of the most bitter aesthetic debates. Since both sides could quote Alberti as an authority, the argument took on the character of a doctrinal dispute—its flames fanned anew by the publication of Sitte's book. Actually Sitte did not argue the point, but merely assumed, axiomatically, that a street with an interrupted view was aesthetically superior (Pl. VIII). It was characteristic of his followers to exaggerate the picturesque beauties of curved and crooked streets, and Martin fabricated the entire seventh chapter of his French translation (1902) out of this theme—a chapter drawn in part from Stübben, although Stübben was in considerable disagreement with Sitte and his followers on the subject.[36]

These matters of straight-line vs. informal planning were not only questions of abstract aesthetic in the layout of new quarters of cities, but were also of fundamental concern in the modernizing of older sections. How to ease traffic and still preserve the quaint character and historic buildings of the old quarters? By 1900 architects and planners in Germany were holding annual conclaves on the subject of the preservation of historic monuments, some of the results of which Stübben printed in his Appendices.[37] Although Sitte was the first to make explicit in a truly analytical fashion the beauty of the towns which they had inherited, he was by no means the first discoverer of their charms. Not only had architectural associations been bemoaning the fact that these ancient quarters were being ruthelessly destroyed instead of serving as models for the new development of cities, but literature of many types dwelt on the superiority of the pre-industrial town.[38] It is therefore not surprising that when Sitte's book appeared he became not only the founder of a school of city building, but also a rallying point in the defense of historic monuments and old towns. He seems to have taken a hand in the regularization of the Königstrasse in old Nuremberg and in fending off a street-railway that was planned for Venice, but he took his most significant action in opposing the official plan for opening up the old city core of Vienna in the 1890's. He lost this battle.

Stübben, who reported the discussions, called Sitte a prophet without honor in his own country. Later commentators considered that following Sitte's advice might have saved the original character of Vienna, which had been unique among the metropolises of Europe.[39]

There was one other partly legal, partly aesthetic topic of this type that should be mentioned because it formed the subject of Sitte's last writing on city planning (Bibl. 88). This was the aspect of expropriation law that dealt with the purchase and redistribution of lots so as to make them usable. Awkward lots could not only result from the layout of new quarters and the design of new thoroughfares for old ones, but also from the constant subdividing of inheritances. (Stübben published a weird lot-plan of Cologne that showed 102 parallel lots, each of which was approximately 6½ feet wide and more than 650 feet long.[40]) Sitte argued that geometrical plans should not be imposed either on an irregular terrain or in a historical situation that had resulted in irregular boundary lines; streets should, instead, conform naturally to such features. His article was essentially a criticism of a policy that had been suggested by Baumeister, Stübben, and Classen (Bibl. 259), and he illustrated his points with his own layout for Olmütz and the way he would correct the plan for Hanover (Pl. IV). This was the old *krumme oder gerade Strassen* theme, of course, and Stübben retorted immediately that Sitte did not understand modern traffic conditions and that to judge each case individually, as Sitte proposed, would be a disastrous procedure.[41] A typical confrontation of these two authorities.

As concerns the practice of city planning in Germany, then, the architects, for whom Sitte was suddenly to become the hero, had been jousting, not too successfully, with the technical and legal experts for several decades. The sociological side of the profession was in its infancy, and the utopians were in eclipse for the moment. Such pressure as the architects exerted seems to have been through their local associations (*Vereine*) whose studies and recommendations we have cited. However, the actual laws that Stübben prints in the Appendix to his *Handbuch* seem to be pale reflections of these recommendations.

One writer (Brix, Bibl. 177) has suggested that modern city planning was launched in Germany (and, practically speaking, this means everywhere) with the principles drafted by Baumeister for the Berlin *Verein* in 1874[42] and that it finished its first phase with the revised principles that Baumeister drew up for the same *Verein* in 1906.[43] To us it is interesting to note that, apart from being longer and more explicit, the 1906 principles differ from the earlier set mainly by virtue of their inclusion of several concepts that Sitte had popularized.[44] However, until 1890 at least, the building offices, to whom the resolutions were directed and who administered the ordinances and did the planning, seem to have been impossibly bureaucratic; the era of enlightened city-architects and far-sighted burgomasters that Horsfall was to write about had not yet dawned. And it was against these city-building offices that Sitte directed his most scathing sarcasm; his suggested alternative was the inclusion of artists of all categories in the design of city plans and the opening of all projects to public competition (cf. his Chap. XI). Herein lay the peculiar 'Viennese' character of his program. Ever since the Altlerchenfeld incident in which his father had figured, open artistic competitions had been the rule in Vienna. Sitte had emphasized the importance of this tradition to Vienna in other writings (Bibl. 111), and the Austrian *Verein* had taken a strong stand on that very subject in its 1877 resolution about the planning of Vienna (Bibl. 457).

It may have been just this principle that accounts for the varied and personalized character of the buildings of Vienna's Ringstrasse. They make up such an incredible panoply of nineteenth-century styles that they have given rise to a number of local adages about themselves and their architects. This variety becomes the more apparent when one compares the Ringstrasse with Haussmann's work in Paris, by which the Viennese plan was supposed to have been inspired. The physical situation in Vienna was, of course, simpler since the Ringstrasse was not *ripped* through its city; nevertheless, the transformation of Vienna gives us none of the sense of having been carried out by a monolithic organization of nameless artists and technical experts deployed like the units of a

Napoleonic army.[45] As an artistic experience Paris was undoubtedly successful; the painters came back into town from Barbizon in order to depict its boulevards. Architecturally speaking, however, Paris offers little to match the impressive lineage of Semper, Ferstel, Schmidt, Sitte, Otto Wagner, and the various Sezessionists whom we associate with the Ringstrasse development. And the impact of this new French image of the metropolis on most building offices in Germany undoubtedly served to reinforce their faceless, dictatorial character and to encourage that emphasis on large-scale technical accomplishments which Sitte criticized so severely.

3

IMPORTANT CONTEMPORARIES OF SITTE: BAUMEISTER, STÜBBEN, BULS, AND OTHERS

FROM what has been said it should be apparent that, although city planning established and perfected itself in Germany through the combined activity of many individuals working on particular problems in a variety of fields, the German profession can at the same time be said to owe its early pre-eminence to the respective efforts of three men: Reinhard Baumeister, Joseph Stübben, and Camillo Sitte. Although they were almost contemporaries—Baumeister only 10 years older than the others—their contributions registered in effect roughly in the order we have listed their names. Sitte was outlived by both the others, who continued for many years with unabated activity but without any further innovations, so that his work, cut short as it was, might be considered the culmination of the triad's efforts. He was also the one who was most imbued with the fervor of city planning as an apostolic mission, a trait of the profession that became so pronounced among twentieth-century advocates like Bruno Taut, Le Corbusier, Frank Lloyd Wright. One is tempted to add to the dramatis personae of our story several others of the names listed in our Bibliography F; however, Semper, Eitelberger and Lichtwark were not enough immersed in city planning per se, Henrici and Fischer were more followers than leaders, and Otto Wagner although of the same generation represents an even later phase.

Reinhard Baumeister (1833–1917) is generally credited with having laid the basis of city planning as a scientific field of endeavor (*Wissenschaft*).[46] He was a man of action who guided professional associations, municipalities, principalities, and, finally, the German Empire itself through the formative years of the new discipline. He lectured and published until the time of his death, producing authoritative handbooks on all those technical and legal branches of the art for which he was so renowned. He is considered to be the first to insist that city planning was a function of vehicular traffic. He was a pioneer in zoning, especially its legal framework. In his work he also emphasized housing problems and matters of public hygiene. Important in the latter was his collaboration with Miquel in framing projects-for-law (cf. Note 31). Although Sitte wrote quite adversely about Baumeister's aesthetic proposals, Baumeister *did* stress artistic considerations in his book *Stadterweiterung* of 1876, and Sitte took over a number of his ideas. For instance the gridiron, radial, and triangular categorizing of planning with which Sitte led off his Chapter IX is right out of Baumeister. But more pertinent is the fact that Baumeister had also criticized the universal use of rectangular systems, had suggested that one look back at the character of ancient squares and the picturesqueness of medieval streets. He recommended that streets be curved for aesthetic effect, and he stressed the importance of the shape and 'walls' of public squares. To use the straight line was to force nature, he said. Sitte had certainly read this book carefully. But Baumeister was subject to a number of pre-Sitte prejudices: he liked churches 'peeled' free, he preferred trees in long orderly rows, and he thought most squares should be square. However, we have already taken note of the difference in the resolutions which he proposed for the Berlin architects' *Verein* in 1874 and those he composed, somewhat retrospectively, for the same organization in 1906 (Notes 36, 42, 43). Not only did he begin the latter with a preamble that reminds us of the Prologue to Sitte's magazine *Der Städtebau*, but he includes a number of Sittesque ideas. The 'turbine plaza' is a preferred type; plaza walls are to be closed when practicable; arches are to be used for this purpose; etcetera. His 1914 summary of the accomplishments of German planning is exemplary and gives due credit to his two contemporaries (Bibl. 264).

Joseph Stübben (1845–1936) was a figure of so great an activity, productivity, and eminence in the field of city planning that it is impossible to summarize his career succinctly.[47] During his lifetime, and owing in part to his efforts, what had been a largely Germanic movement became international in scope, rendering his own contributions even more influential.

He was still participating actively at the age of 86 (at the Berlin Congress of that year), but when he finally expired at 92 his British colleagues (he was a corresponding member of the R.I.B.A.) noted that his writings were dated and belonged to the pre-World War I phase of planning. This is obvious to anyone who scans the three successive and greatly revised editions of his basic *Handbuch* (Bibl. 377–379); despite his efforts to up-date it, the edition of 1924 belongs to an earlier epoch and is mainly of archaeological interest to the planner.[48]

Trained as an architect in Berlin (1864–66, 1868–70), he worked briefly in railroad management and then was placed in charge of the city-planning office of Aachen (1876–81), Cologne (1881 on), and, in Imperial service, he supervised the planning of Posen (1904–20). His plan for the expansion of Cologne was probably his most important, although he was engaged in the layout of more than 30 other cities in Germany and abroad and won a first prize in the Greater-Vienna planning competition of 1892–93. He played a prominent role in professional congresses: those of the German public-health association (cf. Note 31), the first congress of *Art Public* in Brussels (1898), the important R.I.B.A. conference at London in 1910 (p. 94), and then the International Housing and Town Planning conferences. His papers are to be found in the published reports of most of these conclaves. Not only did he, like Baumeister and with Baumeister, draw up many proposals for city-planning ordinances, but he also wrote frequent reports about new city plans in the German architectural periodicals. He was particularly interested in Belgium, on which he had reported in 1878 (Bibl. 374), and he enjoyed the friendship of Buls, who had translated into French his Chicago lecture in 1895. He received many honors and belonged to a number of foreign academies. His name made respectable the masthead of any city-planning venture.

His publications, of which we list only a fraction in Bibliography F, are impossible to summarize because they are crammed with factual information and are encyclopedic in scope. It is not easy to extract an essential point of view from them; even his own effort to give a précis of his ideas in his paper for the engineers at the World's Columbian Exposition is not very successful. His *Handbuch des Städtebaues* (Bibl. 377) was his *summa.* Everything that he had done and published prior to 1890 was incorporated into its first edition—all his reportage and also his early contributions to an aesthetic theory of city planning (Bibl. 372–373). The substance of his later publications was inserted into the two revised editions. Although it is not apparent from his writings, we are told that two of his major interests were opposition to collective housing and, when it came along, promotion of the Garden City movement. Certainly one of the more fascinating parts of his *Handbuch* is his discussion of housing types and his demonstration that the preference for single-house versus 'flat' living quarters is not a reflection of the city-life country-life dichotomy of the nineteenth century but is a built-in cultural preference with a clear-cut geographical distribution in Europe (Part I, Chap. I). The book is not actually tedious to read since it is so informative, but it lacks entirely the vigor and lustre of Sitte's writing. Who today can say he has read the *Handbuch* from cover to cover? All its 6 parts, 30 chapters, 23 appendices, 900 illustrations, and 690 marginal divisions? Stübben's is the cookbook that lists all the ingredients; Sitte's is the soufflé itself.

Although Stübben rightly maintained (Bibl. 385) that he had already treated some of the same artistic problems of the city several years before Sitte's book appeared, it is small wonder that Sitte had paid no attention to his articles, because Stübben's architectural comments and aesthetic critiques always seem platitudinous and hackneyed in comparison with Sitte's insights. For instance, Stübben's own summary of his ideas in 1893, to which we have referred, divides itself into: 1, Practical principles (of which there are a, b, and c); and 2, Aesthetic principles (of which there are a and b). Of the latter, 'a' consists of the 'elegant development' of streets and plazas and sounds like the residue of a Sittesque program; 'b' treats in a cursory way the 'elegant proportion' between streets, squares, and buildings on the one hand and the placement of monuments on the other. He concludes with the meaningless generalization, 'For the irregular arrangements of a picturesque kind, there is no other rule than artistic feeling.' (Bibl. 390, p. 736). Unlike Sitte, he made little immediate use of the study of the towns of the past. During his career our knowledge of the history of the city increased, and this is reflected in the inclusion of more and more historical material in each of his editions, but it is dry except for his own summary in 1920 of the history of modern planning (Bibl. 416). In this last, by the way, he reveals certain of his limitations: he was interested primarily in the world-wide influence of German developments; he had nothing but scorn for the Americans until they produced their Park Movement and began copying German ordinances; and he was, like everyone else, generally uninformed about city-planning theory and practice in Spain in spite of first-hand acquaintance with Barcelona, Madrid, and Bilbao.[49] To us, the most interesting thing is, of course, just which of Sitte's ideas he rejected and which he absorbed and propagated; this is a fairly complicated story, and, as it relates to later events, we will discuss it below as part of the impact of Sitte's book (pp. 82ff).

There is one phase of Stübben's interest in the artistic side of city building that should be mentioned for what it reveals to us of the desire of many planners in his day to arrive at 'laws' or 'rules' by which aesthetic decisions can be made. We are referring to the enthusiasm which Stübben and others showed for the aesthetic theories of Hermann Maertens.

Maertens, a statistician and 'aesthetician', had, since 1877, been promulgating a series of supposedly scientific rules about the proper size of a building or monument in relation to its surroundings, for use in architectural planning.[50] Working with the angle of vision subtended by the building or monument as compared to that of its surroundings, Maertens accumulated long tables of measurements for ancient and modern settings. His system was based ingeniously on Helmholtz, whose scientific experiments had so often impinged on the fields of art and music. His results are rather simply expressed: In order to appreciate best the *details* of a building or a monument, it should be so placed (e.g., its plaza should be so designed) that the spectator ordinarily views it from a distance equal to the height of the object above eye-level, viz., a visual angle of 45°; to appreciate best the *mass or entirety* of the object, the distance of the eye should be twice the height of the object above

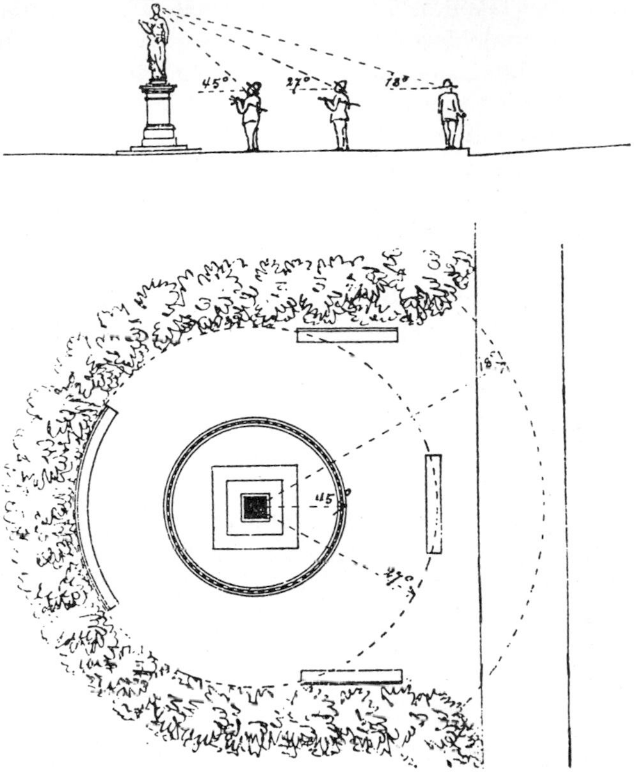

Fig. 1. How to frame a statue beside a walk in order to achieve satisfactory vantage points (Maertens)

eye-level, an angle of 27°; to take in the *ensemble*, the distance should be tripled and the angle 18° (Fig. 1). The outline or silhouette of a group in a panoramic view is best perceptible at a distance of four to five times the height of the object. As Stübben points out, the first rule means that any street must at least equal in width the height of public buildings on it and the best squares for public buildings are two to three times deeper than the building's height (the latter, a simple fact that Sitte arrived at without the use of Maertens). Of course, any one plaza may involve a complex mixture of these angles for its different contents and standpoints. There is also the matter of the maximum allowable horizontal angle, which Maertens seems to have taken as 70° for panoramas. These matters of architectural scale form a hoary problem to which Alberti, Christopher Wren, and others had applied themselves with diligence; the fact that modern perceptual science could solve it with a set of tables seemed delightful, and nearly everyone except Sitte (who does not even mention him) took Maertens' conclusions as gospel. By 1893, Stübben, in his Chicago lecture said, 'According to aesthetic law . . .' and then recited the proportions we have just listed (Bibl. 390, p. 731); others followed suit. Maertens' culminating publication was a large folio volume of 1892 in which he applied his principles to a series of German public statues of the nineteenth century—works of 'art' which present-day taste would require us to look at from the greatest distance possible!

There remains to mention one other important figure of the day who applied himself to practical problems of urban aesthetics, that is to say, to the architectural side of city planning. This is Burgomaster Charles Buls of Brussels, whose story takes us somewhat outside the German ambient, with which we have been concerned so far.[51] Buls, who was personally involved in the preservation of the old parts of the Belgian capital, wrote a small book in 1893 entitled *Esthétique des villes.* Like Sitte's book it was an almost immediate sell-out, and a second edition soon followed. It was translated into German in 1898, into English in an American magazine of 1899, and into Italian (with a special chapter on Rome) in 1903. The American magazine spoke of Buls as being one 'who more than any other man has been the leader of the late worldwide movement in favor of public art.' The amazing thing is that although the little book is in style, organization, and sentiment remarkably like Sitte, it at no point shows any direct influence of Sitte's writing of four years earlier. In the preface to his second edition of 1894, Buls insisted that Viollet-le-Duc had been his major inspiration. He listed seven German aestheticians of these matters, including Semper but not Sitte; in 1895 Buls stated that he had composed his book without knowing of the existence of any foreign work on the subject. He said this on the occasion of his translating into French Stübben's paper for the World's Columbian Exposition (Bibl.

283). It seems that Stübben had written a review of Buls' book for a Cologne newspaper and had sent it to Buls, an incident that led to their friendship and this collaboration. Stübben in turn praised and discussed in detail Buls' restoration of the Grand'Place of Brussels in the chapter on old city districts which he added to his 1907 *Handbuch* (Part II, Chap. 8).[52] Buls was invited to take part in meetings of the German association for the preservation of monuments (Bibl. 286). He seems to have become a staunch supporter of Sitte on this question.

It might be interesting to quote a few passages from Buls' *Esthétique.* It starts:

> 'Old cities and old streets have a peculiar charm for all who are not insensible to art impressions. They may not be called beautiful, but they are attractive; they please by that delightful disorder that here results not from art but from chance . . .
>
> 'When these venerable cities were founded, it would have been useless to have asked whether they were aesthetically planned. They sprang up of themselves; they grew little by little, as needs called for them and conformably to these needs. They drew their beauty both from this conformity and from the local character that was reflected in their building.
>
> 'Today this is no longer the case . . .
>
> 'As one looks at the plan of one of our great cities, one can distinguish at once the ancient from the modern part. The former is made up of a network of streets that ramify, interlacing like arteries and veins in a living body; the latter, with its streets parallel or at right angles, is like an artificial crystallization, dry, mathematical . . . The one aim that has guided the authors of these [latter] plans has been to design the platting most favorable for the sale of the land . . .
>
> 'There is one thing that it has always seemed to me about which architects do not take sufficient pains: that is their tendency to use a bird's-eye survey in their planning. Bent over their paper they devise symmetry which is not visible when one walks about the quarter actually built up . . .
>
> 'Old monuments, old houses of artistic character or recalling historic memories should be preserved, and we should not hesitate to crook a street in order to spare them . . .'

Buls' book confirms Sitte's statement that around 1890 these matters were 'in the air'. And Buls' unique reputation abroad suggests that until it was translated into French in 1902 Sitte's book was little known outside of Germany.

4

THE TRANSFORMATION OF VIENNA

OF all the activities of Germanic city planning, that which bears most directly on Sitte's book is the construction of the Ringstrasse in Vienna. Although the chronicle of the nineteenth-century transformation of Vienna has been dealt with often enough in publications,[53] the details and implications of it are probably not as familiar to the reader as that which transpired in Paris under Louis-Napoleon and the Baron Haussmann.

The old city of Vienna had not undergone any appreciable change in form from the thirteenth century down to this ambitious project that Emperor Franz Joseph launched during Sitte's youth. The town had become a fortified capital of the Babenbergs about 1135, and by the following century, under the first Hapsburgs, it had taken on roughly the perimeter that it still possessed in 1850. Its medieval towers and walls had, of course, been replaced by modern earthwork bastions, fosse (ditch) and glacis (sloping unbuilt land outside) (Pl. XI). The city's suburbs lay at some distance, out past the glacis, and although the latter had been built over with small homes and gardens during the seventeenth century, these were largely cleared away in the eighteenth century; also, in 1704, an outer defense of rampart and fosse (*Linienwall*) was erected for protection against Hungarian raids. The survival of the city until a late date in such a curiously fossilized medieval format can be understood if we remember that for centuries Vienna functioned as Western Europe's bulwark against land incursions from the South and East. Meanwhile it had in the eighteenth century become one of the major capitals of the world and an important commercial center. The illustrations in Max Eisler's historical atlas provide an excellent image of Vienna between 1770–1860.[54]

During the early nineteenth century the major changes in the appearance of the old city had nothing to do with the problem of its exploding urban population: the glacis was planted with poplar trees and the Hofburg area bulged outward because of the addition of the Hofburg Court, the Hofgarten, the Volksgarten, and Peter von Nobile's Burgtor (to serve as a gate in the extended fortifications at that point). But by 1850 there were 34 suburbs lying out past the glacis, in which the new population was settling; these now comprised a far greater area than the inner city itself. As the fortifications had not been able to keep Napoleon out, there was considerable pressure for their removal. Ludwig von Förster exhibited a scheme for this and for the enlargement of the city at a general meeting of German architects held at Leipzig in September, 1842. On December 20, 1857, the Emperor, having decided that the fortifications must go and that the old city core should be more adequately joined to its outlying parts, issued a proclamation which we reprint in full in our Notes (No. 55). In essence, the inner fortifications were to be razed, a Ringstrasse was to be erected on their site beginning in the N.W. at the Danube Canal and running counter-clockwise past the Hofburg and back to the canal; there would be appropriate arterial connections to the periphery of the city. In the Viennese tradition a competition was planned for the architectural layout. The entire operation was to be financed by the sale of portions of the new area to private building interests. Regulatory work was projected for the Danube River and Canal. Förster won first prize in the competition—under the motto: 'Der gerade Weg ist der beste [The straight road is the best]'! Other awards went to Friedrich Stache and to the team of van der Nüll and Siccardsburg;[56] the actual plan employed was drawn up by the new building department of the Ministry of Interior and approved by the Emperor in 1859. The individual buildings that resulted figure so importantly in the text of Sitte's book that we have listed them with some data about their architects—the 'Viennese School'—in our Notes (Note 57 and Fig. 2).

Neither of the big churches of the Ringstrasse was part of Franz Joseph's project. The Karlskirche (J. B. Fischer von Erlach, 1715–37) had been outside the city limits, and it remained for many years a subject of dispute and competitions among architects as to how to integrate it properly into the new boulevards.[58] The Votive Church had been under construction since 1856 and also presented a problem of relationship to the new layout. Buls, in writing about his visits to Vienna, commented on this.[59] The solution that Sitte suggested for its setting formed the crux of his whole scheme of reorganization of the Ringstrasse (Chap. XII); Stübben immediately printed Sitte's proposition for it in his 1890 *Handbuch* (p. 199) as being an excellent arrangement. But the Votive Church had also played another and perhaps more fundamental role in the transformation of Vienna. Ferstel, who won the competition for the church in 1855 at the age of 27, had been faced with the formidable task of producing an archaeologically correct Gothic church with all its sculpture, tracery, and stained glass in a country that had been practicing the *Rundbogenstil* and a decade earlier would have never dreamt of building Gothic (Pl. IX). However, 75 projects had been submitted to the competition, all of them in Gothic! This sudden switch in taste to a Gothic Revival had been precipitated in part by the Altlerchenfeld Church incident, but, as everywhere else, it owed a great deal to the enthusiastic archaeology of art historians (like Eitelberger), to the foundation of a Central Commission for the preservation of antiquities, and similar activities. One of the more remarkable aspects of the Austrian Gothic Revival, however, was the reestablishment, right in the midst of the industrial revolution, of the old masons' lodges (*Bauhütten*). The collaboration in this case between Ferstel and his master-mason was very close, and the undertaking served as both stimulus to and market for a first-rate artisanship that persisted in Vienna long after the short-lived Viennese neo-Gothic phase had spent itself. Ferstel was Camillo Sitte's teacher, and it was apparently to this revival of sculptural art that Sitte is referring in his Chapter I (pp. 17ff).[60] This tradition may explain in part the mixed styles of the Ringstrasse buildings, some of which are Gothic with classicizing ornament, others Renaissance with Gothic ornament. The whole is an exceedingly rich example of nineteenth-century 'artistic city building,' and it is ironic to think that the vast enterprise was carried out in those very years when Austria was beginning to lose its cosmopolitan character by reason of adverse military and political events.

The Ringstrasse project elicited much professional comment as it progressed, some of which relates to Sitte's own critique of it. In 1858 Eitelberger, who was to be his teacher, delivered a public lecture in Vienna on city planning and city building that was obviously prompted by these current events (Bibl. 290). Humanist that he was, Eitelberger took the occasion to give a sketch of the way in which the form of the city had served as an expression of culture and social systems from classical times to the present. It is clear that for Eitelberger city planning was a very serious and important matter. He emphasized the role of the architect as planner and the function of public buildings as the spiritual essence of the city—drawing copious examples from Greece, Rome, and the Middle Ages. Vienna in 1858 did not measure up to the status of a metropolis in these terms, he observed, but the project before them could produce the great artistic buildings necessary to fill the need. His lecture was a solid historical presentation and one that would do credit to a speaker a century later. It was not composed in Sitte's abstract analytical terms, but it does demonstrate the wealth of erudition that was available (for instance, Sitte's citations of Aristotle and Pausanias on his p. 8 are right out of Eitelberger). Eitelberger's nostalgic description of Pompeii recalls the opening of Sitte's book, and, as Sitte would do later, Eitelberger already bemoaned the indiscriminate use of the ruler in laying out the new Vienna.[61]

Chronologically the next event in the Ringstrasse work that had reverberations in Sitte's book was the calling of Gottfried Semper in the late 1860's to advise on the further development of the Hofburg area which, being the royal palace, had always posed special problems. Semper's suggestion for the layout of this complex of large buildings serving a variety of purposes was virtually the same he had proposed for the Zwinger at Dresden, an arrangement which Sitte called an 'Imperial Forum.' This consisted of an immense oblong court open at one short end and provided with symmetrical bulges or exedras near the closed end to give the court area a varied and subtle spatial effect. (See *Sitte*, Pls. XX, XXI, and Fig. 95.) As the Ringstrasse would bisect the new Hofburg plan, Semper

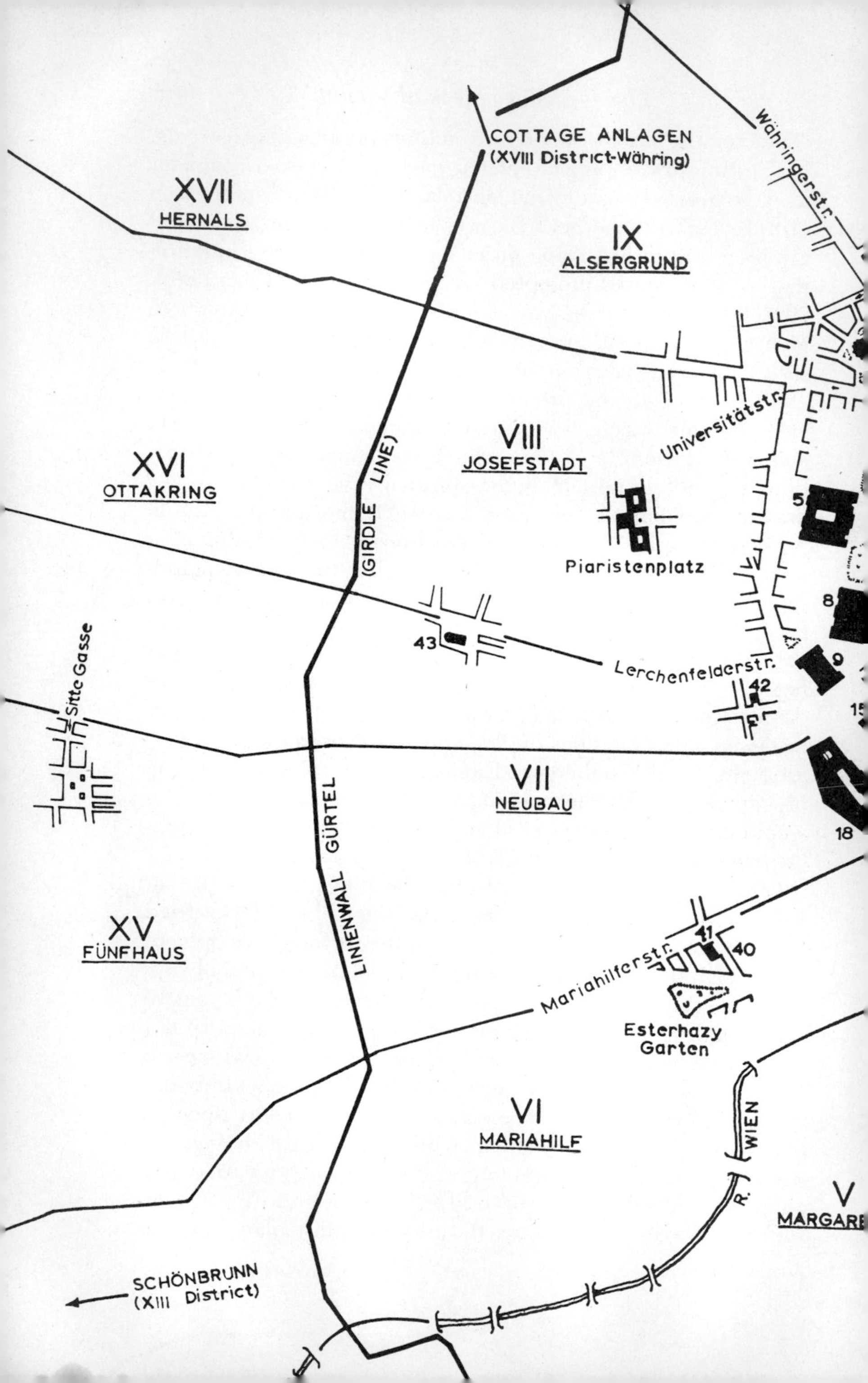

COTTAGE ANLAGEN
(XVIII District-Währing)
Währingerstr.
XVII
HERNALS
IX
ALSERGRUND
Universitätstr.
VIII
JOSEFSTADT
XVI
OTTAKRING
(GIRDLE LINE)
Piaristenplatz
5
8
9
43
Lerchenfelderstr.
42
15
Sitte Gasse
VII
NEUBAU
18
LINIENWALL GÜRTEL
XV
FÜNFHAUS
41
40
Mariahilferstr.
Esterhazy
Garten
VI
MARIAHILF
WIEN
R.
V
MARGARE
SCHÖNBRUNN
(XIII District)

Fig 2. Plan of Vienna, showing the location of buildings and monuments mentioned in this book. For key, see p. 40

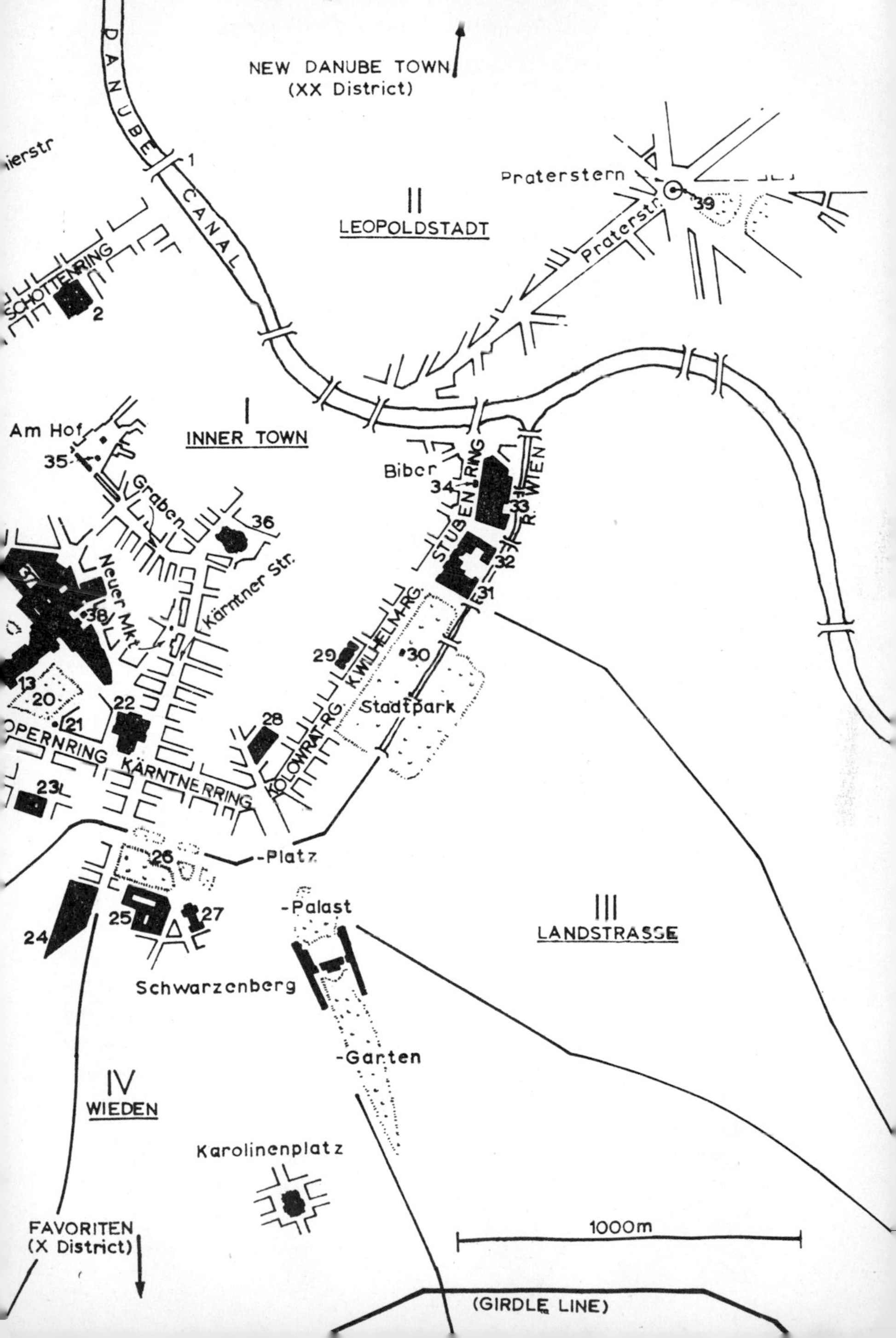

Key to Fig. 2. RINGSTRASSE AREA:

1. Augarten Bridge.—2. Bourse.—3. Votive Church.—4. University.—5. Rathaus.—6. Rathausplatz.—7. Burgtheater.—8. Parliament.—9. Palace of Justice.—10. Volksgarten.—11. Theseus Temple.—12. Hofburgplatz.—13. New Hofburg.—14. Burgtor.—15. Natural History Museum.—16. Maria Theresa Monument.—17. Art History Museum.—18. Imperial Stables.—19. Gänsemädchen Statue.—20. Hofgarten.—21. Goethe Monument.—22. Opera.—23. Academy of Fine Arts.—24. Freihaus.—25. Technische Hochschule.—26. Karlsplatz.—27. Karlskirche.—28. State School of Applied Arts.—29. Gartenbau-Gesellschaft.—30. Schubert Monument.—31. Austrian Museum of Art and Industry.—32. Kunstgewerbe Schule.—33. New War Ministry.—34. Radetzky Monument (now)

INNER TOWN:

35. Radetzky Monument (formerly).—36. St. Stephen's.—37. Old Hofburg.—38. Josefsplatz

OUTER DISTRICTS:

39. Tegetthoff Monument (Distr. II).—40. Mariahilf Church (Distr. VI).—41. Haydn Monument (Distr. VI).—42. Mechitaristen Church (Distr. VII).—43. Altlerchenfeld Church (Distr. VII).

---

planned to screen it with triumphal arches and eventually to remove the old Burgtor at that point so that the enclosed court could become a spatial entity. To what extent Semper and Sitte considered this format to have been drawn from Rome of the Caesars or from Rome of the Popes is not quite clear, because it is similar to both and identical with neither; it certainly has nothing of the medieval about it. It was apparently imposed on Vienna to emphasize that the 'K.u.K.' empire was the legitimate heir to Rome, in rivalry with upstart Paris and Berlin, to which Vienna was actually losing ground at the time. The failure to carry out Semper's plan was both architecturally and symbolically catastrophic for Vienna, as it had been earlier in Dresden.[62] Sitte seems always to have cherished the hope that it would be completed; he made no changes in his remarks about it for the later editions of his book. We know how strong an influence Semper's planning ideas had exerted on him from the repeated comments on Semper in his book and from the earlier essay on Semper's theory which he incorporated into it.[63]

Progress on the Ringstrasse project occasioned one other intervention which has generally passed unnoticed in planning literature but may have done much to help formulate Sitte's ideas about the practical aesthetics of planning. In 1877 the Austrian Engineers' and Architects' Association published in its magazine its considered opinion (*Denkschrift*) about the state of the works and the future of the city.[64] This was a remarkable document for its time in the extent to which it stressed the artistic factors in city building, and one could hardly deny its effect on Sitte. To quote but one passage that sounds like Sitte speaking:

> 'The design of a city plan in its entirety as well as in its detail is an eminently artistic matter. City plans and city expansions are not accomplished with compass and ruler; needed are, as in all artistic tasks, ideas first of all and secondly a thorough understanding of the requirements of a metropolis and the demands of modern living—but also, and especially so, a sensitive feeling for space and an understanding of form.'

Among other things, the group recommended a comparative study of city plans—those of Antiquity, of the Middle Ages, and even of old Vienna—in order to observe the importance of art in city building. They felt that, in general, variety is the basis of civic beauty: e.g., variety in streets, which should be curved when traffic allows it. They considered that planting and public gardens are vital, but that the planting of squares should be subordinate to the architecture; water should be treated as an aesthetic element in the city. They regretted the piecemeal way in which Vienna was being transformed and the lack of a long range overall building plan. There should be a more organic relation of the Ringstrasse to that which already existed in the ancient core and in the suburbs. There was a lack of understanding of public transportation and of the urgency of regulation of the Danube. They called for more open competitions. Much of this appears in Sitte.

Sitte's major objection to the Ringstrasse in 1889 was not, however, to be found in any of the critiques or activities that preceded him, but evolved instead from his own highly original analysis of old-time urban spaces—probably the most unique contribution of his book. He was upset about the clumsy handling of space around the major buildings and the method of placing public monuments. It seems certain that his effort to determine just what was amiss and precisely how to repair it was what caused him to publish his ideas. As Alfred Lichtwark later remarked: 'The entire layout of the Ring is basically unsuccessful. It is no wonder that the observation of this monstrosity has led a man like Camillo Sitte to the study of old streets and squares. If only one had learned something from him! . . .'[65]

That which we have been describing and Sitte dealt with in his book was, actually, only the first stage of the transformation of Vienna—down to about 1890. What followed was called the 'Second Viennese Renaissance' at the time (Bibl. 179), although it was later accused of having destroyed the charm of the city, in part because of ignoring Sitte's warnings.[66] The major undertakings of the 1890's were the improvement of street connections to and through the inner city, transformation of the outer girdle of fortifications (*Linienwall*) into a series of ring-boulevards (*Gürtelstrassen*); construction of the network of the metropolitan railway; treatment of the valley of the River Wien, (Pl. X). Twenty of Vienna's numbered districts (the old town is No. 1) were thus incorporated into the city, seven within the *Gürtelstrassen*, ten outside, and two across the Canal. The broad bed of the little River Wien was split in two: one half was deepened for the stream and vaulted over almost completely, the other was walled off and used for the city railway. Meanwhile work proceeded on the Danube. The final results were 1) the Danube Canal, at the site of the original town, made into a harbor by means of a lock; 2) the main stream (*Donau Strom*) regulated as a navigable and controllable waterway; 3) the old Danube, isolated as a loop on the far side of the stream. Sitte was particularly interested in how to employ for commerce and housing the thousands of reclaimed acres near the Danube.

The third phase of Viennese planning, and the last to be of concern to us here, took place after 1904 when municipal control was extended across the Danube and a ring of woods and meadows (*Wald- und Wiesengürtel*) was provided as a buffer outside the suburbs. This ring, a prototype of our modern green belts, contained an 18-mile circumvallating road within it.[67]

An international competition had been held in 1892–93 for the various works of the second phase. Winners of the overall plan for Greater-Vienna were Joseph Stübben and the Viennese architect Otto Wagner. The brothers Mayreder submitted the winning design for the completion of the Ringstrasse development. A new city planning bureau was established to combine the best elements of the various competition entries and to prepare definitive programs for all phases of the work; Karl Mayreder was put in charge of the architectural aspects of this undertaking.[68] From time to time during the rest of the 1890's detailed plans of the various projects were exhibited by the planning bureau (*Stadtbauamt*) and were subjected to public discussion in meetings of those professionally interested. As Sitte played an active, if somewhat marginal role, in all these proceedings, it behoves us to examine some of his writings of the period. He died before the third Viennese phase got under way, and it would appear that his role as maverick in the city-planning activities of Vienna was assumed by Otto Wagner (1841–1918), whose principles of planning were anti-Sittesque, but who also based his effects on visual principles and, under the influence of Semper, likewise stressed the architectonic character of the city plan. Wagner's concept of beauty was, however, of a much more twentieth-century cast; for him beauty arose out of a scrupulous compliance with the purpose (*Zweck*) of a project. Wagner was given the responsibility of designing the entire metropolitan railway system which, with its stations, overpasses, tunnels, and elevated sections, was a perfect demonstration-piece for his ideas. Wagner's credo of planning was summed up in a slight, Sezession-styled book on the Metropolis (*Grossstadt*) of 1911.[69]

Sitte reacted with enthusiasm to the new phase of Viennese planning, since it was going to tackle several of the problems that he had outlined in the conclusion of his book. Already in January 1891 he gave a lecture on 'Vienna of the Future,' in which he discussed the accomplishments of the first phase and outlined the tasks ahead (Bibl. 57). The lecture was based largely on his book, but it paid somewhat more attention to practical matters such as traffic, and it also gave a brief summary of the character of recent city planning events, including a complimentary reference to Stübben's *Handbuch* and praise for Henrici's Dessau plan (Pl. XV–a). He then wrote a number of newspaper articles on different phases of the Viennese project during the next three years, ending up with a series in 1894 that enlarged on the theme of his 1891 lecture and evaluated the recent competition (Bibl. 58–66, 69–73). Although Abercrombie considered Sitte to have exerted a beneficial effect on the work of the *Stadtbauamt*, it certainly did not come about through any direct intervention since he was too critical of that body to work with it, having inherited his father's dislike for bureaucratic control of architectural matters. Art, he observed (cf. Frank Lloyd Wright), cannot be created by committee but only by individual artists (*Sitte*, p. 122). That his criticism was not appreciated, we know from the discussion of the *Stadtbauamt*'s plan in which he took part and about which we have already remarked above (p. 22). In early 1896 Mayreder put on exhibit his office's project for the reorganization of the old inner city; he lectured about it and then a public discussion followed in several sessions, lasting through an entire month. The details were reported faithfully in the magazine of the Austrian *Verein* and were summarized in that of the Berlin *Verein*, by Stübben.[70] Sitte apparently spoke so heatedly about Mayreder's plan and was received with such hilarity and ridicule for his 'impractical' suggestions, that he refused to have his remarks recorded and instead submitted a list of twelve principles as a summary. He stated in them that the destruction to the old buildings of the town was monstrous and that the old plazas would be ruined by directing traffic arteries through them. That the parallel system of uniformly-wide streets was absurd, that there should be a variety of street types and also of building-block types. That the garden areas were poorly designed and unprotected. In short, that there was no trace of artistic beauty to be found in the project, although it could have been obtained at no extra expense.

Perhaps this experience embittered Sitte. Only once again did he apply himself to matters of Viennese planning—on the occasion of the competition for the Kaiser Franz Josef City Museum in 1901–02 when he wrote, and published separately, articles of criticism about the various entries (Bibl. 83–84).

5

SOME OTHER SOURCES OF SITTE'S IDEAS

IN addition to his reactions to events in the planning of cities in his day, there are other components that went into the making of Sitte's book. Among these could be cited the ancient, medieval, and Renaissance writings on the city. There is a great body of such material, but it is largely composed of utopian writings that are cosmic or reformist in nature and are often concerned with geometrical abstractions that may be rich and fascinating in their own right but have nothing to do with Sitte's interests. Of 'practical' texts inherited from older times, the majority are preoccupied with matters of fortification and frequently, although for different reasons, are also absorbed in geometry. That delicate balance between the practical and the aesthetic which we find in Sitte has few precedents in the writings of the past, and where it does occur, the precepts must be isolated from a compendium of information on many other things besides city building proper.

The first of these early sources is Aristotle, who was, actually, not too fruitful in this respect. Among the things that Sitte extracted from Aristotle's writings was the principle that a city be designed so as to make its people secure and happy (*Sitte*, p. 1), an idea which was drawn rather freely from parts of Book VII of the *Politics*. Oddly enough Sitte did not pick out the passage about safety and beauty (Book VII, Chap. 11) which many others quoted.

The second authority from whom Sitte drew was Vitruvius, on whom, incidentally, his friends considered him to be particularly well informed.[71] On pp. 5–6 he cited many of Vitruvius' comments about city layout, mentioned the Dinocrates anecdote, and took over verbatim Vitruvius' differentiation between Greek and Roman forums as everyone else did. Then on pp. 50–53, when criticizing an overreliance on symmetry, he launched into a learned philological discussion of the term, starting with the Greek and with Vitruvius' passages on the subject. Finally on p. 131 he held up the example of Vitruvius to his contemporaries on the matter of paying attention to the direction of prevailing winds in laying out city plans.

Sitte's third such source was Alberti.[72] Although he is seldom named by the writers (and never by Sitte), several ideas of the Renaissance theorist became part of the argumentation of modern city-planning theory. Basically Alberti had much in common with the 'city-building' phase of planning with which we are concerned. For instance, he remarked, 'the principal ornament of the city will arise from the disposition of the streets, squares and public edifices, and their being laid out and contrived beautifully and conveniently . . .' (VII, I, p. 134). Most famous was Alberti's observation that winding streets add to the beauty of small towns (IV, V, p. 75). Nevertheless, in the case of large cities he recommended straight and broad streets treated as an architectural whole (IV, V, p. 75 and VIII, VI, *passim*). He also has been accused of originating the use of street intersections as public squares and emphasizing the traffic nature of streets (Bibl. 178, p. 23). An Albertian simile taken over by many is that of classifying plazas by types and likening them to the usage of different rooms in a house (I, IX, p. 13); apparently the comparison of a public square to a festival hall (in Stübben and Sitte) is out of this tradition. Alberti also gave attention to the thorny problem of the proportion of the size of public buildings to that of their squares (VIII, VI, p. 173), and he recommended using arches to close off streets where they entered plazas (VIII, VI, p. 174).

As writings on the history of planning began to proliferate over the turn of the century, authors sprinkled their texts with classical allusions in order to add humanistic dignity to the new profession; it is characteristic of Sitte that he did not employ such quotations as literary status symbols, but as live arguments in the solution of current problems, much as he marshaled his visual data.

The remarkable popularity of Sitte's book can be explained in part by the way in which he substantiates each point, in modern art-historical fashion, by a clear visual image of his idea drawn from the plan of an existing European city. The very over-simplification of some of the plans renders his points more graphic. The 'source' of this aspect of his book is, then, the actuality of old European towns and cities as he had himself observed them on his travels. An additional air of legitimacy was lent to his arguments by his insistence on discussing only those places which he had seen in person, although at the same time this blinded him to the virtues of certain things he had never seen (cf. Note 183 on the *Plaza de Armas*). Old Vienna itself harbored superb instances of the ancient beauties which he sought out and documented throughout Europe; he seldom used it to illustrate his points, but what it may have contributed to his ideas we can gather from the plates of Eisler's *Atlas* (1770–1860), which we have already mentioned (Bibl. 458). He assembled instead a corpus of foreign material for his Viennese audience, and the way in which he did this is instructive. We quote from an account of his procedures that appeared at the time of his death in a Chicago newspaper, written by an American member of his following:

> '[Sitte's] study of towns, especially of medieval cities, was encyclopedic in scope, and there is an agreeable suggestion not only of practical sense and thoroughness, but also of good living in the following programme, which he followed on visiting a strange town. Alighting at the station, he would bid the cabman drive immediately to the central square. There he would ask for the leading bookstore, and there he would inquire for three things, namely: First, the best tower from which to view the city; second, the best map of the city; and, third, the hotel where one could eat the best dinners. Then, having cut the map into small squares, easily handled in the wind, he would betake himself to the outlook tower, and there spend several hours analyzing the plan of the town. Later he would study in detail and make sketches of the cathedral square, the market place, and perhaps other capital points in the city's organization.
>
> 'In 1889, after thirty years of such observations, he wrote a book on the subject.' (Bibl. 156).

It should be noted that a view of a town from a tower is one that is more concerned with the present morphology of the town than with its form in any one of its prior incarnations, such as the year 100, 1000, or 1500. 'Medieval' Vienna as Sitte saw it or as any of the other artists in Eisler's *Atlas* depicted it was a Baroque town, as yet only slightly scarred by 19th-century incursions; Vienna had been a marvelous Baroque city.

Sitte, then, to judge from his sources and his methods, was not simply a romantic medievalist as he has so often been pictured, but, like his English contemporary William Morris, he reached back quite indiscriminately for anything of beauty from before the deluge—before the incidence of urban explosion and mechanized technical methods that marked his own day. His was a sort of Queen Anne Revival in city planning.

6

SITTE'S POINT OF VIEW AND ANALYTICAL PROCEDURES

ONE of the compelling features of Sitte's book as a treatise on city planning was his manner of extracting universal principles out of the array of concrete examples that old cities present. It is proper to ask, therefore, from what standpoints he generalized . . . what are the premises that underlie his analyses and that made the volume so timely a document?

He himself claimed in the preface to his 1901 edition that 'the basic idea of this book . . . is to go to school with Nature and the old masters also in matters of town planning.'[73] That is to say, city planning is an art and as such its practitioners would profit from the same advice that teachers have given painters and sculptors since time immemorial. This slogan, however, has meant different things at different times, and, considering the artistic ferment of the years 1889–1901, it may have had a slightly different meaning for Sitte at the beginning and end of that period. Certainly by 1901 an artist would consider any painter from Polygnotus to Delacroix an 'old master;' 'Nature' no longer necessarily meant landscape but for many had taken on, during the Art Nouveau period, the idea of an inner force or an organic consistency. By 'Nature,' then, Sitte was apparently referring to the natural functions of the city: the environment of man as a social and artistically sensitive being. The question was not one of mere sanitary drainage or traffic flow as others had insisted, but of how to shape the accretion that a city is so that it would be psychologically and physiologically adequate for the needs of successive generations of city dwellers—specifically, for their open-air assemblies and their promenading, for the satisfaction of individual contemplation, etc. This was, admittedly, an image of the metropolis free from the sinister character that seemed to be attributed to it everywhere in the nineteenth century. For Sitte the example of cities of the past was instructive not for any particular style of architecture or city building—in writing about church architecture in 1887 (Bibl. 111) he had observed that modern free eclecticism had rendered 'style' meaningless —but rather for basic ideas about the art of living. Sitte's contribution, like that of Riegl and Wölfflin in other arts, was notable for his reduction of the urban environment to essentials that underly any or all period styles. Like those other two theorists he based his analysis on the mode of perception of the modern spectator and of the period in question. One senses after reading Sitte's 1887 essay that, as an artist, he was tiring of architecture and was ready to turn to city planning because the latter provided him a unique opportunity to speak in terms of abstract artistic concepts rather than details of particular historical styles. City building was an art of pure arrangement. To label this man medieval, Baroque, or romantic is absurd; although the results might vary in each case, Sitte's method is equally applicable to settlements in Central Europe, China, or the Highlands of Peru. In this respect he was thoroughly modern.

His favorite type of cityscape is discussed in our critical notes to his text (Notes 163 and 237), and needs no more than brief recapitulation here. He was fascinated with perspective, especially as provided in Baroque vistas, but himself preferred rather limited panoramas of a picture-like (*malerisch*) character (cf. Note 163 and *Sitte*, p. xii). His contemporaries called this a 'closed architectonic effect' (*geschlossenes Architekturbild*).[74] We have likened this taste to that of late Impressionism, a similarity that is well illustrated in the cityscapes by his contemporary, Camille Pissarro (1831–1903). Pissarro delighted in the use of perspective, but often displaced its axis to the side of the observer so that the vista became closed off (Pont Neuf series); he also depicted the closed beauties of curved streets (*krumme Strassen*), e.g., in his Rouen etchings of the 1880's (Pl. VIII). A city view (*Stadtbild*) that is so contrived gives the effect of being more a function of the spectator's eye, than of either an a-priori pictorial structure (perspective) or of an a-priori town plan (gridiron); Sitte constantly speaks of what the spectator can take in at a glance (see Note 163). All of this led him to a rather personal interpretation of the idea of 'orientation' in the city, which we have discussed in Note 237, and which city planners evidently never understood since they have nowhere commented upon it. They seized instead on his use of the word *malerisch* as if it meant only picturesque medieval effects of a somewhat ramshackle character and proceeded to pin the term romantic on Sitte and his followers. Indeed, many of the latter were as guilty of the same misunderstanding as were his critics; a lot of strange and romantic things were perpetrated in Sitte's name.

Although it might appear at first glance to be inconsistent with the two-dimensional vision just described, a second basic premise of Sitte's and one that produced a profound revolution in city planning was his insistence that the city was a work of architecture, to be conceived of three-dimensionally. After his book had appeared, no self-respecting city planner in Germanic lands would ever work out a new city section by means of a flat survey. Had it not been demonstrated that the towns of old had grown by slow steps, without plan perhaps, but under the supervision of an uncanny spatial sense on the part of successive generations of builders? Sitte, singlehandedly, had given city planning back to the architects.

However, his architectonic image of the city was a somewhat personal one, not shared by all his contemporaries. He sought a special sort of continuity of effect in the fabric of the city. For Sitte, plazas, whether singly or in groups, should provide spatial unity and containment, as expressed in the closure, perhaps by overlapping, of their wall sections—like a Wrightian living room (*Sitte*, pp. 33–34). There were to be no loose elements standing about, such as freed-up churches or central monuments; the furniture was to be built-in, as it were. To ensure closure, arches and colonnades could be used across major openings, as Vitruvius and Alberti had counselled. Despite this concern about the 'walls' of plazas and streets, however, it was not the architectural container that interested him as much as that which was contained: the space. For Sitte, the character of a town or a city lay in the public spaces that it could provide for its citizens, and its beauty lay in their rhythmic interrelationships. As for plazas, he definitely preferred a chain of dissimilar types, joined. His eloquent description of Venice in Chapter VI demonstrates this (cf. Pl. XIV). It has, in fact, become an accepted architectural idea; in 1950 Walter Gropius explained his new graduate quadrangle to the Harvard alumni in just such terms.[75] Sitte's delight with Venice is testimony to the abstract character of his analytical method: in that city he could treat bodies of water as the equivalents of paved streets and squares (*Sitte*, p. 58).[76]

Sitte did not discuss the spatial character of streets in any detail (the chapter dealing with this in the French edition was not his), except for the fact that space in neighboring streets should be screened off from the plaza wherever possible. Planted squares and parks, unlike ordinary squares, should be located at a distance from each other, separated by the intervening mass of buildings, much as the inner court of one building is separated from the next (cf. Notes 247, 277). To Sitte, then, urban design consisted of the arrangement of spaces in appealing and useful patterns and sequences, rather than the division of a site into building blocks separated by traffic arteries, as in a grid-system (*Sitte*, p. 87). Stübben disagreed with him on this from the very beginning (Bibl. 4), but his admirers felt that Sitte had made civic art a truly spatial art (*Raumkunst*).[77]

It is characteristic, moreover, that Sitte would eventually address himself to that other intangible of the urban scene—greenery. About this his ideas were, as we might expect, different from those usually held in his day.[78] Whether they were intended to serve a 'sanitary' or 'decorative' purpose, he considered the arranging of trees and shrubbery to be a matter of judicious taste, not of geometric consistency. The large single tree, over whose civilizing influence he rhapsodized, should be placed, like a monument, at the edge or corner of a space. Quantities of trees and bushes should be arranged in clumps or islands in instinctive rhythms rather than in a meaningless geometrical file. For Sitte these elements formed part of the architectural apparatus of the city and should therefore be designed in harmony with buildings, monuments, and façades rather than in competition with them or so as to obscure them. He also speculated on the ways in which plantings could best offer recreation and contemplation to modern city dwellers: in parks and squares, well protected from traffic, and even within the interior courts of buildings. As it happened, these ideas had little influence in Germany until after his death, since the periodical for which he wrote them was an obscure one and the essay was not generally available until his sons printed it as an appendix to the 1909 edition of his book. The French translation had included some fragments of it as early as 1902; English readers have never seen the material in its original form.[79]

Thus architecture and nature and solids and voids were for Sitte the building elements for making the city into that total work of art (*Gesamtkunstwerk*) toward which we know he always aspired: the city as 'a popular synthesizing of all the visual arts' (his p. 185). So abstract a point of view prepares us for his frequent comparisons of the city with other types of artistic composition: his use of musical analogies, his likening of town views to stage sets (Note 163), and his speaking of the perfect town as if it were an exhibition arrangement (his p. 120). His biographers emphasize that a favorite theme of his was the relationship between architecture and music.

It is clear, then, that Sitte's theoretical contribution to the new German science of city planning was that of a rather subjective set of principles. He was apparently not comfortable himself when 'on axis' or 'in the center,' and he knew that many people felt skittery on large open squares (Note 186). A careful clinical scrutiny of the form of the towns of past ages suggested to him that these phobias were not personal with him but were almost universal, and that the old masters had kept such considerations in mind as their towns grew. His description of promenaders 'craving for protection from the flank,' etc. (*Sitte*, p. 95) calls to mind the figures in contemporary street scenes painted by Edvard Munch. We can understand why for one with such a Freudian sensitivity to matters of internal adjustment, geometrically exact checkerboard plans are not necessarily evil, but simply meaningless and banal, because they are at best neutral and can never be human. To Sitte it was obvious that the growth of the modern city could not be left to technicians, municipal offices, pattern books, or chance: it was a creative task for the individual artist.

The need for the intervention of artists in city planning was obvious in 1889, and the architects had already shown themselves eager to move into the field for some time. But when Sitte justified the participation of artists in matters of city layout by virtue of his having detected the artist's hand in the irregular features of old cities, he provoked an argument that has still not resolved itself today. Brinckmann and many others considered him impossibly romantic on this count. Sitte had mixed in allusions to child art and primitive art with his discussions of city-building principles (his p. 21). To discover and to verbalize the artistic properties inherent in things previously considered to be sub-artistic or accidental, and to postulate that behind them lay deep-seated, intuitive creative drives, was to subvert the inherited aesthetic dogma of the nineteenth century in dangerous fashion. Yet to do so was quite characteristic of the years in which Sitte wrote; we inevitably think of his Viennese confrère Alois Riegl and of the concept of will-to-form (*Kunstwollen*). The atmosphere of Vienna in those days for both psychological and art-historical theorizing must have been a heady one.

To sum up here the rules by which Sitte suggested that his ends might be achieved would be superfluous. Such a précis can be obtained by scanning the titles of his chapters or by consulting the passages in which Sitte recapitulates his own arguments.[80] It should, nevertheless, be emphasized that the book falls roughly into two halves. The first part (through Chapter VIIB) is one of analysis. In it he examines admiringly the structure of the pre-industrial town of western Europe. The flavor of these chapters is largely, but not entirely, medieval since the towns he chose were old settlements that had been cast in medieval format. Many of his squares, however, including his favorite in front of S. Marco in Venice, had had a sizeable portion constructed as late as the nineteenth century (cf. caption to his Fig. 46). In the second half of the book, which is one of synthesis, he criticizes many of the modern procedures in city planning, which we have described above, and suggests how, in his opinion, the inevitably mechanical systems of modern times can be ameliorated. His cures are based on just those utilitarian matters with which his contemporaries were obsessed—land-usage studies, frontage lines, traffic flow, building density, etc.—except that they are considered by him in terms of their aesthetic potentialities. The devices he suggested were drawn mainly from the late Baroque period or from Semperian derivatives of the Baroque, since only the Baroque period had developed urban forms of sufficient power and magnitude to cope with the scale of the modern metropolis. The highly irregular tendencies of the medieval period that he had described in the first part of his book he himself used only rarely and with great simplicity—as around the neo-Gothic Votive Church. (*Sitte*, Fig. 112.)

Sitte suffered the fate of many prophets in that his own disciples, as well as his opponents, did not really understand his message. For instance, he himself warned against indiscriminate copying of the ancient towns, especially as regards their irregularities, e.g., *Sitte*, pp. 16, 105, 111, 174. His followers, especially Henrici and Gurlitt, fell into exactly that habit, and he was eventually blamed for it. The misunderstandings of Sitte are legion, and might best be studied in connection with the later editions and summaries of his book—especially the French editions and the English summaries.

7
THE SUCCESSIVE EDITIONS AND TRANSLATIONS OF THE BOOK

No less important for us than the details of Sitte's life and professional ambient is the story of the various editions of his book, of how the volume was originally put together, and what the consequences have been of certain modifications made by its translators.[81]

While it is true that he wrote with great verve and conviction, which was certainly one of the main factors in the instantaneous success of his book, even the most casual reading of the German text will reveal how redundant and repetitious Sitte can be. He continually repeats, sums up, and reiterates, often for no apparent purpose. This makes translation difficult, because it seems as though the second or third statement of the same idea must have been meant to indicate something that was not contained in its first phrasing, although the words are always more or less the same. Camille Martin, in his preface to the first French edition (p. 67), explained that Sitte had drawn up 'these notes hastily at the request of friends who wished to see propagated the ideas expressed in his talks and lectures.' A plausible explanation, but careful study of Sitte's life reveals no lectures on subjects treated in his book before the volume was actually in press (see Bibl. 54). The American George Hooker gives an explanation that fits better our notion of Sitte as a worker of prodigious energy, namely that the whole book 'was written at seventeen night sittings' (Bibl. 156). In any case, Sitte himself seems never to have been bothered by the creakiness of literary construction, and neither he nor his sons made any modifications with regard to it in later editions. Martin edited out such repetitious passages ruthlessly in the French.

The book first appeared in May of 1889, and, as is well known, a second printing was already necessary in June. Apparently no changes whatever were made at this time.

Reviews of the book on this, its first appearance, were few, but two of them hold interest for us; they appeared in Germany rather than in Austria. Stübben reviewed it for the Hanover *Verein* with great enthusiasm, calling it a work of tremendous importance, many of whose criticisms of modern practices gave him great joy (Bibl. 4). He found its method of analysis remarkably perceptive and marvelously clear. His main reservations were, as one might expect, that Sitte declined to give traffic matters first priority and that he concentrated almost solely on squares, which Stübben considered to be only a part of city building. The other critique appeared over a year later in the art magazine *Kunstchronik* of Leipzig. As this writer already dealt with the sensational professional impact of the book during its first year, his comments are discussed below in that connection (p. 76).

The third German printing appeared in 1901, although the author had already signed its preface in August of the previous year. It is clear from the remarks in this preface that the little book had indeed exerted a remarkable effect on the profession. A Berlin magazine noted that it was unnecessary to review it because it was already a classic (Bibl. 8). It was now published simultaneously in Leipzig. The author saw no need to make any changes in the text, which is almost identical with the earlier editions except for certain modernizations in spelling.

Revisions came only with the fourth German edition, which was published posthumously by his sons in 1909. By this time the book had appeared in French with considerable modifications, and the sons imply that their father had intended to make similar revisions in the German edition before his death. These may have been in line with his increased concern with the practical matters of planning during the 1890's (as seen in Bibl. 57, 73, etc.), or it may be that he intended to clear the air after the controversies in which his followers had become involved (e.g., the Henrici-Stübben disputes). It is odd that he never added the former materials; perhaps he intended to treat them in his never-to-be-published Volume II. In any case, revisions were slight. Following the cue of the French edition, Sitte's article on Greenery in the City was added as an appendix. Wording and spelling underwent further modernization, and all the chapter headings and ornaments that we have employed in our translation for their period-flavor, were dropped. Many of the old prints and heliogravures were replaced by modern photographs, and certain plans were redrawn or substituted, but basically the book remained the same. Goecke, Sitte's co-editor, reported that the teachings, still unheeded, read as freshly as ever. In one of the most interesting reviews that the book has provoked, Goecke attacked those who, like Brinckmann, had accused Sitte of two-dimensional picturesqueness, and went on to demonstrate that Sitte's was a spatial theory of planning (Bibl. 14). He also made interesting distinctions between what study of the medieval town and study of Baroque layouts can contribute to modern methods—a clarification of Sitte's rather eclectic method that we have discussed above.

The last German edition appeared in 1922, its preface dated December 1921, again by the sons. This was an exact reprint of the fourth edition, apart from a slight re-writing of the preface and the substitution of photographs for the last remaining prints of city views. Hermann Jansen, an admirer of Sitte and editor of the magazine *Der Baumeister*, wrote at that time:

> 'This book is still a revelation—like a constellation gleaming in the dark sky, unaffected by the passing of years and fashions. It still retains, without effort, its position among the great number of books that have appeared in city planning and related fields during the last decades. That nothing had to be changed is witness to the accuracy of his elaboration of a problem that needed to be recognized, formulated, and then defended against the numerous errors into which city planning had fallen in his day . . . It is precisely in this field, seriously under-rated in importance and badly neglected, that the emphasis on quality of work becomes the more urgent.' (Bibl. 18.)

Here it seems appropriate to mention the Spanish edition of 1926 which, being the most faithful of foreign translations, is essentially a sixth edition of Sitte's original. For it Siegfried Sitte wrote the following preface, which we reprint in its entirety:

PREFACE TO THE SPANISH EDITION

The first edition of my father's book *Der Städtebau*, published in 1889, awakened great interest, reaching beyond the narrow circle of professional experts; it was exhausted in a few weeks, leading to the publication of a second edition that same year, followed in 1900 by a third; after his death (November 16, 1903) there came a fourth in 1908, and the last one in 1921. [These are preface, not publication dates.]

In 1902 appeared the French translation by Camille Martin under the title *L'art de bâtir les villes*; on this occasion my father expressed his desire to revise somewhat the next edition; an idea that was partially carried out in the fourth, and completely in the last edition.

These changes are limited to adding the plans of the festival precinct at Olympia, the Acropolis of Athens, and the Forum Romanum, according to the results of latest research. Some plans were redrawn and other drawings were replaced by the fifteen photographs which can be found at the end of the present edition. Added as well, in order to make it available to a greater number of readers, was his essay on 'Greenery within the City' which appears here as an Appendix. The text itself has not been changed, as its basic intention, *to study town planning under the tutelage of Nature and the Ancients*, did not require it.

Since then his principles have become basic. Every day the congresses, societies and periodicals are more numerous that are dedicated to studying various aspects of city planning—the economic problems related to planning and, in particular, those of housing in the city.

We record with satisfaction that the interest in the book which initiated this movement is increasing and that among the several editions in other languages that are being contemplated at present,[82] we can already welcome the Spanish, by the architect D. Emilio Canosa, who is a specialist in these matters and knows our language. We hope that it will be as well received in Spanish speaking countries as it has been in others.

Vienna, October 25, 1926 Siegfried Sitte
Professor and Architect

It might be of interest to point out that the architect Emilio Canosa, who translated the book, was also responsible for publication of the Spanish edition of Banister Fletcher (c. 1928) and the basic monograph on the Catalan architect Antonio Gaudí (1928, 1929). Siegfried Sitte's confidence in Canosa was justified; he produced a fine and lively version of the fifth

German edition, adhering to its chapter structure and omitting only those few passages that were of very local interest or were too dated. His plans and photographs were almost entirely taken from the German edition; from the French edition he employed only the line-drawings of city views, which we have also incorporated in our translation.

Of reactions that have been expressed in Spain to the teachings of Sitte, the most interesting came nearly a decade after the appearance of the Spanish translation, when he was pilloried by the young moderns of the Republican period, along with Stübben, the Frenchman Hénard, and the Garden City. This group of architects, which called itself G.A.T.E.P.A.C. and functioned as the Spanish unit of C.I.A.M., was in revolt against the academic teachings of Spanish architectural schools. During the years of the Republic they maintained an excellent and lively periodical, *A.C.*, and were in close touch with the international developments in architecture and planning. In 1934 *A.C.* (III, No. 13) struck out at academic planning, printing a passage from Sitte (pp. 106–107)—somewhat out of context—and illustrations from Stübben as examples of 'old principles still in vogue in our schools.' A great X is drawn across the page with the remark that *A.C.* is utterly opposed to the embellishment of public streets.

A year before, in 1925, Sitte had been translated into Russian at the behest of the Office of the Moscow District Engineer. The Engineer himself, P. A. Mamatov, wrote a special foreword to the translation in order to demonstrate the value of Sitte's message to the New Order in Soviet Russia. This foreword is a remarkable testimony to the free and experimental character of Soviet planning practice before the intensification that set in with the first Five-Year Plan (1928–33). It seems to represent a middle road among the competing theories that marked the reconstruction period in Soviet history; cities are appreciated for their historical traditions rather than slated for abolition as the decentralists demanded. Nor is this the pompous veneration of the capital and its colossal civic monuments that was to triumph in the 1930's after decentralization was suppressed as a planning policy. The keen sympathy that

Mamatov exhibits for the artistic heritage of Russia's past and his emphasis on the artistic aspects of planning in his day come as something of a surprise.

Mamatov understood Sitte's role as the champion of individuality and ingenuity in the face of the routine formulations of his time. And the realization that, although Sitte's was ostensibly a book on aesthetics, its critique of the short-sighted technical practices of the nineteenth century made the book a 'fresh and lively' exemplar for technical solutions in the 1920's would rank Mamatov's statement among the most perceptive analyses of *Der Städtebau.*

We include a complete translation of this preface which, we presume, is unknown to readers outside the Soviet Union:[82a]

From the Office of the Moscow District Engineer:

FOREWORD TO THE RUSSIAN TRANSLATION

In pre-Revolutionary times Russia's legislative bodies paid little attention to the matter of city planning. Their legislation, when compared with the extensive Western-European codes, exhibits an extreme poverty, not only in thought but also in relation to purely legislative standards. Our literature on questions of building, town planning, and the organization of public services in cities was just as poor. Therefore it is not surprising that the pre-Revolutionary past left us a painful heritage in this respect; it can be overcome only by means of an expenditure of great time and effort.

A certain enlivening has come about only with the liquidation of the tragic aftermath of the Imperialist [i.e. First World] and Civil Wars. Soon after the October Revolution many of our cities and settlements contemplated wide programs of reconstruction in those areas that had been destroyed, basically transforming them by means of new planning and by the creation of new and independent settlements of an urban type. To that epoch are related in particular the large-scale treatment of questions relating to the planning of Moscow, Saratov, Yaroslavl', Kiev, and a number of other cities.

But apart from the formulation and broadening of the complicated problems involved in construction of cities as a whole, in many cities at the present time partial changes of former city plans are being carried out. This relates not only to existing streets and squares, but also to the as yet unbuilt lands which are included within the city perimeter. These kinds of changes are, for the most part, based on very local circumstances or individual problems; often they are completely unrelated to the general scheme of the city, and their basic intention may contradict former established principles. Thus, under the banner of the Industrial Revolution, rails are being laid along streets so as to intersect construction blocks, plots of land are being used to enlarge extant factories and for the construction of new buildings of a commercial or industrial character in boroughs that were intended exclusively for residential use; monuments of art and of antiquity are being destroyed—not only those which constitute the intrinsic beauty of the city but those which have over-riding historical significance, etc. Such purely haphazard decisions in city planning can be the cause of evils which will remain uncorrected for years to come. Western-European practice provides us with innumerable instances which bear witness to the extreme cost to our heirs of such mistakes and lack of attention on our part. Examples are to be found in Berlin, Paris, Rome, and other cities, especially those that have survived from the Middle Ages.

But of all that one can say about contemporary planning, the artistic side of the question has special significance. In the absence of firm legislative regulations and well-established views about the aesthetics of cities, this aspect of the question exhibits, for the most part, the greatest number of omissions and inadequacies in execution and most frequently is the source of misunderstandings and errors. In our present condition of social life, however, we find ourselves in a position of unanimous agreement in theory and regarding the positive legislative measures that should be taken at the moment about the aesthetics of construction; the arbitrary, unprincipled projects and layouts for city streets, squares, green parks, construction of public buildings and monuments in pre-Revolutionary Russia, as well as in Western Europe at the end of the nineteenth century, and frequently in our own time are hardly admissible.

It is undeniable that precisely now most serious attention must be paid to questions of city planning in the widest sense of the word, not only from the viewpoint of higher official circles, but also on the part of scientific and social theory. These questions must be posed as widely and variously as possible and, together with the working out of the legal aspects, must be thoroughly discussed from the standpoints of theory, social hygiene, art, and the like. This is especially important for our country at the present when, according to all the symptoms, we are experiencing a noticeable quickening of building activity, particularly as concerns Moscow. This ancient city, abounding in the precious heritage of ancient monuments of the people's history, way of life, traditions, has become the bright capital of the powerful might of the workers and peasants—the center of a new political, social, industrial, and cultural life of world significance. . . .

But a sharp break with the past must be established. New conditions, the many demands that accompany the rapid growth of Moscow, the increase in her population, and the generally increased tempo of planning and construction of the city urgently demand changes in the city's layout and building—even in her external outline. But at the same time Moscow demands special consideration and attention so as not to destroy that which preserves her lively character and in order, under these new conditions, to avoid anything that might preclude artistic and scientific interest.

The Moscow District Engineer invites attention to Sitte's *Der Städtebau nach seinen künstlerischen Grundsätzen.* The choice of this book is not accidental. In his time the author was a decisive opponent of that routinely formulated policy in the area of town planning and city building which ruled in Europe during the second half of the nineteenth century, when, under the sway of false goals of practical expediency, the basic laws of aesthetics were ignored, resulting in the distortion and even the deformation of the outlines of many ancient cities.

It would be a mistake to search for scientific theory in Sitte's book. The thought of the author turns primarily on the aesthetic and the artistic—which are discussed from the most varied points of view and which, in the opinion of the author, are not at variance with the demands of contemporary conditions in the city. By contrasting artistic and practical principles, the author actually evokes a whole series of technical problems in contemporary city planning. We find, moreover, detailed discussions on the question of the city plan, the layout of blocks and independent structures, the economics of urban construction, social hygiene, traffic movement, the improvement of living conditions of the working classes. Many of Sitte's views are still fresh and lively, so that they may serve as excellent guidance for the solution of problems in construction, town planning, and the organization of public services.

P. A. Mamatov

How influential this Russian translation may have been we do not know: Peets (Bibl. 363) implies that the new Moscow plan of about that time was based on picturesque effects of the Sitte type. Unwin's *Town Planning in Practice* (Bibl. 215) was also translated, suggesting that there was considerable interest in the City-Building tradition of planning in Russia.

The version of Sitte's book that deserves our most careful attention is the French, since it was largely through this translation that his ideas were propagated outside of Germany. During the period of greatest interest in Sitte's theories among city planners and architects, most non-German-speaking people had recourse to the French editions, which appear to have been printed in large quantities. Sad to say, the French edition is a completely different book, not only poorly translated, but actually enunciating ideas that are diametrically opposed to Sitte's principles. Nothing has done more to confuse the name of Sitte with the short-sighted picturesque techniques of his followers. In fact, considering the universal distribution of the French edition, a more heinous literary crime could hardly be perpetrated against an author by his translator.

This circumstance is the more remarkable because the translator, Camille Martin, was a member of the master's closest following; he and the illustrators of his volume were city planners and architects in their own right; two of them (Martin and Puetzer) collaborated in the founding of Sitte's periodical.[83] Although the misunderstandings to which Martin's translation gave rise are legion, the major damage can be summed up under three headings.

First, Camille Martin put the strong feelings, the colorful expressions, the many asides, and the complex Germanic phrases of reservation in Sitte's book through what can only be called a Gallic filter, and out came a handbook of logical principles, nicely ordered into a coherent series of chapters. What had been the conversational reveries of an informed traveller with sensitive taste and perfect recall, became exactly that sort of logically-coordinated treatise which Martin promised in his preface it would not be. This process began on the title page where the name of the book, *Der Städtebau*, was rendered as '*The Art of Building Cities*; Notes and Reflections of an Architect.' To the French public this immediately identified Sitte's little volume of essays with the familiar lineage of French handbooks that had been published on architectural subjects throughout the nineteenth century, all of them entitled The Art of Building This-or-That, Here-or-There; Choisy's publications are outstanding examples of the scholarly how-to-do-it series with which Sitte thus became associated. It is by this title that Sitte's book is known to English readers.

The matter of titling and simplification of ideas was by itself an innocent means of selling the book to the French audience. Actually, Sitte, when shown the new French edition, was impressed. He shook his head sadly and remarked, 'My book reads, I regret to say, better in the French than in the German'

(Bibl. 155, p. 126). What he did not notice, and what a reader of only the French edition does not realize, is that in order to make the book more palatable to the international audience, Martin had wherever possible cut out German examples and discussions of Vienna and had substituted 'more familiar' French or Belgian ones. He had not only suppressed the examples of 'too local an interest' as he promised in his preface, but had actually made Sitte's book, which on its original title-page claimed special reference to Vienna, into a vehicle for perpetuating the primacy of Paris (for good or bad) as the focus of city building in the nineteenth century. This is our second indictment of Martin. It is clear that the transformation of Vienna, although a much less familiar story on the whole, is of an importance to us today matching that of Paris, if only because it produced Sitte. Martin could not root out all that pertained to Vienna, of course, because the book was built around it. A later French authority, Pierre Lavedan, could do this, however. In his monumental *Histoire de l'urbanisme* (3 vols., 1926–1952), the greater part of volume III on the modern period is given over to Paris and France; there is precisely one paragraph (in 446 pages) on Vienna—which is brushed off as not being based on Paris, but on Louis XIV!

An amusing and more understandable aspect of this Gallicizing of Sitte's book occurs in the second French edition of 1918. As this was published at the end of the war and Martin hoped that its principles would assist in the reconstruction of devastated areas, he carefully removed all traces of Sitte's Germanic origin, such as the word Vienna at the signature of the Author's preface. Both Adshead and Peets (Bibl. 152, 363) say that Sitte's ideas were followed in rebuilding the destroyed towns of France; although we have been unable to find any evidence that they became official policy.

Third, and by no means least of Martin's crimes was his misrepresentation of Sitte's intent by playing up the medieval all through the book and suppressing Sitte's interest in the Baroque. Martin was himself a medievalist; with one exception his major publications were textbooks or monographs on medieval architecture. As a writer he showed himself to be of exactly that picturesquely-medieval faction of Sitte followers who were to bring down so much opprobrium on their master. His Chapter VII on streets, a complete fabrication which he added to the French edition, is a good instance of this, as we have explained in Note 196. Martin even attempted to correct Sitte. For example, on Sitte's page 4 where he said that we would study monuments of the Renaissance and Baroque periods, Martin changed it to read 'the Middle Ages and the Renaissance.' Another interesting 'correction' of this sort was Martin's use of Rohault de Fleury's plans of Italian towns to augment Sitte's. Rohault de Fleury's interest seems to have been to re-enact medieval life as it once was: his drawings of buildings include people in period costume, and a number of his town plans were 'reconstructions' to the 12th or 13th centuries. Such was the case with his plan for Lucca which Martin drew on to make graphic an unillustrated point in Sitte's discussion of related squares. (See *Sitte*, Fig. 42, and Note 192.)

As we know, Sitte was not exclusively interested in how towns appeared during the Middle Ages. His interests were more catholic, since he was seeking to demonstrate that up to a certain critical point in the nineteenth century towns and cities had grown organically, alluvially, through the sustained effort of centuries of administrators and builders. Thus plans taken from contemporary Baedeker guidebooks were of more use to him than were antique prints or accurate reconstructions of the towns of earlier days. Lucca is a good case in point. Its cluster of squares is an admirable illustration of Sitte's thesis about plaza groupings, but the major square mentioned by Sitte, the Piazza Grande, had been designed under the rule of Napoleon's sister, and so could not possibly be found in the twelfth-century plan on which Martin drew to illustrate the point! To read Sitte with medievally-tinted glasses is to miss the lessons that he was trying to teach his contemporaries about their own day.

The other side of this medievalism of Martin is the fact that he seems to have disliked the Baroque, not only the style, but even the word (apparently a common French prejudice of the day). It is amusing to note that the word 'Baroque' was *completely* expurgated from the French editions of Sitte. Martin ignored it, substituted something medieval for it, or said '18th century'—often implying French 18th century, which is not usually what Sitte had in mind. To read Sitte in French is like travelling through Europe with an old *Guide Bleu* in hand; the Baroque does not exist or is simply the degenerate excrescence that crops out on top of a medieval façade!

In addition to these liberties that Martin took with Sitte's basic ideas, he made innumerable other changes in the book which we have tried to indicate in our critical notes as they occur. The visual material was radically changed. The old prints that the German editions were still using were replaced by line drawings made by the group of Sitte followers whom we mentioned above. (Those that are of views not included in the German edition we have added to our translation.) Many German plans were omitted or were modified (frequently after Stübben), and many new plans were added; we have included the additional French plans and any changed ones that represent an improvement. The adding of illustrations to any text enriches it, but modifications made to the text itself can become a bit sinister; not only was Sitte's phraseology often changed so that the idea comes out the opposite in French, but large sections of his later chapters were so juggled about that resemblance to the original book is slight. However, before going into these modifications, which are so intricate that they must be explained in table form, it might be interesting to read how Martin explained these and other matters in his prefaces:

TRANSLATOR'S PREFACE TO THE FIRST FRENCH EDITION

The present work, of which the first German edition appeared in Vienna in 1889 (second edition the same year, third edition 1901), has inaugurated a new era in the art of building cities. The principles set forth by its author have since been applied on many occasions, and in this way their practical value has been clearly demonstrated. It has, therefore, seemed useful to us to offer a translation of the book to the French public. This is certainly not the sort of manual that discourages non-professionals, although to the technician it will perhaps seem to lack precision, and the scholar will no doubt find more than one error of detail. Indeed, M. Sitte drew up these notes hastily, at the request of friends who wished to see propagated the ideas expressed in his talks and lectures. It is not our intention to take away the spontaneity and zest to be found in his reflections by coordinating them logically and thereby making such a suggestive study into a complete but arid treatise. We have permitted ourselves the suppression of only those examples that are of too local an interest, replacing them with plans of towns that are more generally known. Chapter VII, dealing with streets, did not exist in the German edition. Chapter XII has been augmented with some examples of modern city planning, designed according to the rules stipulated in this work; their authors have permitted us to publish them. The appendix is a resumé of an article by M. Sitte which appeared in the periodical *Der Lotse* under the title, 'Grossstadt-Grün.' The plans illustrated here have been for the most part improved with the aid of publications by Stübben and Rohault or by means of official town plans.[84] The views have been drawn especially for this French translation and will certainly increase its value. May their authors, as well as all others who have assisted us with their advice, accept here this expression of our gratitude.

Geneva, October 1902 C.M.

It should be noted here that there was no French edition of 1912. The reference to it in the following preface was a typographical error that has precipitated mistaken entries in a number of important bibliographies, including Lavedan's *L'Histoire de l'urbanisme* and Hegemann & Peets' *Civic Art.* Martin's preface to the second French edition of 1918 follows:

TRANSLATOR'S PREFACE TO THE SECOND FRENCH EDITION

When we published in 1912 [no, 1902] the first French edition of this work, the Latin countries were still not granting proper attention to the eminently social art of city planning. Since that time France, rich as it is in great urban ensembles, has awakened from its indifference, and today, under pressure of contemporary events, the architects, artists, and city officials are trying to revive the long-neglected art of building cities. In the course of the last few years a number of publications have clarified the different phases of this problem that is each day of greater preoccupation to those municipal administrations that are concerned about the future of the cities entrusted to their care.

Although the present work was drawn up before this revival in city planning, it has been, in a certain way, the starting point for the revival, and it retains even today all its value and current interest. It is not a systematic and complete treatise intended only for professionals. Nor is it an arid manual and précis for the use of technicians. It is a book written with much warmth and enthusiasm, from which those everywhere who work for the coming of a better city can gather instruction and suggestions.

L'art de bâtir les villes is the vigorous defense by an idealist of a cause that had too long been reduced to the level of purely material problems.

All our cities can be proud of their transportation networks, their sewage systems, their means of communication, their electric installations and all the practical improvements that modern science has brought to the conditions of communal living, yet they cannot lay claim, in the great majority of cases, to any dignity on the part of their works of art. They resemble a body that is more or less well organized, but is devoid of a soul.

In analyzing the structure of ancient and modern cities and in studying the way in which they came about, Sitte has revived those principles which must guide the builders of cities in all times. On the dawn of a day when so many destroyed homes must be reconstructed, it is important to listen to the voice of those who wish to give to the modern city, in addition to the comfort to which we have become accustomed, the stamp of beauty, of order and of harmony.

Geneva, January 1918 C.M.

The differences between Martin's book and what Sitte really said are so great that it is difficult to consider them under Martin's rubric of 'translated and completed' which appears on his title page. Our own translation follows Sitte except for Chapter VIIA; wide divergencies or omissions in the French editions are indicated in our critical notes. Other sizeable French insertions are translated and printed in the critical notes, along with any new illustrations that Martin employed with his insertions. Where Martin added illustrations directly to Sitte's text we have printed them there with a note of explanation. When we know the source we have indicated where Martin (and Sitte) obtained an illustration. As the reshuffling of the later chapters is so great—Martin must have used scissors and paste—we supply here a table of concordance that indicates the way in which the French text was composed from the German. We have used the page numbers of the second French edition of 1918 and of the fourth German of 1909 as being the most comparable and easily obtainable editions.

2nd French edition (1918)		*4th German edition (1909)*	
page 1	Half-title		
2	(blank)		
3	Title page	page I	Title page
4	(blank)	II	Copyright
5–6	Martin 1918 preface	III–IV	German prefaces of 1–4 edits.
7–8	Sitte 1889 preface (1st ed)	VII	Table of Contents
		VIII	(blank)
9–17	Introduction	1–12	Introduction
19–28	Chapter I	13–23	Chapter I
29–40	,, II	24–37	,, II
41–47	,, III	38–47	,, III
49–57	,, IV	48–57	,, IV
59–66	,, V	58–64	,, V
67–73	,, VI	65–71	,, VI
75–85	French Chapter VII (our Chap. VIIA)		(This is not in German editions)
87–109	French Chapter VIII	72–91	of German Chapter VII (our Chap. VIIB)
109–110	,, ,, ,,	126–128	of German Chapter XI
110–112	,, ,, ,,		(This is not in German editions)
112–116	,, ,, ,,	128–132	of German Chapter XI
116–118	,, ,, ,,	125–126	,, ,, ,, ,,
119–120	French Chapter IX	92	of German Chapter VIII
120	,, ,, ,,	94	,, ,, ,, ,,
120–121	,, ,, ,,	93–94	,, ,, ,, ,,
121–132	,, ,, ,,	101–110	of German Chapter IX
132–133	,, ,, ,,	94–96	of German Chapter VIII
133–137	,, ,, ,,	97–100	,, ,, ,, ,,
137–138	,, ,, ,,	114–115	of German Chapter IX
139–143	French Chapter X	116–120	of German Chapter X
143–146	,, ,, ,,	122–124	,, ,, ,, ,,
147	French Chapter XI	125	of German Chapter XI
147–170	,, ,, ,,	134–158	,, ,, ,, ,,
171	French Chapter XII	159	of German Chapter XII
171–179	,, ,, ,,	160–180	,, ,, ,, ,,

(French 1st edition has 6 pages here that do not appear in 2nd French or any other editions)

(Not in French editions)		181–186	German Conclusion
181	French Appendix	187–193!	of German Appendix
181–183	,, ,,	111–112	of German Chapter IX (!)
183–185	,, ,,	193–204	of German Appendix
185–186	,, ,,	112–113	of German Chapter IX
186–188	,, ,,	207–211	of German Appendix
189–192	Indices	213–216	Indices

Some lesser insertions and deletions not indicated in this table will be found described in the critical notes to the text. The rather considerable condensations in the French edition can be detected by comparing the span of page numbers in our table. The only difference of any substance between the French editions of 1902 and 1918 lies in the six extra pages of the earlier edition that describe some town plans by Sitte followers (see table and Note 286); presumably these were omitted in 1918 because they were all in Germany.

All of this has led to a number of comical errors and misunderstandings about Sitte. Very few writers seem to have realized that the French and German editions are actually different books. Elbert Peets is one who has noted this, but even he and Werner Hegemann got tangled up in their *Civic Art.* The confusion in the illustrations between the two versions is such that in *Civic Art* they inadvertently printed both Sitte's plan for Regensburg and Martin's plan for Ratisbonne, the same town. (See Note 208.) Lavedan used only one picture in his discussion of Sitte's principles, our Fig. 9 of Notre Dame in Paris, which is part of a long passage that Martin had inserted; Lavedan actually employed this plan in both his medieval and modern volumes. Many of those who later discussed Sitte, favorably or unfavorably, did so in terms of Martin's chapter about Streets, which was not even based on Sitte, having been drawn from Stübben and from the arguments during the 1890's about straight-or-crooked streets. An example of this is the important critique by Adshead in 1930 (Bibl. 152) in which considerable passages (pp. 90–91) are quoted from the apocryphal chapter.

It is remarkable that the differences were not commented upon when the French edition first appeared. One would expect any reviewer at least to spot-check a translation against its original, and the most cursory glance would have revealed these startling transformations. The three reviews that we list (Bibl. 10–12) are spirited and enthusiastic summaries, but offer little critical comment; it is clear that the French were not yet prepared professionally for the richness of Sitte's analysis, even though they had been previously exposed to Buls' writings. The Clerc 'review' was actually a public lecture to a Marseilles civic-improvement society, for which both Sitte and Martin appear to have provided illustrative material.[85]

It was originally expected that an English translation—by George E. Hooker of Chicago—would appear shortly after the French one. Hooker, a man deeply involved in municipal reform, was named on the masthead of *Der Städtebau* and seems to have formed part of Sitte's circle.[86] His translation never appeared. The project was revived in the 1920's when it was thought that Nils Hammarstrand, a historian of city planning, would carry out the task; this also fell through.[87] It has been reported that a translation was under way in England in 1945, but was abandoned (Bibl. 154). Considering the eagerness of the architectural and planning professions to secure a complete version of Sitte in English and the willingness of his heirs to comply, it is surprising that the work was not translated into that language until nearly 60 years had passed. This might be taken as testimony to the fact that the little book, albeit disarmingly simple in appearance and supplied with plentiful explanatory illustrations is, nevertheless, a hard nut to crack. Although easy enough to read, Sitte's mellifluous prose is difficult to render into English, and it is full of allusions to things literary and scientific that are remote to us today.

Consequently, we are not surprised to find that when Sitte was finally published in English in 1945 (Bibl. 21) the American translator relied wherever practical on the French edition rather than on the original German. Although it was sharply criticized when it appeared for its faults in translation, it should be recognized that many of the deviations represent liberties that Martin had already taken with the German text forty years earlier. The American translation follows the French text closely, with the latter's numerous omissions and insertions, up through German Chapter VII (our VIIB). After this point French and German texts deviate markedly, so the translator worked more directly from the German. The illustrations are, consequently, a mixture of the French and German ones. Martin's tendency to cut out Germanic examples and to substitute 'Middle Ages' for 'Baroque' carries over into the American translation, at least in the earlier part of the book. The French chapter on streets and the Appendix are omitted. The prefaces to the first four German editions are printed at the end. The volume also included the following essays:

Eliel Saarinen, 'A Note on Camillo Sitte', on pp. iii–iv;

Ralph Walker, 'Introduction to the English Translation,' on pp. vii–ix;

Arthur C. Holden, 'Present Significance of Sitte's Artistic Fundamentals,' on pp. 114–120.

The translator's preface to the American edition reads as follows:

TRANSLATOR'S PREFACE TO THE FIRST AMERICAN EDITION

A literal, if cumbersome, translation of the title of this book would be 'City Building According to its Artistic Fundamentals.' It was written by Camillo Sitte, a Viennese architect, and first appeared in 1889 to burst like a demolition bomb on the city planning practices of Europe. Its attack upon monotony and dreariness in city arrangement precipitated a revolt against unimaginative formality which Mr. Eliel Saarinen regards as the 'informal revival' in city planning—the effort to restore fundamental but forgotten principles in civic design.

Sitte's work has been translated into French and Spanish. Although it has not previously appeared in English, it has exercised a persistent, although necessarily a diminished, influence in English speaking countries. It is presented, even half a century late, to American readers because it has much that is timely to say to us in a day that is marked for the structural rebirth of our cities. Sitte's mighty scorn for the uninspiring practices of his day retains its cauterizing sting for ours. While some of his specific suggestions may need reappraisal in the light of new elements in urban living that have been introduced since he lived and wrote, the essentials of his book, the 'artistic fundamentals,' have not been invalidated by the passage of time.

Rebuilding of cities has become a vital subject in America. It has a prominent and urgent place on our post-war agenda. Preparations being made for it are largely legalistic and financial. When the decks have been cleared of these fiscal preliminaries, we shall be face to face with the practical problem of rebuilding our cities in good taste as well as for efficiency and economy. We shall then find *The Art of Building Cities* as timely as the morning paper.

. . .

Washington, D.C. Charles T. Stewart
September 17, 1944

Of the numerous reviews that greeted the appearance of an English edition of Sitte, two are noteworthy: those by Rudolf Wittkower and by Nikolaus Pevsner (Bibl. 22, 32). Most of the commentators addressed themselves simply to the question of whether Sitte was relevant to the 1940's. These two, however, after brief, cogent statements about Sitte's place in the firmament of city planners, dealt with the translation as such. Wittkower's lengthy indictment of the book on this score has led, indirectly, to the present translation.

Meanwhile, in 1953 there appeared quietly in Milan, on the 50th anniversary of the death of Sitte, the first Italian translation of his book (Bibl. 35). It was carried out by a writer on city planning, Luigi Dodi, who carefully adhered to the original intentions of the author. Chapter divisions and plans are identical with Sitte's, and the city views are very much the same. The volume contains the first of Sitte's Prefaces and his Appendix on Greenery. Sitte's Conclusion is omitted, the Appendix is cut to about one third its original length, and a considerable amount of the discussion about local Viennese problems is left out. In his only comment on the text, Dodi suggests rather apologetically that Sitte's scheme for the Ringstrasse did not take into account the exigencies of modern traffic and that it is of importance only as a general example of harmonious urban effect. The translator added a preface which gave, briefly, an account of the life of Sitte, the circumstances under which his book appeared, and a homage to his memory. Although a handy and useful translation of the original German text, the volume appears to have attracted little attention in professional circles. Sitte's writing was in this instance presented more as a historical document than as a message with current implications.

Likewise the reviewers of the 1945 edition in English had

acted as though Sitte was a somewhat alien figure of another era, from whom the English-speaking world had been too long cut off by reason of language. It has not generally been realized how imperceptibly and thoroughly Sitte's ideas, however twisted, have by a process of osmosis become an integral part of modern city-planning theory. The manner in which his teachings took root in Germany and then spread abroad in the twentieth century is the next subject to which we shall turn.

8

SITTE'S IMPACT ON GERMAN CITY PLANNING

A REMARKABLE thing about the influence of Sitte's book on the building of cities is the rapidity with which it took hold in Germany and Austria.[88] A reviewer in Leipzig, who did not get around to his task for a year, found himself in the unusual situation that, instead of being called on to describe the contents of the volume to the public and explaining its importance, he was faced with writing a history of the events that the book had already precipitated and trying to explain them to his readers (Bibl. 5). He pointed out that many municipalities had completely redrawn their plans for new city sections on the basis of Sitte's theories; Ludwigshafen and Altona were cases in point. That Henrici had already won a prize with a plan for Dessau based on Sitte's principles (see Note 295 and Pl. XV–a). That officials of Olmütz, Brünn, and Linz had approached Sitte for advice. The reviewer attributed this largely to the enthusiasm with which Sitte wrote and the ingenious simplicity of his presentation. By 1891 Sitte was illustrating his lectures with reproductions of current plans such as Altona and Dessau (e.g., Bibl. 57, p. 29). When the first edition of Stübben's *Handbuch* came out in 1890, we find that not only did the author enthusiastically describe and illustrate Sitte's plan for the setting of the Votive Church, and use a dozen of Sitte's plans of old squares, but Sitte's theories had worked their way into the very fabric of the book; within a year, Stübben, who had recognized at once the epoch-making character of Sitte's ideas, treated them as established elements of planning, incorporating many—with acknowledgment—and debating the merits of others.

More important plans were actually made by followers than by Sitte himself. Chief among these in the decade of the 1890's were Karl Henrici (1842–1922), a contemporary of Sitte, and Theodor Fischer (1862–1938), a member of the younger generation. As both of these men were, in turn, distinguished teachers, they did much to propagate Sitte's ideas among succeeding generations of German architects and planners. Henrici, already an architect in his own right—he was a professor of architecture in Aachen for many years—was turned into a city planner by the reading of Sitte's book. He became one of Sitte's most vocal exponents, though later he was much criticized for having over-emphasized the romantic, picturesque, and medieval aspects which were characteristic of the Sittesque school. He won numerous prizes for his city-extension projects, foremost among them being that for Dessau (1890), which we have already mentioned, and that for Munich (1893), on the jury for which both Sitte and Baumeister had served.[89]

Munich occupies a very special place in this story, since the extension of that city was from 1893 on under the supervision of Theodor Fischer, details of whose work were often illustrated: e.g., by Martin in the first French edition (Note 295 and Pl. XV–b) and also by Stübben. Fischer served as a bridge between Sitte and the progressive architects of the twentieth century. As a dominant intellectual force at the *Technische Hochschulen* of Stuttgart and Munich, he was the teacher or mentor of as heterogeneous a group of architects as J. J. P. Oud, Walter Gropius, Paul Bonatz, and Bruno Taut. He took an active part in the formation of the *Deutsche Werkbund* and in the designing of its 1914 exhibition at Cologne. Fischer held unqualified admiration for Sitte, whom he considered to be 'the father of modern city planning.' The article which he wrote at the time of Sitte's death (Bibl. 297) and a later lecture which was translated into English (Bibl. 298) are stirring testimony to Sitte's position in the profession.[90]

Following the publication of Sitte's book, German city planning can be divided into several tendencies. There remained a number of individuals who were so involved with pressing problems such as traffic and rapid transit, housing conditions, legal technicalities, and statistical surveys, that Sitte meant nothing to them. Rudolf Eberstadt is an example of such a city planner. Our interest lies rather with the aesthetic-architectonic faction, which was assuming an important role in all modern countries during the 1890's, but especially in Germany and

Austria. From 1889 until well into the twentieth century, Sitte's became the dominant manner of laying out city expansions by those in the German orbit who took architectural considerations into account, and who in turn, divided into two groups: Sitte's followers and his critics. Those who, like Otto Wagner, worked within the architectural tradition but were unaffected by Sitte seem to be rare. Moreover, an interesting fact is that, just as this crisis in city planning (or beginning of city planning, as some would have it) was precipitated by an art historian—Sitte—writing what was essentially an art-theoretical treatise, we find that any discussion of his subsequent influence must be undertaken without differentiating between practitioners like Stübben and historians of the art such as A. E. Brinckmann.

Of Sitte followers we have already mentioned Henrici and Fischer. The most doggedly faithful of all was, however, Theodor Goecke, who collaborated with Sitte in the founding of the periodical *Der Städtebau*. Goecke, a planner, seems to have been a rather dry and prosaic person in comparison with Sitte. His writings are technical and reportorial except when, piqued, he answered an attack on his colleague by such a clever critic as Brinckmann; then he waxed eloquent and, as in his review of the 1909 edition, showed that he grasped better than anyone the essence of Sitte's teaching.[91] Then there were a number of planners who, like Henrici, can be designated as the 'Sittesque school' or as exponents of the '*Sittesche Stil*'. It is not always easy to distinguish those who were really trying to adhere to Sitte's principles from those who were simply caught up in the fad for picturesque eccentricities that marked the 1890's. German planning of the day was nearly always informal (Otto Wagner, a decided exception) even when designed by Sitte's opponents; later writers referred to this as the 'romantic period' of city planning. Characteristic examples of the work of the Sittesque school will be found in our Note 295, analyzed by Camille Martin, or in Raymond Unwin's *Town Planning in Practice* (1909, pp. 99–110) where they are also carefully explained. Some names that might be mentioned as followers of Sitte are Eugen Fassbender, Felix Genzmer, Karl Hocheder, Hermann Jansen, Otto Lasne, and Friedrich

Puetzer.[92] If we were to check on the centers of activity of the leading Sitte exponents, we would find that by about 1905 Berlin, Munich, Stuttgart, Aachen, Danzig, Darmstadt, Dresden, Vienna, and Karlsruhe, among other major cities, had such persons either as their official architect or as professor at their Technische Hochschule.

Finally there were those who were active primarily as writers—either architectural historians or city-planning reporters. The writings of some of these individuals carried so much weight that they have actually done more to shape our later image of Sitte than have his own book and the city plans by his followers. One notices a number of things about the impact of Sitte on studies of the city and city-history. To begin with, the substance of the first half of his book, in which he discussed the morphology of the older city, seemed, when he said it, to be so patently clear, so obvious, that it became accepted as historic fact except for a few details on which later research proved that he had over-generalized in his enthusiasm. By about 1910 the published lectures of the important Berlin city-planning seminar—in particular those of his follower Felix Genzmer—are quite Sittesque in thought, yet often give no acknowledgement to him; this means that either the audience realized it was Sitte without its being footnoted, or Sitte's ideas were public domain and even scholars did not bother to credit them. Especially in this seminar and in the first years of the magazine *Der Städtebau* there appeared particularized studies based on or extending Sitte. A good example of this is the analysis of the town of Buttstedt which Unwin picked up from the magazine to read first as a paper before the R.I.B.A. and to use later in his book (Bibl. 215, pp. 215ff.). All such authors and lecturers might be considered, in a certain sense, to be followers of Sitte. There are two of these *literati* who merit special attention.

The first of these, and the elder, is Cornelius Gurlitt (1850–1938), a well-known German art historian who was almost a contemporary of Sitte. Of his large bibliography, we list those of his writings that bear directly on city planning. (See Bibl. 313–319.) Gurlitt not only edited an important city-planning periodical, *Die Stadtbaukunst*, for a number of years following World War I, but he also had taken a fling at planning itself; a project of his near Dresden is illustrated by Unwin (Bibl. 215, p. 109). In his early years Gurlitt had been a devoted Sitte follower, and an admiration for Sitte's innovations and activities lies at the root of his writings. His little book on architecture of 1904 (Bibl. 316), a jewel of Jugendstil graphic design, illustrated Sittesque points pictorially by comparing 'good' and 'bad' photographs of cities, much as Unwin was to do later in his book. Gurlitt was one of those remarkable art historians who, by keeping abreast of contemporary creative movements, could relate his own studies of historical problems to the pressing issues of his day. Already by 1903 one finds a new theoretical point of view expressed in his writings, which is characteristically modern (Bibl. 314); he insists that between art and technics there is no antagonism; only the useful can be beautiful, and only the beautiful can be useful (Otto Wagner's adage reading backwards and forwards). The city plan—an architectural matter—develops out of the problem itself, he insists (cf. *Sitte,* p. 148). This was prophetic enough that Gurlitt had only to amplify it to handbook-size in 1920 in order to produce a teaching manual for the post-war decade (Bibl. 317). This manual is a learned and stimulating demonstration of the ability we have ascribed to him, as was the new periodical he founded that year (Bibl. 483). Although the title of the latter, translated 'City-Building Art,' would at first glance label it as a purely Sittesque conception, it was not quite so. In its first issue Gurlitt pointed out that the most promising result of the exciting architectural developments of the last years of the German Empire had been the art of building cities.[93] He was hoping to continue with that tradition, banking on the spirit of enthusiastic reconstruction that followed the 1918 debacle. He wanted this new magazine to be more art-historical, more modern, and more international than *Der Städtebau.* That it was very avant-garde is evidenced by the fact that he endured the antics of Bruno Taut and his friends for fourteen issues in their 'Frühlicht' supplement before throwing them out of his magazine.[94]

The other author of significance was A. E. Brinckmann (1881–1958). Brinckmann, almost as prolific a writer on art history as Gurlitt, professed to have been a Sitte follower in his youth, and had actually designed town extensions. He published a series of articles and books which superseded Sitte in a sense, and he eclipsed Sitte considerably by virtue of his sharp criticism of the latter's theory and methods. The books in question, which apparently had a much greater circulation among the general public than any of Sitte's early editions, were respectively: Bibl. 267 on plazas and monuments, 1908; Bibl. 273 on old German planning, 1911; reprint of No. 267 on plazas and monuments in 1912; Bibl. 276 on city-building art past and present, 1920; revision of No. 273 in 1921; reprint of No. 276 in 1922; and revision of No. 267 in 1923. Brinckmann levelled the following criticisms at Sitte, which were then frequently repeated by later writers: That Sitte, the 'Romantic of City Planning', had been much overrated. That Sitte was primarily concerned with the medieval city, of which he had made only a partial examination. That Sitte as well as his followers had laid upon planning the curse of contrived irregularities. (Brinckmann reproduced and ridiculed the *Stadtbild* renderings with which Henrici had illustrated his Munich project.) That Sitte thought in terms of theatrical two-dimensional images, not in terms of a spatial art. That in the matter of planted squares Sitte did not take sufficient account of their physiological merits.

The reaction of Sitte's most objective admirers—Goecke and Werner Hegemann—was immediate and bitter. Why, they asked, should such excellent publications as Brinckmann's be made the vehicle for unjust attacks on Sitte? They then proceeded to demonstrate that Sitte was an innovator of truly spatial planning, that he was a Baroque enthusiast, and that his own layouts were often quite regular in character. Brinckmann's comment about planted squares seems strange to anyone who has read Sitte. It is interesting, moreover, to examine Brinckmann's writings. Stimulated perhaps by Sitte's observations, there had been an increasing number of studies made of the architectural form of older towns and cities. Brinckmann's are acknowledged to have been among the most significant and systematic of these.[95] In particular he continued Sitte's tendency to analyze abstractly in terms of space and rhythm.

Platz und Monument, which is dedicated to Heinrich Wölfflin, is to a large extent an application of the latter's precepts to plaza design—an elaboration of Sitte's own analyses according to a new approach. Brinckmann's work on old German planning, under cover of a sharp denunciation of Sitte, is essentially a Sittesque analysis, spruced up with later research and twentieth-century terminology. The book on the city-building art of past and present is more of the same—a series of essays including one, entitled 'Der Optische Maassstab,' which is an elaboration of Maertens' system. Brinckmann, a writer of brilliance and of great academic prestige, inflicted on Sitte's memory as mischievous a crime as Camille Martin had. He built a twentieth-century superstructure upon Sitte's ideas and then, instead of the customary acknowledgement, made out the man whose teachings he had preempted to be an antiquated fool. He even used an opening gambit similar to Sitte's about travel impressions in his introduction to the book on old German planning of 1911.

The significance of two further members of Gurlitt's generation, Werner Hegemann and Bruno Taut, will be discussed below in other connections. There remains, however, to chronicle the interrelationships between Stübben and Sitte and his followers.

Stübben and Sitte had greeted each other's books with enthusiasm (Bibl. 4, 57). Sitte declared that Stübben's *Handbuch* formed the basis for a good comprehension of the history and problems of city planning, and that there was now no excuse for errors. In addition to their differences over traffic (see pp. 17–18), traffic intersections (see Note 234), and central placement of monuments (see Note 154), which we have discussed already, Stübben's *Handbuch* differed from Sitte on several points. Stübben did not believe that the irregularities of the medieval city had been an artistic intention, and he criticized those who imitated them. He also claimed that Sitte's disapproval of isolated buildings was not substantiated by the actual history of old towns. However, he praised Sitte's invention of the 'turbine-plaza' and his ideas about the proportions of deep and broad squares. Stübben's discussion of 'Architectural Squares' was derived largely from Sitte, and they came to agreement on the need for variation in street frontage lines, for sequences of plazas, etc. In his second edition of 1907 Stübben commended Sitte heartily both in his passage on public squares (p. 203) and in his conclusion; he used four illustrations of town extensions that had been planned by Sitte.

Relations between Stübben and the self-appointed followers of Sitte were not cordial. In 1891 Henrici, who had just won the Dessau competition with what everyone took for a Sitte-type plan, reviewed Stübben's *Handbuch* in the magazine of the Berlin *Verein.*[96] His major criticism of the book was that while it summed up current practice it only pointed to the future where Stübben had relied on Sitte: that Stübben's chapter on the art of public squares (Part II, Chap. 9, in 1890 edit.) did not fit in with the rest of the book, being based so much on Sitte. Henrici then proceeded to lay down some rules about street design, which Sitte had neglected in his concentration on the matter of plazas. Stübben replied heatedly, referring to his earlier writings on the aesthetics of streets and plazas, questioning whether the picturesque beauties of old towns had come about by design or by accident, and attacking Sitte's way of treating traffic intersections (as we have described in Note 234). Henrici replied in turn and then Stübben again, the former always pleading the virtues of individual creativity in planning and Stübben forever reminding him of the practical restrictions. Then in 1893, after Henrici had won the Munich competition, the argument broke out again in the same magazine.[97] Sitte did not intervene, and it was becoming clear that a faction somewhat independent of him had arisen—the Sittesque school—whose basic preoccupation was with whether streets should be straight or curved (see above p. 22 and Note 22). Henrici's Dessau plan had many formal aspects (as we might expect from Sitte himself), whereas the Munich layout was a net of almost exclusively curved and wriggly streets. The later project had also been accompanied by a quantity of renderings of picturesque views of its streets and plazas—a device that was to become standard with the school in its effort to follow Sitte's stricture about three-dimensional conceptualization of the building plan (*Bebauungsplan*).[98]

Their 1893 exchange had opened on the subject of boring (straight) vs. lively (curved) streets, and a fitting conclusion to the two years of locked struggle between Stübben and Henrici over this essentially Jugendstil doctrinal matter was provided by the words of the Munich artist Adolf Oberländer on viewing Henrici's Munich project:

> 'The whole empty, bare, vacuous spirit of our modern world is expressed in the endless, geometrically straight street. The curved line is the line of Life. It awakens the imagination. The straight one is that of Death. It causes stagnation of the mental processes. This is not merely a painter's whim, holding no interest for the layman; it is a basic human feeling that calls our attention to the qualities of a variegated line . . .' (Bibl. 340).

In general Stübben always held that although much of Sitte's planning was based on practical adjustments to irregular terrain, odd boundary lines, and existing roads, his followers had carried the picturesque too far, forcing it. This attitude characterized his final dispute with Sitte over boundary lines, which we have discussed above (p. 23). In his obituary notice about Sitte (Bibl. 406) he was a bit cool and suggested that Sitte had had primarily a literary importance; he may still have been smarting from the criticism that Sitte had heaped on his winning Vienna plan, accusing him of plagiarizing Henrici's ideas for Munich, etc. (Bibl. 73). Sitte's plea for artistry and individuality in planning was largely lost on Stübben who always considered Sitte's interests to be only one ingredient in the large body of practical matters with which the German science (*Wissenschaft*) of city planning was concerned. This attitude of Stübben conditioned in part the way in which Sitte was received abroad, as we shall see.

9

THE INFLUENCE OF SITTE AND GERMAN PLANNING ABROAD

In discussing the influence of Sitte and the German city-planning movement on other countries, there are several points that should be kept in mind. First of all, German city planning, when other nations became aware of it, came as a package, as a whole body of municipal matters of which Sitte was only one component. The differences in aesthetic doctrine that had been so hotly disputed within the German profession during the 1890's were relatively meaningless to this foreign audience. Also the entire 'package' was received abroad fairly late, and certain of the arguments had by then resolved themselves.[99] The French had available their own edition of Sitte by 1902, but the English seem to have been unaware of these aesthetic developments in Germany until after Horsfall's report of 1904. The United States awakened to it even later. Although the 1890's were characterized by a revival of interest in civic art in all countries, the non-German areas were mainly acquainted with Buls—in part because of the importance of the first Congress on Public Art that was held in his city in 1898. In any case, the earliest reports about German city planning tended to be published by individuals who were more interested in other aspects of municipal reform than the city as a work of art. We can expect therefore that the influence of Sitte abroad was late and very diffuse.

It is astonishing with what a lag in time and how haphazardly this new German science became known abroad, considering the momentum it had been gathering since Baumeister's pioneering efforts of the 1870's. One hesitates to attribute this entirely to difficulty in idiom. It is rather that Paris was the paradigm of planning for all, not only the French, and other cities of Europe were simply measured up to it. France had isolated itself from German traditions after the events of 1870–1871. In Belgium Buls, after his surprise discovery of Stübben, published him in translation and was probably the one who invited him to speak at the 1898 Congress. But England and the United States are of more concern to us. In both these countries students of municipal reform visited the Continent during the 1890's and made reports that emphasized the technical and administrative excellence of German cities.[100] Horsfall, in particular, caught the attention of the R.I.B.A. and of Unwin, which, in turn, led to the permeation of English planning with German theory by the time of World War I.

In the United States, contacts with the German city-planning movement were earlier and more frequent, but erratic in their results. The fact that our first architectural school, at the University of Illinois, had been founded (1868) under essentially German auspices did not seem to lead to a consistent interest in German studies. In 1891 the *American Architect* printed the translation of a good survey by Semper's son of Austrian nineteenth-century architecture and the Ringstrasse, but it had been written prior to Sitte's book (Note 57). The appearance in 1891 of an American translation of Baumeister's *Cleaning and Sewage of Cities* was a fluke (Bibl. 258). Likewise without repercussions was the paper that Stübben delivered before the engineers at the Columbian Exposition of 1893; a glance at the Table of Contents of their *Transactions* will testify that he could not have been more miscast. This was no Berlin *Verein* of architects and engineers, and to judge from the uninformed comments that Stübben provoked, his audience was not prepared to discuss the artistic implications of building cities. Albert Shaw (Note 100) was a mine of information on municipal affairs in Europe during this same period, but he was not very sensitive to matters of urban aesthetics.

The contradictory state of affairs in the United States is apparent from the periodical *Municipal Affairs* published in New York City by the 'Reform Club' from 1897–1902, years of special interest to us (Bibl. 471). Although short-lived, this was a fine little magazine with outstanding contributors from many walks of life here and in England. However, it had a split personality. Robert C. Brooks (Note 100) provided a bibliographical index for each number, drawing from as many as 60 foreign periodicals, nearly half of them German; the issue of March 1901 (346 pages) was given over entirely to bibliography. The issue of December 1899 had been devoted to 'The City Beautiful,' and for it someone, probably Brooks, provided a translation of Buls' *Aesthetics of Cities* (Bibl. 281) and a translation-summary of Stübben's chapter on 'Municipal Memorials'—a key passage in which the ideas of both Sitte and Maertens are described (Part IV, Chapter 7). Meanwhile the articles on civic art contributed to the number were made up of rather vague, undisciplined sentiment, spiced up with adulatory remarks about the Parisian boulevards, but without the slightest awareness that Buls, Stübben, Baumeister, Sitte, et. al., had by this time evolved an extensive body of organized theory on the subject.

Students of art history may be puzzled why in the period 1880–1910, which was characterized by so phenomenally rapid an international interchange of ideas in the arts of sculpture, painting, architecture, and design that it is hard to determine who was borrower or lender, this new art of city building should experience so faltering a transmission. Perhaps it is that, although the books of both Sitte and Stübben were outstanding for their wealth of illustrations, these were not visual images of the sort that communicate themselves without words, nor, in fact, without intricate argumentation. Yet ideas do not have to be purely visual to emigrate rapidly. In our architectural magazines of the period there were constantly appearing articles translated from all languages on a wide variety of subjects of more conventional interest to the profession—architectural education, vaulting procedures, the use of brick, ornamental theory, etc. —regardless of whether these were rich in pictures or not. An excellent instance of this, and one that bears on our field of interest is the fact that Otto Wagner's essay on Modern Architecture, first published in Vienna in 1896 was made available in English in the American *Brickbuilder* a mere five years later (Bibl. 426, 427). Wagner's meteoric rise to architectural eminence in Europe, coupled with the brevity, clarity, and radicalism of his remarks, had led to his immediate recognition in America. Thus his ideas about planning that chronologically came after Sitte's, actually arrived here first and most likely rendered the eventual reception of Sitte's theories somewhat more difficult.

As an English translation of Sitte was not available until the 1940's, anyone interested abroad had to read it in the original (unlikely), in French (somewhat more likely), or in summary form. Even those who could handle the German language were inclined, in all innocence, to rely on the French translation, with the result that curious misinterpretations cropped up in the literature. As for summaries of Sitte's ideas, it is easy enough to reduce the first part of his book to a series of principles, albeit playing down his Baroque interests somewhat. But more often Sitte was diluted—forming part of a condensation or an extract of Stübben or appearing in a handbook of current practice which was not always able to acknowledge fully his contribution. Unwin's book is a good example of the latter, although he cited Sitte as often as possible. Most of these 'summaries' of Sitte had limited circulation, but it might be worthwhile to enumerate them.

First via Stübben: His *Handbuch* appeared in 1890, 1907 (containing more of Sitte), and again in 1924. The Columbian Exposition paper with its enumeration of his artistic principles for city building was available in three languages by 1895. The gist of his ideas about the history and design of plazas was printed in the *American Architect* of 1894, although with no indication that it was Stübben speaking (Bibl. 382). In 1898 he addressed the Brussels Congress (in French) on the subject of streets and plazas, and the following year, as we have seen, *Municipal Affairs* printed an extract from his *Handbuch.* His participation with Buls and Unwin in the seventh International Congress of Architects at London in 1906 was also significant. Then from 1911 there was on hand for students at Harvard a good translation of almost his entire *Handbuch* in its 1907 edition (Bibl. 380).

More general analyses of the German movement, of strongly Sittesque character, were also prepared. They included the transactions of the aforementioned session on 'Streets and Open Spaces in the City' at the 1906 London Congress. The *Architectural Record* of New York in 1908 printed a translation of Gurlitt's short history of modern German planning (Bibl. 315), and the same translator, Sylvester Baxter, also made available a lecture by Theodor Fischer that focussed on Sitte.[101]

Sitte's essay on Greenery in the City, which most Germans did not see in its original publication, was summarized for their benefit by Henrici the following year in *Deutsche Bauhütte* (Bibl. 343), and was then reprinted in the German editions of Sitte in 1909 and 1922. A garbled version of it appeared in the French editions of 1902 and 1918 (see table, p. 70), and the latter was then printed in English in the first volume of *Park International* (Washington, D.C.) in 1920 (see Note 299).

Regarding the message of Sitte's book itself, transmittal was weak and often muddled. First came the French edition of 1902, summarized in that country by lectures and articles; Harvard students were provided almost immediately with a translation in typescript of the first chapter (only) of the French by a faculty member. The periodical *Der Städtebau* became a very important source from 1904 on, and probably received more attention than the book itself. Horsfall cited Sitte's book in 1904, and the R.I.B.A. was given an excellent summary of the French edition the following year by John W. Simpson. Simpson's report was reprinted in full in the American periodical *House and Garden.*[102] Then came Unwin's and Triggs' books of 1909 and Geddes' accounts of his German tour of that year.[103] The widely-reported Berlin Exposition of 1910 brought Sitte and his followers considerable renown.[104]

Thus it is clear that until the early 1920's a purely English-speaking city planner would have had little clear notion of Camillo Sitte unless he were a faithful member of the R.I.B.A. or had been trained at Harvard's school of architecture and planning. But even then his image of Sitte would probably be a 'Stübbenized' one or a medievalized one. In 1922, however, Hegemann and Peets published their monumental *Civic Art*, and a new era began.

This book presented in sumptuously graphic form the whole spread of city building from antique times to the present. Its opening chapter, 'The Modern Revival of Civic Art,' is a summary of Sitte's book. Accurate and well illustrated, it was the most complete presentation of his ideas in English until the translation of 1945. The remaining chapters deal with plaza and court design, grouping of buildings, architectural street design, garden art, unified city plans, and an essay (by Peets) on the planning of Washington, D.C. With its handsome folio format, 298 pages, 1203 figures in the text, it outdid even Stübben's *Handbuch*; the store of knowledge that went into its assembly was incredible. Its full title: *The American Vitruvius; An Architects' Handbook of Civic Art*, tells us a good deal. It was apparently designed for the school and office of American architects who had been pursuing the rather vaguely defined 'City-Beautiful' concept. Its authors—Hegemann, an architectural historian and planner, and Peets, a landscape architect—were great admirers of American accomplishments in planning, but they could see that the isolation which was symptomatic of the American profession needed the corrective of European travel sketches (Peets), European tradition (Hegemann) and historical perspective (both).[105] Furthermore, the writers explained that their 'American Vitruvius' reflected the character of Colen Campbell's *Vitruvius Britannicus* of 1717; 'Modern civic art,' they wrote, 'can learn most from a study of the achievements of the seventeenth and eighteenth centuries, which in turn were deeply influenced by classic antiquity' (p. 29). This was, of course, a very conservative architectural policy for the year 1922, especially when expressed by two individuals who were so well situated internationally and one of whom was soon to edit a most perceptive magazine about the contemporary architectural scene: *Wasmuths Monatshefte*. The picturesque tendencies of Olmsted and other American planners were strongly criticized in the book, and there is not a single contemporary-looking building included—nothing of Sullivan or Wright among all the American material.[106] However, it is interesting to observe that when Hegemann returned to the United States a decade later and brought the book up to date with supplementary volumes (Bibl. 334), their character was completely different. American architecture and planning, now in step with international movements, had become absorbed with housing and other sociological problems; 'art' as such got short shrift, and there are many illustrations of the bare modernity of the 1920's.

We have noticed that Sitte was open to quite contradictory interpretations by his followers. Hegemann and Peets, between them, focus our attention on an old disagreement: was Sitte primarily a Romantic medievalist or an admirer of the Baroque? Hegemann had always insisted, since his early quarrels with Brinckmann (see p. 81 and Bibl. 321), that Sitte was the latter, and *Civic Art* is clearly an effort to encourage the revival of Renaissance and Baroque principles in America. Peets disagreed with Hegemann, however, as is clear from a guarded statement in the introduction to the volume, and from his 1927 article in the *Town Planning Review* (the only biographical sketch of Sitte ever published in English), wherein he demonstrated by systematic analysis of Sitte's own planning that he was a medievalist in taste. One gets the impression that Peets relied on the French text—which was used for quotations and illustrations in their book—while Hegemann worked from his early memories of the original German. Actually Peets' attitude mellowed with time, and his latest critique of Sitte takes a middle position in the controversy:

> 'Most of the differences of opinion about Sitte, however, have been differences of interpretation. The reason for this doubtless lies in the broad scope of Sitte's appreciation. His worship of art was non-sectarian; he had no professional vested interest in any planning style. Very diverse types of design aroused his superlatives and different people linger over different pages.' (Bibl. 365, pp. 5–6.)

The last important summary of Sitte before the American edition of 1945, was that of Eliel Saarinen (1873–1950). Saarinen was a Sitte follower in the most fundamental sense. He searched behind Sitte's statements and 'rules' for his underlying philosophy, disregarding the storms that raged over matters of detailed interpretation of the master. Sitte's book had a formative influence on Saarinen (certainly by the time of the European trip that he took to prepare himself for the planning of Helsingfors), and throughout his life his planning projects—city extensions, civic centers, campuses—all reveal a basic understanding of Sitte's principles. His early articles written after he came to the United States are Sittesque in terminology and concept, but do not mention Sitte's name. On the other hand his 1943 book about the city summarizes Sitte's contribution aptly and confronts him interestingly with Baron Haussmann. The quintessence of Sitte was to Saarinen: 1) an emphasis on the informal nature of classical and medieval town building; 2) an emphasis on the coherent organism of the town, achieved through proper correlation of building units; 3) a stress on the function of plazas and streets as organic, spatial enclosures (Bibl. 204, p. 118). In his introduction to the 1945 translation, he insisted that Sitte had pioneered in placing the expression of contemporary conditions above any particular style-form; Saarinen was probably unaware that Sitte had actually made such remarks (cf. our pp. 49–50).

Besides his immediate followers, other aspects of international city planning reflect Sitte's influence. We have so far, in discussing the history of the profession, followed a particular thread of artistic considerations. This is no place for a review of all facets of the modern designing of cities, but a few other key tendencies might be listed, in order to suggest the relation of Sitte and other phases of German planning to them.

To start with, there is the matter of how the internationalism that characterizes advanced planning in the present century came about and how the previously separate and somewhat autochthonous movements became merged and mixed. The milestones in this process were a series of important international meetings and the appearance of new, widely-circulated periodicals, all of which served as sounding boards for divergent views. The motivating spirits were men like Patrick Geddes—whose Outlook Tower that surveyed the world-scene represented better the new state of mind than did Sitte's Holländer Turm that was to epitomize Germanic culture only. Viewing this development from our rather special interests, we find that the progression of events was roughly as follows.

The important international conclaves begin with the first Congress of Public Art, held in Brussels in 1898 and attended by well-known figures from all of Europe and America (Bibl. 455). *Municipal Affairs* of New York in that year reprinted text and pictures from the reports of the Congress. We have already mentioned several times the participation of Stübben and Buls in the meeting. The next significant event would appear to have been the Cities Exhibition at Dresden in 1903 (Bibl. 489). To judge from its catalog, this was Stübben's *Handbuch* in the flesh, with all imaginable categories of city activities represented, including an exhibit of firemen in uniform. City plans that were shown (and described by Gurlitt in the catalog) were largely Sittesque in character. In 1904 appeared Sitte's magazine *Der Städtebau*, the first periodical devoted exclusively to problems of city planning.[107] Its ample, attractive format and the seriousness of its articles did much to spread the gospel of German city planning as well as Sitte's method of historical analysis. The next event of consequence to the German profession was the opening of the Berlin–Charlottenburg Seminar on City Planning (1908–1920) under Joseph Brix and Felix Genzmer; the scope of its lectures on city building has probably never been surpassed (Note 95). The printed lectures were widely circulated (*Städtebauliche Vorträge*, Bibl. 485).

The *Town Planning Review* commenced publication at the University of Liverpool in 1910 under the direction of Abercrombie, Adshead, and others. During that year important articles appeared in it on the transformation of Vienna and on German Garden Cities. The year 1910 also featured international gatherings in London and Germany. In Berlin and Düsseldorf there was held in May–June of 1910 the Universal City-Building Exhibition, whose *leit-motif* was the Greater-Berlin planning competition but whose displays, arranged by March and Hegemann, were world-wide in coverage. Numerous projects by Sitte and his followers were shown, and the Greater-Berlin prize was captured by his disciple, Hermann Jansen (Pls. XII–XIII, Notes 104, 108). Hermann Muthesius, inspired by this event and by the appearance of Sitte's fourth edition, wrote a stimulating piece on city building for a Berlin magazine, in which he made many discerning remarks about city planning, past and present, but especially he praised Sitte and condemned the cheap, speculative exploitation of his ideas.[109] City planning, he observed, is a matter of Form; without Form there exists only chaos. Largely the same cast repaired to London in October of that year, where, as guests of the R.I.B.A., they took part in an impressive series of sessions on the history and practice of city planning. The international competition for Canberra, which was to electrify the profession, grew out of this conference.[110] The influence of Germany on this occasion was quite strong, as one might expect from recent developments in England. Hegemann chaired one of the sessions, and it would have been amusing to have been in attendance, if only to observe one confrontation: Brinckmann and Stübben were among the Germans who delivered papers, Brinckmann castigating the recent 'romantic' style of German planning and praising the American Burnham's new-found 'French' spirit; Stübben, meanwhile found himself showing with pride a series of very practical and quite lovely new German communities that had been laid out according to Sittesque principles—including several of his own design!

The sessions on city planning at the International Congresses of Architects during the decade 1900–1910 were also crucial; we have already referred to their gathering at London in 1906. At Vienna in 1908 Otto Wagner was in charge, and Sitte's grave was honored in a special ceremony.[111] In 1913 at Ghent an even more international conclave occurred—the first International Congress and Comparative Exhibition of Cities—with speakers from Latin America included. The preponderance of German theory was not so noticeable, although Stübben gave two papers, citing Sitte in one. (Bibl. 414.) Germany was even more dislodged, of course, at the Conference on Reconstruction at Brussels in 1919. As this was a function of the International Garden Cities and Town Planning Association, the English pretty much took over. Then, beginning with its 1923 congress at Gothenburg (exhibits arranged by Hegemann), the same Federation's conferences became an annual clearinghouse, held at different world capitals. Its only serious competition for years came from the progressive moderns in the C.I.A.M. meetings, from 1928 on. Actually, after World War I all these congresses became so absorbed with problems of housing and land use that they have little bearing on our study. Built-in social reform was to

I. Vienna: Mechitaristen Church, 1873–74, by Camillo Sitte

BEBAUUNGS-PLAN
VON
MARIENBERG.
STRASSEN
PROFILE
ARCHITEKT: CAMILLO SITTE

III-a. Church plaza at Marienberg (Sitte)

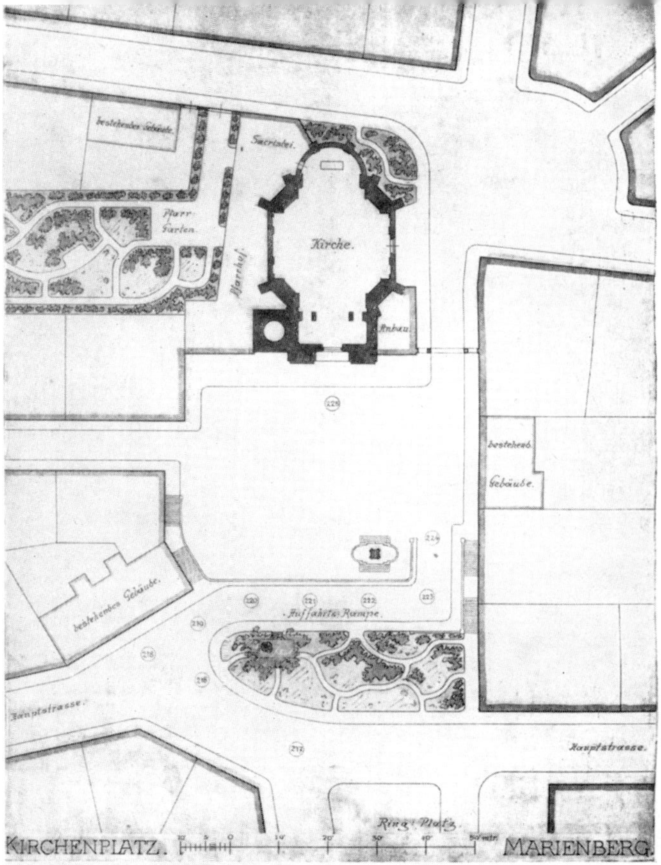

III-b. Plan of the Church plaza at Marienberg (Sitte)

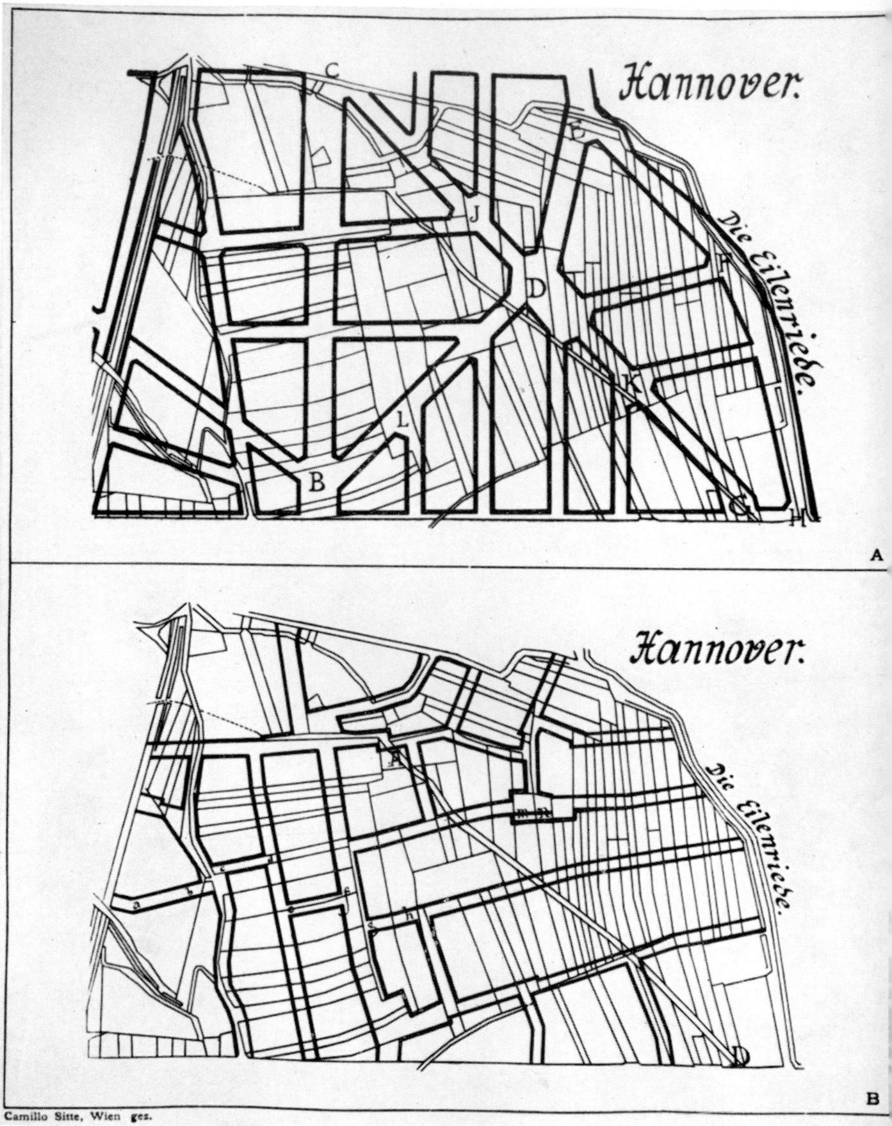

Camillo Sitte, Wien gez.

IV. Layout for the Eilenriede in Hanover
A. Without regard for the old property lines.—B. According to Sitte's proposal

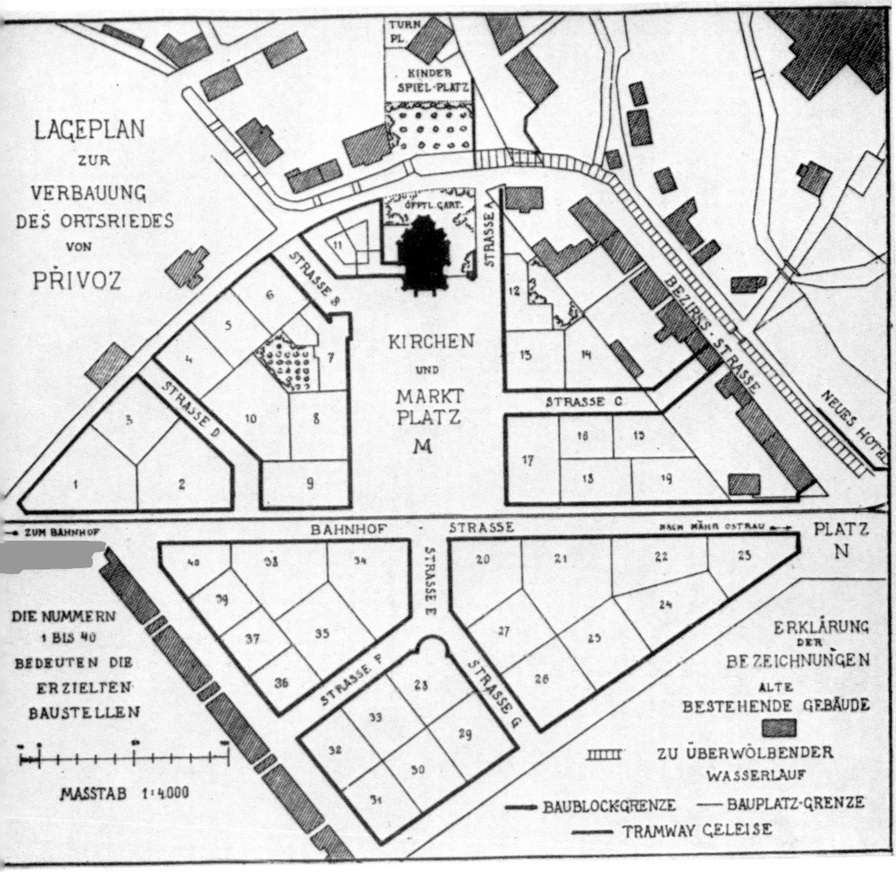

V. Plan for a new section of Oderfurt-Přivoz in Silesia (Sitte)

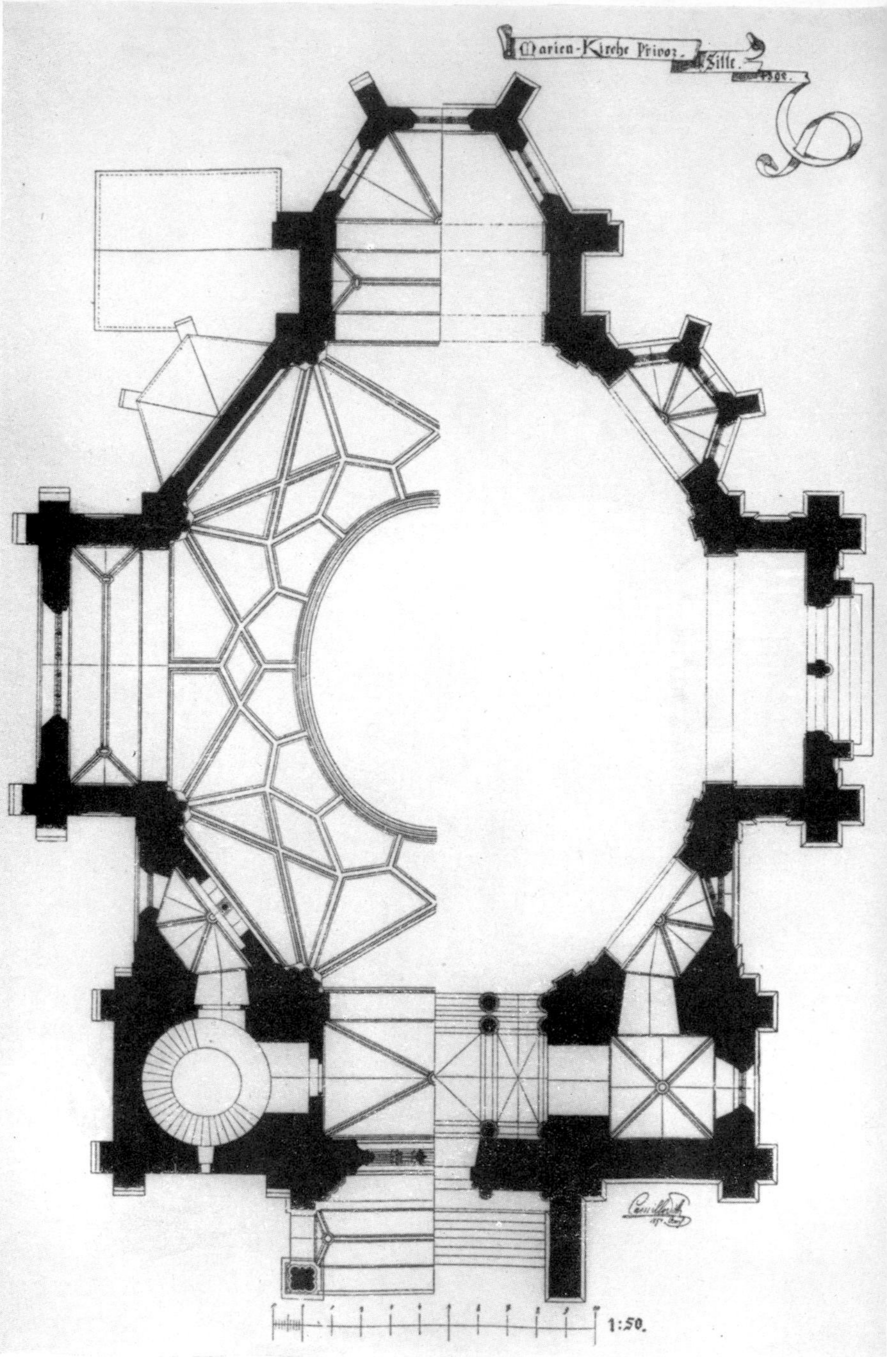

VI. Plan of Sitte's church at Oderfurt-Přivoz

VII. Façade of the church at Oderfurt-Přivoz

VIII. Camille Pissarro: Rue des Arpentes, Rouen. Etching, 1887

IX. Vienna: Votive Church, 1856–79 (Ferstel)

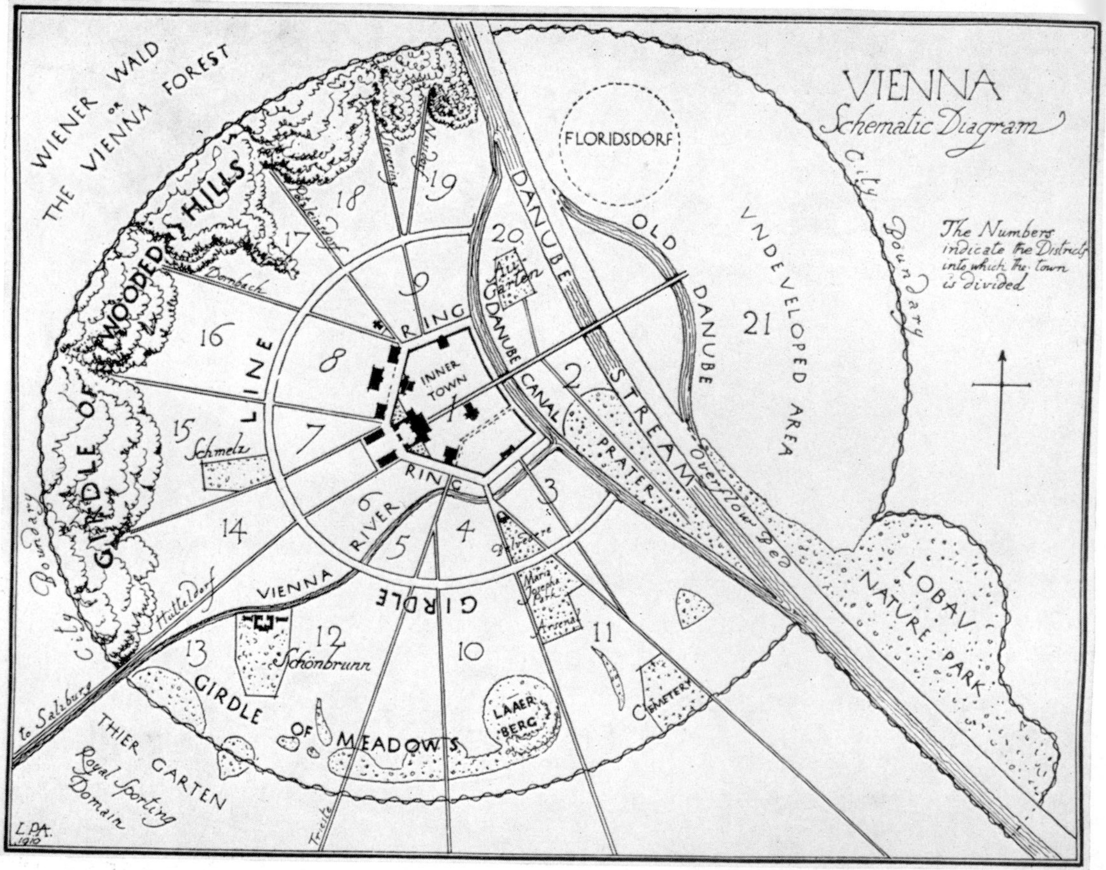

X. The growth of Vienna by 1910 (area of the Inner Town is exaggerated in comparison with that of the whole city)

XII. Bird's-eye view of a projected resort at Marienthal in Lower Austria, by Sitte.[108]

XI. Vienna in the eighteenth century with its old ramparts. The Hofburg is at the top, River Wien at the left, Danube Canal at lower right. From J. D. Huber's bird's-eye map of the city and its surroundings (1769–77)

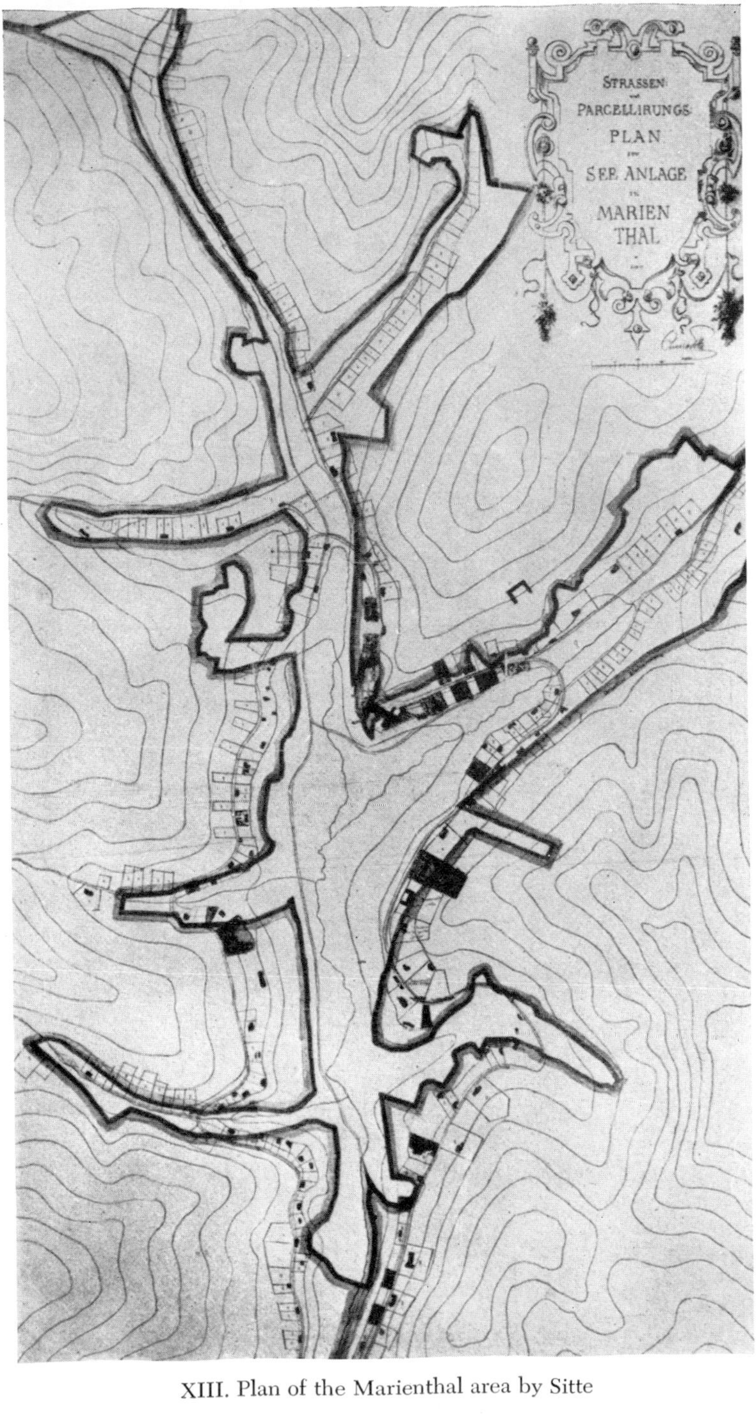

XIII. Plan of the Marienthal area by Sitte

XIV. Venice: air view of Piazza S. Marco

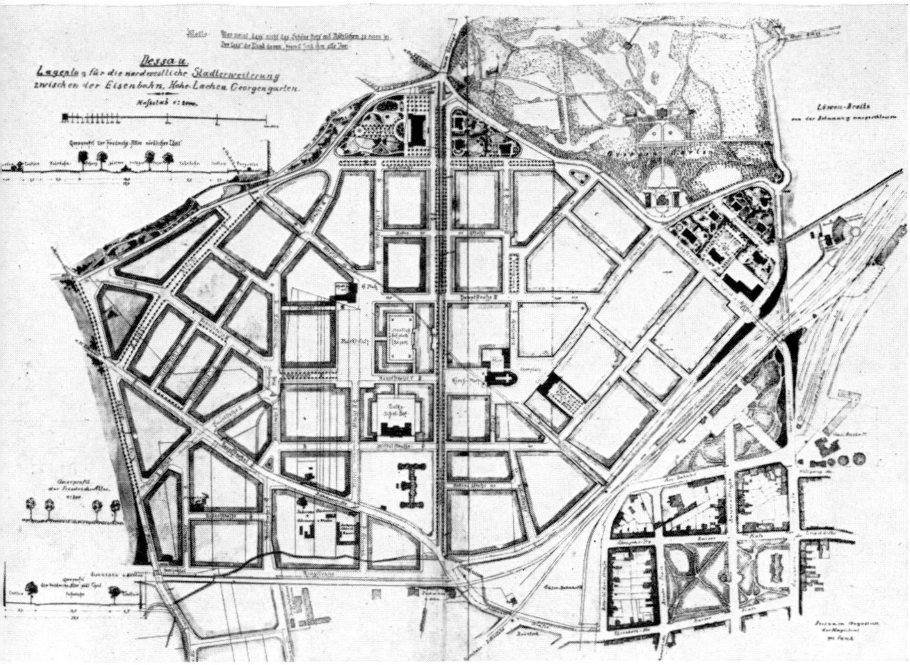

XV-a. Projected plan of extension for the city of Dessau (K. Henrici)

1

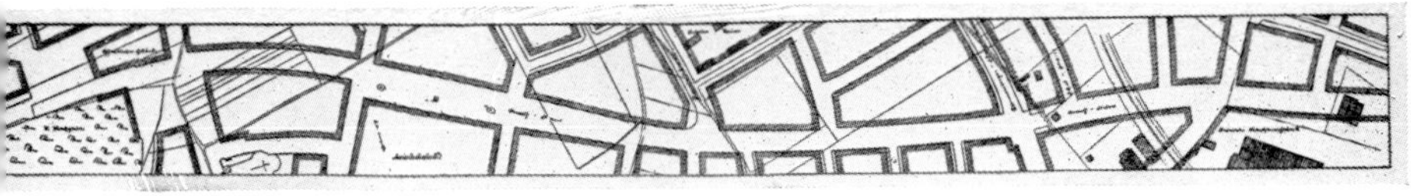

2

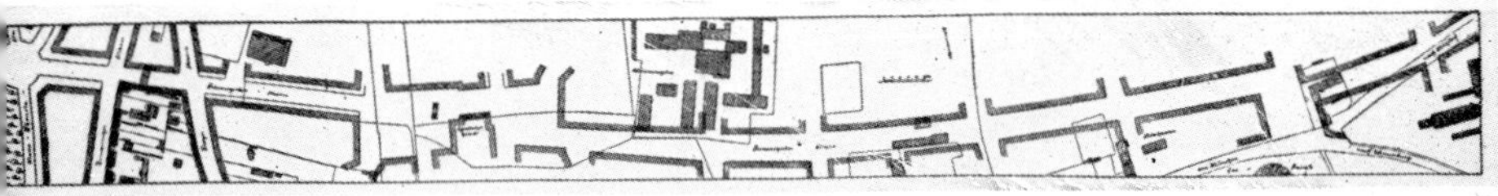

V-b. Details of the plan of extension for the city of Munich (Th. Fischer). 1. Arnulfstrasse between the railroad and the Nymphenburg canal.—2. Prinzregentenstrasse, on the bank of the Isar opposite the city

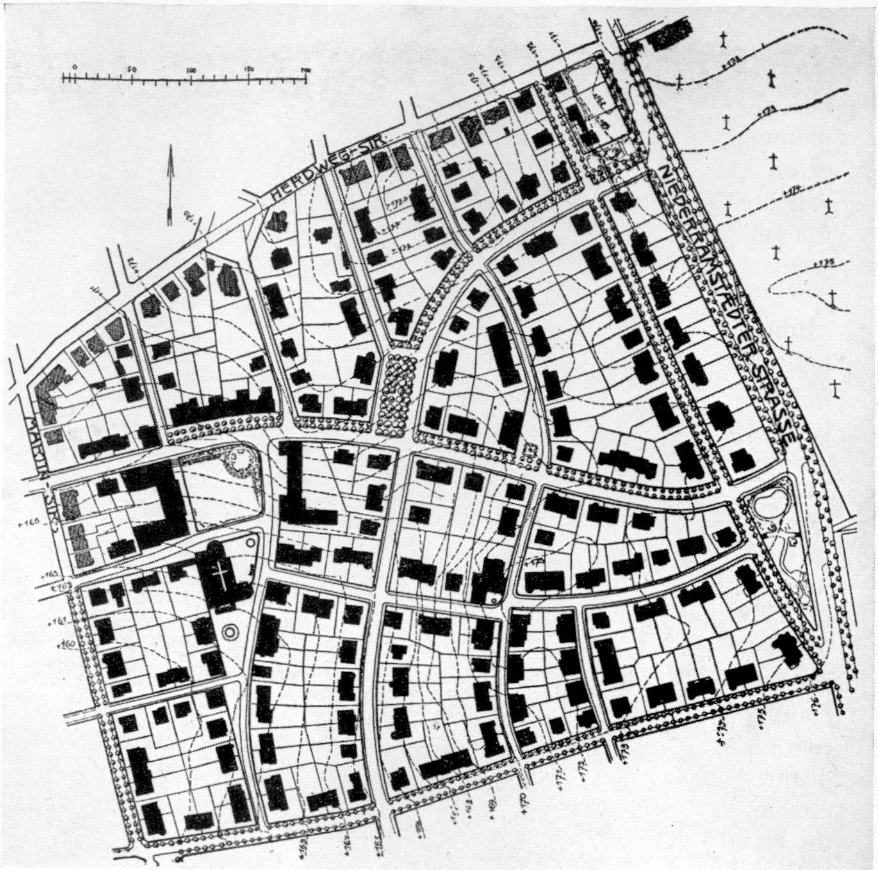

1

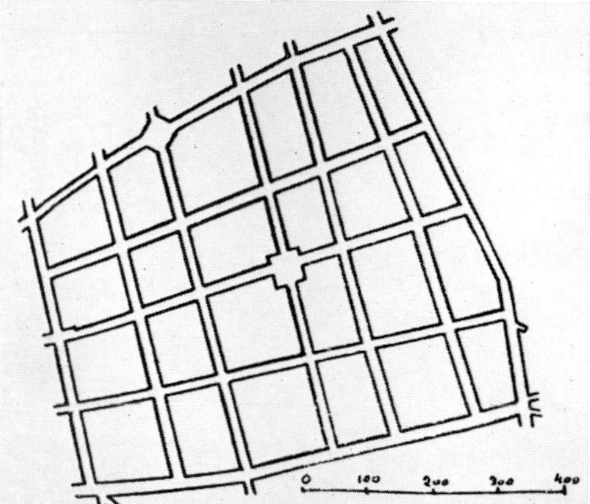

2

XVI. 1. Plan of a villa suburb at Darmstadt (F. Puetzer).—2. Plan of the same district as laid out earlier under the direction of the municipal administration of the city of Darmstadt

become a basis for theorizing about architecture and city planning now for several decades. With the frontiers gone and exotic lands like New Zealand filling up, the social utopian was driven back into the suburbs, as it were, and began to use the rebuilding of our cities as the laboratory for his experiments with human destiny. He turned architect and planner.

Additions to the body of aesthetic principles in planning during the early twentieth century seem to have been few. Some speculation in all countries went into the matter of adjusting to modern use the theories of beauty and function that had developed during the nineteenth century. Otto Wagner, Muthesius, Gurlitt, Hegemann, and many others dealt with this in the realm of city planning, as we have mentioned. It was distinctly a post-Sitte argumentation, although his book was an important ingredient in it. As planning itself expanded to a regional scale, the city and the town began to be considered less important in themselves, and we find an increasing preoccupation with the relation of the urban nucleus to its countryside. Architecturally this proved to be a problem in two ways: there was a good deal of talk about the silhouette of the town as seen in its landscape setting (mountains, rivers, etc.) and also about the way in which city fringes merged with the hinterland. Oddly enough, Sitte had not concerned himself with either of these factors, in spite of their being a logical outcome of the *Stadtbild* craze he had started. The Berlin Seminar lectures were full of the subject, and certain favorite silhouettes occurred frequently in their publication. The matter of *krumme oder gerade Strassen* in this century became a dead issue, lost sight of in the life-and-death struggle between medievalists, renascentists and modernists.

During these years the English Garden City idea spread like wildfire. It proved naturally attractive in Germany, where its reception had been prepared for by several precedents: Germans were proud of their own record of wholesome, if somewhat paternalistic, workers' colonies like those of Krupp (well illustrated in Stübben's 1890 *Handbuch*). Also, as we noted earlier, numerous cities in Germany and Austria had been for some time expanding in the form of garden suburbs like

Vienna's Cottage Anlagen. The idea of a ring of greenery around a metropolis, not unrelated to the satellite theory, had been under consideration in Vienna for a number of years and had been suggested for Berlin as early as 1874.[112] Furthermore, certain aspects of Ebenezer Howard's scheme had been anticipated in Theodor Fritsch's *Die Stadt der Zukunft* two years earlier (1896).[113] However, considering the emphasis in German planning on matters of city-extension rather than on model social communities, it is not surprising that the Garden City was employed there more as a device for city suburbs or for workers' settlements (including later ones for Krupp) than as a philosophy of life. The union of the Garden City theory, then, with Sittesque street layouts was a natural one for Germany, especially as Unwin, the form-giver of the Garden City, was going Sittesque himself.[114] Also Berlepsch-Walenda, a leading promoter of the Garden City in middle Europe, was an enthusiastic Sitte supporter.[115] As early as 1905 Sennett's handbook on Garden City building showed a number of German pictures, although the author apparently had no knowledge of Sitte.[116]

Through the efforts of Georges Benoit-Lévy and his Association des Cités-Jardins de France, the idea of Ebenezer Howard received early and sustained propagation in France, although the French, like others, tended to extract mainly its potentialities for suburban growth. French planning, under the spell of Paris, seems to have continued to concentrate on the transformation of its cities along the lines of Haussmann. Most interesting of the successors to him was, perhaps, Eugène Hénard (born 1849), who was active in all the early congresses and received a great deal of attention in German planning literature, especially for his planning in terms of traffic, his invention of the traffic circle, and his futuristic projects.

Most isolated from Germany was Spain, a curious situation when one considers the usual pre-eminence of Germans as students of Spanish culture. Spain's modern city-planning tradition extends back to the efforts of the engineer Ildefonso Cerdá in Barcelona in the 1850's; he is presumed to have invented the word *urbanización,* and his is one of our first technical treatises on planning. It was eventually a German, Oskar

Jürgens, however, who provided us with our most scholarly treatment of Spanish cities.[117]

The United States, prepared as it was for utopias by its countless nineteenth-century experimental colonies, and actually as advanced as England with regard to garden- and park-suburbs (owing to the work of Downing, Olmsted, and others), absorbed the British Garden-City style without argument. Just what part a twentieth-century suburban street system in the United States owes to Olmsted, to Unwin or to 'Sitte' remains to be seen. Newton, Massachusetts, for instance, possesses only a few clusters of regularly shaped blocks although hardly any of its many curved and crooked streets bear any logical relation to their terrain as Sitte had suggested they should.

Before leaving the matter of British contributions to the planning movement, it should be pointed out that England also had its 'City Beautiful' phase of artistically oriented planning, growing largely out of the Arts and Crafts movement in her case. A number of influential lectures were delivered on that subject during the period in question, and the *Town Planning Review* was launched more or less on the same note, what with Abercrombie's reports on the beauties of various world capitals, including Vienna, and Adshead's long series on civic art.[118] One important element which Great Britain contributed at that time but has never been picked up—unless by Bruno Taut—was the cosmic one present in W. R. Lethaby's *Architecture, Mysticism and Myth* of 1891–92.[119] And then there was, of course, the venerable British tradition of verdured squares which had been amplified in the mid-nineteenth century by its public parks. Both devices served as an example to all nations, as we have already observed.

During this period of ferment—from c. 1900 to c. 1920—city planning became involved with a number of tendencies that would at first glance appear to have nothing to do with Sitte or with the German tradition of city building.

For instance, there developed a technological mania about future cities—Vernian metropolises—based on transit systems that bear little resemblance to the street networks that so occupied the German and British planners. Its roots are many and are as yet largely unexplored. France, for instance, produced at this time the imaginative schemes of Hénard and Tony Garnier for which one can find native forerunners like Mathieu.[120] In England, a novel of H. G. Wells, *When the Sleeper Wakes* of 1899, was printed with science-fiction illustrations whose prototypes probably had appeared in the engineering (rather than architectural) magazines of the day. The Germans did, in fact, contribute to this tradition in a number of ways. To begin with, their architects and engineers often shared the same periodicals—to wit, those of the Berlin *Verein* and the Austrian *Verein.* Such magazines reported from time to time about progress in elevated R. R. systems, subways, monorails, moving belts, etc., matters which in other countries were lost in the more technical journals.[121] In 1909 the Berlin publisher August Scherl caught the public imagination with his project for a centralized high-speed monorail transportation system for all of Germany.[122] The following year, at the Berlin city-planning exhibition P. Wittig, director of Berlin rapid transit, displayed sensational cutaway sections of the London Underground, New York City's Hudson Terminal, and other metropolitan railway systems, which were then reprinted in many magazines. In London, Hénard caused a stir at the city-planning conference of 1910 with his illustrations of a 'City of the Future' that consisted of many-tiered streets flanked by high-rise buildings and hovered over by airplanes. In 1911 the *Town Planning Review* reprinted a dramatic cutaway of the new Grand Central Terminal in New York City which emphasized its many levels of vehicular and pedestrian movement. Surprisingly enough, it was the Italians who took over at this point, with an employee in the works department of the city of Milan, the architect Antonio Sant'Elia, whose Futurist fantasies of 'La Città Nuova' were then propagated throughout Europe. The next step in this progression was, of course, Le Corbusier, who had been in Berlin the year of the exhibition, was well enough acquainted with Hénard's ideas to criticize them in his *Urbanisme,* and whose project for a city of 3,000,000 is, in plan, essentially a squared-up Mathieu metropolis. In America this tradition veered off in another direction—that of the endlessly-long, snaky 'Roadtown' plan by Chambless and Hastings in 1910, a characteristically American agrarian program.

As the Germans had been so concerned with the rather hard-headed practical and aesthetic matters of what is often called the 'city-building' phase of modern planning, we would not expect them to relate very much to these more ideal and radically utopian schemes that form such an important ingredient in twentieth-century planning theory. And this proved to be the case until after World War I. Germany has nothing to match the dreams of the French, English, and Americans: Papworth's Hygeia, Buckingham's Victoria, Mathieu's *Capitale Modèle*, Bellamy's *Looking Backward*, Tony Garnier's *Cité Industrielle*, Hébrard and Anderson's World Center of Communication.[123] But immediately following the war, and as part of the German Expressionist idealism of that moment, Bruno Taut produced a series of projects that outdid them all.[124] Taut, a student of Theodor Fischer and an admirer of Sitte, saw the planning of the whole earth itself as a purely artistic task. His group's idea of the *Stadtkrone* (crown to the city) was a characteristic twentieth-century outgrowth of Sitte's image of the town as a social-architectonic entity. It derives in part from the town-silhouette idea we have mentioned above, but is essentially a sacred intellectual civic center surrounded by a cluster of plaza-courts. This desire for a towering accent in the skyline is a post-World-War I symbol with which we are acquainted in the more conservative planning of our own country: the Nebraska State Capitol, the Pittsburgh Cathedral of Learning, the pages of Hegemann and Peets' *Civic Art*. Unique about Taut's new world, however, was its Scheerbartian glassiness and its aerial pyrotechnics, which are still futurist to us today. Taut far outdid Sitte's dream of a Holländer Turm!

The scope of Taut's projects indicates to us that by 1920 our conception of architecture and planning had expanded to include interrelationships covering entire regions. Of this there was, of course, little or nothing in Sitte. It derives instead from the tradition of the sociological and ecological surveys instituted by Patrick Geddes, the Reclus brothers, and others. Thinking on this scale was greatly stimulated by the work of

Daniel Burnham, especially his Chicago plan that had been featured by Hegemann at the 1910 Berlin Exhibition. Nothing was so surprising to the Germans as to find that instead of being frontiersmen living in little checkerboard settlements that had been set out by railroad surveyors, the Americans were actually advanced over the rest of the world in three respects:

1) The concept of a regional plan involving vast transportation networks. Geddes had lectured in Chicago in 1900, but it is not at all clear what this American innovation owed to his influence.

2) The design of city parks and green spaces on a large metropolitan scale for the reclamation of land, the insulation of residential areas, recreational purposes, etc. Olmsted and Baxter, whom we have mentioned, were pioneers in this development, which was now outstripping the British.

3) The City Beautiful movement, stemming from the 1893 World's Fair, which more than anything else had succeeded in applying to city planning the Beaux-Arts principles of assemblage, symmetry, and *point.* Again, Burnham.

This last, being essentially a Renaissance-Baroque practice attracted the attention of Brinckmann, Hegemann, and others of the later Sitte following. It was, however, quite free from German influence, having already evolved in the 1890's under the impact of our French-educated architects and intellectuals. A series of lectures in Boston in 1889 had touched off the movement, and our periodicals were suddenly full of articles about civic beauties, as we have already noted.[125]

Thus, while we have no desire to overstate the importance of Sitte in the face of many other, sometimes more exciting, contributory ideas it is not hard to demonstrate that many branches of twentieth-century planning are descended in one way or another from him and the German 'city-building' tradition, so that it is not without reason that Sitte has been so often called 'the Father of Modern City Planning.'

It is of interest to examine how Sitte has been evaluated in general works on modern architecture and city planning. This is, of course, too detailed and secondary a study to go into here at any length, but a few observations might be in order. Modern literature on the history of city planning usually mentions Sitte. With few exceptions, however, such remarks are second-hand or even uninformed; professionals tend to use him as a whipping boy for something they do not like. Errors are frequent: some have him born in Trieste, one writer assumed his book had been translated from the Italian. Several have called him a 'bohemian type,' for which there is no evidence other than his family's having come from Bohemia! More surprising are, actually, the total omissions of Sitte's name. A number of otherwise excellent surveys of the history of city planning and of architectural history make no reference at all to his existence.

Out of deference to the authors concerned, we have listed in Bibliography E those whom we have noticed to have made interesting comments on Sitte or on his influence, in the course of some larger study they were conducting.

On the famous controversy that developed in the mid-1920's between Le Corbusier and the ghost of Camillo Sitte, much has already been said and we have little to add. To begin with, the two men did not speak the same language, for reasons that we have outlined above in our discussion of the sociological and technological utopias of our century. In this instance, it seems that they did not read the same language either. Although Le Corbusier had studied in both Berlin and Vienna, it would appear that his idea of Sitte's being 'the winding road' and 'the Pack-Donkey's way' had come from his using the French edition, printed in his own French-speaking section of Switzerland. Le Corbusier's dislike of picturesque planning derived from many sources, of course, but not the least may have been the fact that one of Camille Martin's major city-planning commissions had been to lay out a new section for Le Corbusier's home-town, Chaux-de-Fonds—a town that had long been famous for the exactitude of its original gridiron layout, a long, thin lattice such as Tony Garnier used.[126]

The young Spanish critics of Sitte whom we have mentioned took their cue from Le Corbusier, and another member of the international C.I.A.M. group, Sigfried Giedion, added fuel to the fire. Giedion was well aware of the importance of Sitte and described it clearly, but concluded his remarks with the statement that '. . . the town planner had lost contact with his period. He was a kind of troubadour, ineffectually pitting his medieval songs against the din of modern industry.' (Bibl. 181, pp. 505–506.)

Certainly some of the best writings that we have on Sitte and his period are by the Hamburg architect and city planner, Fritz Schumacher. Schumacher was of the old school (1869–1947) and had read Sitte's book as a student in Munich (1889–1891) when it first appeared, but his own writings on city planning and city-planning history date from after World War I, so that he belongs at this point in our chronicle. In his retrospective writings of the 1930's (Bibl. 205, 206) he expressed remarkable enthusiasm for Sitte and a keen and objective insight into his contributions, considering that Schumacher had himself always been concerned with the social problems of planning. He considered that Sitte, in dealing with artistic matters, had made city planning comprehensible to the layman by removing it from the arcane realm of technicians. His analysis of Sitte's aesthetics is perhaps the best we have. He was a defender of Henrici who, he felt, had through his own efforts secured the entree of the architect into the city-planning coterie of the day.[127]

The most recent studies and summaries of Sitte with which we are acquainted are, unfortunately, not easily available to readers. The master's essay of Alvin S. Boyarsky (Cornell University, 1959) contains interesting insights, but has remained unpublished. Equally inaccessible, because of idiom, is an analysis of Sitte's aesthetics and impact which appeared in Yugoslavia in 1961.[128]

CONCLUSION

THERE are certain things to point out about the relevance of Sitte to the practice of city planning in our day. A number of developments within the profession since World War II suggest that his ideas are still viable in the context of the later twentieth century. As has always been the case, his influence can be seen in both the actual building of cities and in historical and critical writings.

In recent years tendencies have been observable in architectural and planning practice that could be termed 'latter-day Sittesque.' Some of the more popular recent books on urban design are illustrated according to the custom initiated by Sitte, Henrici, and Brinckmann (Note 98), and the same tradition is echoed in certain of our most perceptive modern architectural photography, e.g., Bibl. 208 and 218. As for actual city-planning projects, the urban renewal work in Philadelphia is usually described and illustrated by its administrators in terms of what are basically Sittesque *Stadtbilder.* A city-building complex like Eero Saarinen's new Yale dormitories is the epitome of Sitte's *Bebauungsplan.* The centers of several of Britain's New Towns have their squares and pedestrian malls laid out in ways of which Sitte himself would have approved. It is hardly necessary to remind our readers that this period has also seen two editions of Sitte in entirely new languages, English (1945) and Italian (1953). Whether these and the many other instances of Sitte's taste that could be cited are actually due to his influence, or merely indicate that his book stands for a particular mode of vision that is a constituent and periodically recurring phenomenon in our culture, is hard to decide.

But that all these are manifestations of a certain feeling about the city which we share with Sitte is unquestionable: a yearning for human scale in our urban environment in the face of relentless technological advances. As one reads the pages of his book the question ever arises as to whether Sitte's precepts —conceived as they were in a horse-and-buggy era—still hold true for us today. He wrote when our lives had not yet experienced the high speed of airplanes or the towering city-silhouette of skyscrapers.[129] It is not clear, however, whether these extended dimensions of our century have actually invalidated his point of view. Sitte, as well as Stübben and many Sitte followers, actually accepted the enormity and the technology of the modern metropolis as given conditions, but they were convinced that if its open spaces were to be scaled to the gigantic size of its buildings they would be too vast for human comfort. They insisted, therefore, that at certain key points, the foci of human conviviality, there should be moderately-sized, enclosed plazas—'islands in the endless sea of buildings,' in their words. The size and manner of decoration of these 'hypaethral assembly halls,' as the classically-trained Sitte termed them, were for him the very qualities that distinguish city from town, that make a town stand out from its countryside, and that cause certain metropolitan centers like Vienna to be world-cities belonging to us all—not just to their own residents. Vienna's Ringstrasse, he felt, could still be saved; that is why he spoke out. Sitte also pleaded for diversity in the face of the standardization of 'building blocks,' etc., an argument that is very topical today (Bibl. 468). Picturesque irregularity he recognized and praised as being characteristic of the townscape of other days, but as we have seen, he did not necessarily recommend that it be imitated in his time. Where it did hold current interest for him, as it does for us, was in the preservation, wherever possible, of old streets, old squares and the low building height of former times. We are reminded of the torments of conscience that venerable cities like Boston are now experiencing over the future of such residential streets as Commonwealth Avenue. One feels that even the insistence on Sitte's part that the plans in his book be in identical scale was an effort to preserve a sense of recognizable, human dimension in his discussion of his ideal city of the future.

Sitte saw that a single-minded concern with traffic conditions would make impossible the preservation of humanistic values in the city, and so he fought bitterly with his contemporaries on that score. The battle is not yet over, although a great deal of the damage has been done or is under way. Some of these teachings of Sitte have been summed up neatly in recent years by the Goodmans (who draw on Sitte for a number of their suggestions for the city as a Way of Life):

> A city is made by the social congregation of people, for business and pleasure and ceremony, different from shop or office or private affairs at home. A person is a citizen in the street. A city street is not, as Le Corbusier thinks, a machine for traffic to pass through but a square for people to remain within. Without such squares—markets, cathedral places, political forums—planned more or less as inclosures, there is no city. This is what Sitte is saying. The city esthetic is the beauty proper to being in or entering such a square; it consists in the right choice and disposition of structures in and around the square and in the relation of the squares to one another. This was the Greek, medieval, or Renaissance fact of city life. . . .
>
> It is possible that this urban beauty is a thing of the past. . . . If this is so, it is a grievous and irreparable loss. . . . If it is so, our city crowds are doomed to be lonely crowds, bored crowds, humanly uncultured crowds. (Bibl. 182, pp. 49–50)

If, then, the principles that Sitte stressed as intrinsic to the city as a vessel of humanity and as a work of art no longer apply today, it follows that the city as we have always known it and the city of the future are antithetical, and the thread of historical continuity has been broken. But even if this is, tragically, the case, Sitte will still serve us as a key and guide to the character of the city of another era as Dr. Leete did in Bellamy's *Looking Backward.*

The reader should be warned, however, that in travelling through Europe or other parts of the Old World with Sitte's book in hand, a tourist will probably find many squares, streets, buildings, and monuments that never conformed exactly to the standards which the author enunciates so clearly. But such exceptions, in a sense, prove his point. He did not claim to acquaintanceship with all the towns of Europe, nor does he anywhere insist that the examples which he selected for illustration are 100-per-cent representative. In his search for an underlying beauty he must have been aware that the ancients, too, had tolerated intersections and spaces that were unsuccessful or ungainly, a fact that in no way detracts from the general validity of their organic, three-dimensional procedures of city building. He was, after all, searching for the motivations of our ancestors discernible in those parts of towns that lingered most vividly in his own memory; he was not attempting an exhaustive, statistical study of the morphology of the city. As we pointed out to begin with, no one was more surprised than himself when his little volume of essays provoked such universal enthusiasm and touched off a profound revolution. His concern had been with the subconscious, the memories, dreams and other intangible variables of the human mind. As Elbert Peets wrote,[130] 'Whether Sitte can guide our hands in these matters of planning may well be doubted—but he can certainly guide our hearts.'

NOTES

NOTES

(The word *Sitte* indicates that the pages or Figures referred to are in the companion volume; *Collins* refers to the present volume in any case where there might be a confusion. For explanation of abbreviated periodical titles see pp. 199, 200.)

Notes to Chapter 1

CAMILLO SITTE'S BACKGROUND, LIFE, AND INTERESTS

1. For biographical data on Camillo Sitte consult the following (publications of 1903, 1904 are mostly obituaries):

C. von Wurzbach, 1877 (see Bibl. 161).

Ludwig Eisenberg and Richard Groner, *Das geistige Wien*, Vienna, Brockhausen, 1893, I: 5.

H. C. Kosel, *Deutsch-Oesterreichisches Künstler- und Schriftsteller-Lexikon*, Vienna, Gesellschaft für graphische Industrie, 1902, I, p. 29.

A. Birk in *Biographisches Jahrbuch und Deutsche Nekrologie*, VIII, 1903, pp. 225–226.

DB, XXXVII, 1903, p. 604.

Allgemeine Zeitung (Munich) CVI, Nov. 17, 1903, Abendblatt, p. 1 and Beilage No. 263, Nov. 18, p. 335.

Schweizerische Bauzeitung, XLII, Nov. 21, 1903, p. 249.

J. Stübben, Nov. 28, 1903 (see Bibl. 406).

Julius Koch in *ZOV*, LV, Dec. 11, 1903, p. 671.

H. Schmidkunz in *Deutsche Kunst und Dekoration*, XIII, 1904, pp. 309–314.

Berliner Architekturwelt, VI, 1904, p. 323.

Th. Goecke in *StB*, I, 1904, p. 5.

Othmar v. Leixner in *Der Baumeister*, II, Jan. 1904, pp. 44–46.

Geo. E. Hooker, Jan. 15, 1904 (see Bibl. 156).

Theodor Fischer, in *DB*, XXXVIII, Jan, 20, 1904, pp. 33–34.

Karl Henrici, Jan. and Mar. 1904 (see Bibl. 344, 345).

Theodor Bach in *ZOV*, LVII, May 12, 1905, p. 298.

L. Bauer, April 1923 (see Bibl. 153).

F. v. Feldegg, June 1923 (see Bibl. 155).

Heinrich Sitte, 1929 (see Bibl. 160).

Wasmuths Lexikon der Baukunst, IV, [1932] p. 396.

Thieme-Becker, *Künstler-Lexikon*, XXXI, [1937].

Erwin Ilz, 1943 (see Bibl. 157).

Josef Schwarzl, 1949 (see Bibl. 158).

2. For more biographical data on Franz Sitte consult the sources listed under his name in Thieme-Becker, *Künstler-Lexikon*, and Schwarzl, Bibl. 158.

3. On J. G. Müller (1822–1849) see *Sitte*, p. 160 and Notes 296, 297. For biographical details about him see Thieme-Becker, *Künstler-Lexikon*; Förster (as cited in Note 296); and J. M. Ziegler, *Aus dem künstlerischen Nachlasse von Johann Georg Müller*, Winterthur, Wurster, 1860. The Altlerchenfeld church incident is related at length in Förster, *op. cit.*, chap. 8.

J. G. Müller, poet, draftsman, and architect, merits a modern study of his work and influence.

4. This plaque was designed by the sculptor Anton Brenek, a friend of Sitte who had worked with him at Olmütz (cf. Note 19). It was displayed at the Berlin city-planning exhibition of 1910.

5. L. Tržeschtik, 'Weiland Architekt Johann George Müller und der Altlerchenfelder Kirchbau,' *ABZ*, LX, 1894, pp. 7–8. Most of the later clique will be found listed in Note 57; van der Nüll had actually been a pupil of Sprenger, the villain in this case. Camillo Sitte discussed this situation at length in his article on church architecture (Bibl. 111), dealing in particular with the tyranny of Sprenger and his own father's teacher Nobile. He emphasized that the year 1848 marked a turning point in the Austrian medieval revival and that Müller's winning design had actually been much more Gothic in style than the North-Italian *Rundbogenstil* church that resulted. For a monograph on the building see Franz Rieger, *Die Altlerchenfelder Kirche*, Vienna, Gerlach and Wiebling, 1911.

6. The following is a partial list of works by Franz Sitte:

- 1849–61, Vienna, Completion of Altlerchenfeld Church.
- c. 1849 on, Vienna, Parish house of Piaristen Church (Ledergasse 8).
- c. 1852, Vienna, Priests' hospital in Ungargasse.
- 1853, Vienna, Tomb of Archbishop Milde in the Catherine chapel of the Church of St. Stephen.
- 1860, Jedenspeigen (Lower Austria), Parish church.
- 1860, Vienna, Piaristen church (Maria Treu), façade work and the Baroque towers; the church itself dates from 1716.
- 1860–70, Vöslau (near Baden, Lower Austria), parish church of St. James the Greater.
- c. 1873, Vienna, enlargement of Mechitaristen monastery.
- ?, Erlau (Upper Austria), restoration of the Cathedral.

He also took part, unsuccessfully, in the Votive Church competition of 1855, published a piece on Austrian civil architecture in 1868, and held a retrospective exhibition of his designs in 1877.

7. Rudolf Eitelberger von Edelberg (1817–85) and his student Albert Ilg (1847–96) are best known, perhaps, for their *Quellenschriften*, a collection of art-historical source materials that we refer to in Note 214.

Eitelberger was a moving force in the development of medieval art history and archaeology in Austria. Those of his publications which concern us here are his lecture on city planning, his opinion about the Vienna Ringstrasse competition, and his articles on Viennese architects (see Bibl. 290–292). He also wrote (with Heinrich Ferstel) about moderately-priced housing: *Das bürgerliche Wohnhaus und das Wiener Zinshaus*, Vienna, Gerolds Sohn, 1860. Camillo Sitte described the great debt that he owed to Eitelberger in an oration he gave and in articles he published at the time of Eitelberger's death: 'Rede am Grabe Eitelbergers,' *NWT*, April 20, 1885; 'Rudolf von Eitelberger,' *NIZ*, April, 1885.

Ilg, among other distinctions, was the 'discoverer' of Fischer von Erlach, the Austrian Baroque architect. (Eitelberger, incidentally, disliked the Baroque.) Writings by Camillo Sitte relating to Ilg include 'Offenes Schreiben an Dr. Ilg,' *SGB*, 1879, and an obituary in *NWT*, Dec. 2, 1896.

8. Sitte wrote the following on drawing, anatomy, etc. (As it is not clear whether they were all published, we have not included them in Bibliography C):

'Geschichte des perspektivischen Zeichnens,' before 1877.
'Neue Methode des perspektivischen Construierens,' between 1879–1884.
'Die Perspektivlehre des Pietro degli Franceschi,' May 1879.
'Zur Geschichte und Methodik des elementaren Körperzeichnens,' April 1884.
'Zur Methodik des Zeichenunterrichtes,' 1885.
Grundzüge zu einer Reform des Zeichenunterrichtes, 1899, with the following appendices:
'Das Entwerfen im Freihand-Zeichenunterricht,' 1884;
Über Schreib- und Zeichnenstellung der Hand,' 1890;
'*Lehrgang für das ornamentale Freihandzeichnen . . .*, von Gebrüder Hein (1896), Eine Besprechung';
'*Das Zeichnen nach der Natur* von A. Kornhas (1898), Eine Besprechung.'

9. The renderings were done for the K. K. Oesterreichisches Museum für Kunst und Industrie. Some were used by the K. K. Central-Commission zur Erhaltung der Baudenkmale. A number were said to have been used for Bucher and Gnauth's *Kunsthandwerk*, Stuttgart, Spemann, 1874–76, 3 vols.; although only plate 30 of vol. III bears Sitte's name, it may be that the unsigned renderings from Viennese collections were also by him (I, pl. 16, 37; II, pl. 37, 72; III, pl. 54). Others apparently served as plates for Custos Lippmann's *Über Chinesische Emailvasen,* Vienna, Rosner, 1870, not being used, however, for its original publication in the *Mittheilungen* of the Museum in 1870.

10. This monastery with its church stood on the site of a 17th-century Capuchin establishment that had come into the hands of the Mechitarists in 1813. The monastery had been rebuilt, 1835–37, after plans of Josef Kornhäusel; Franz Sitte was retained to enlarge it in the 1870's and relinquished the construction of the church to his son. Camillo apparently drew all the cartoons for the paintings himself and carried out as much as possible of the figure painting with his own hand, reserving his holidays for that work.

The Mechitarists are an Armenian offshoot of the Benedictine order. They have their headquarters in Venice, important establishments in Vienna and Constantinople (where Camillo was also employed by the order). They have been responsible for a series of learned publications on Armenian manuscripts by Stryzgowski and others.

11. Aided, in particular, by Eitelberger and Dumreicher. Armand von Dumreicher (1845–1908) had been installed in the Austrian Ministry in 1871 to build up the teaching of the industrial arts. Sitte wrote a review of Dumreicher's study of the French art-educational methods for the *Norddeutsche Allgemeine Zeitung* (Berlin), Nov. 22, 1878. Dumreicher seems

also to have been responsible for the organization of the Vienna school to which Sitte was called in 1883.

12. Sitte's articles for the *Salzburger Gewerbeblatt* (*SGB*) include the Ilg letter (Note 7), the Semper obituary (Note 15), and the 'Die deutschen Gewerbe-Ausstellungen von 1879,' all in 1879.

At one time or another he wrote the following items on arts and crafts, some of which may have appeared in the *Salzburger Gewerbeblatt*. It is not known exactly how all of them were published:

'Kunstbericht zur Ausstellung im Neuen Museum für Kunst und Industrie,' *NWT*, Nov. 30 and Dec. 19, 1871.

Über Zweck und Nutzen des Gewerbeschulwesens: Ein Vortrag . . . Salzburg, 1875. (See Bibl. 103). This also appeared as a supplement to the 1899 item listed in Note 8.

'Die Lehrmittel des gewerblichen Unterrichtes,' *SZ*, April, 1875.

'Die gegenwärtige Lage des Bau- und Kunstgewerbeunterrichtes in Deutschland und Oesterreich,' *SZ*, Nov., 1875.

'Erneuerung alter Ledertechnik bei Bucheinbänden,' 1877.

'Die Ledergalanterie seit der Pariser Weltausstellung,' 1878.

'Zur Lehrmittelausstellung der Gewerbeschule,' April, 1878.

'Zur Geschichte der Salzburger Weissgeschirr-Fabrikation,' 1882.

'Grundzüge zu einer keramischen Formenlehre,' 1883.

'Über Technik und Ausbildung der Rundeisengitter der Renaissance, 1885.

'Schlösser und Schlüssel,' June, 1885.

'Formenlehre des Möbelbaues,' 1885.

'Über Öesterreichische Bauernmajolika,' 1886.

'Das Salzburger Filigran,' 1887.

'Zur Geschichte der Gmunder-Majolika-Fabrikation,' 1887.

'Die Entwicklung der Schmiedekunst in alter und neuer Zeit,' Oct. 1887.

'Die Grundformen im Möbelbau und deren Entwicklung,' 1888.

'Bericht über die Ausstellung kungstgewerblicher Schüler des Königreiches Sachsen,' 1888.

'Referat über die Frage: Empfiehlt sich die Einführung von Lehrbüchern an gewerblichen Lehranstalten,' 1895.

'Kunstgewerbe und Styl,' *NWT*, Dec. 15, 1898.

'Das Verhältnis der Bürgerschulen zu der höheren Gewerbeschule' and '*Die Erziehung in Schule und Werkstätte . . .* von Frdr. Graberg (1894), Eine Besprechung,' (supplements to the 1899 item listed in Note 8).

A discussion of the lecture, 'Die Moderne in der Architektur und im Kunstgewerbe,' reported in *ZOV*, March 17, 1899. See Bibl. 120.

13. Camillo Sitte's endeavours on behalf of the preservation and restoration of monuments and old sections of cities are impressive.

In Salzburg he described the restoration of a famous fountain: 'Der restaurierte Marktbrunnen,' 1879.

He published the following studies:

'Auszug aus dem Vortrage über die Baugeschichte und Restauration der gothischen St.-Wolfgang-Kirche bei Kirchberg a.W. im Alterthums Verein am 2. Nov. 1885,' *Berichte und Mittheilungen des Alterthums Vereines zu Wien*, XXIII, 1886, pp. 248–50.

Über die Erhaltung des Gurker Doms und dessen Malereien,' *Mittheilungen der K.K. Central-Commission zur Erforschung und Erhaltung der Kunst- und Historischen Denkmäler*, n.s. XVIII, 1892, pp. 53–56, 75–80.

'Aus der Burg Kreuzenstein,' *Kunst und Kunsthandwerk, Monatsschrift des K.K. österreichischen Museums für Kunst und Industrie*, I, 1898, pp. 3–15, 95–104, 155–164. Note that this was the lead article in the first issue of one of the most lush Sezession-style publications of its day.

When he became established as an authority on city planning, he intervened on several occasions to try to preserve old city cores. See pp. 22–23, 43–44.

14. Hans Richter (1843–1916), a horn player, had attended the Löwenburgisch choir school. Taken on by Wagner as his copyist and general assistant, he became the leading Wagnerian conductor. His popularity and influence was immense in England where he resided from 1897 on.

Sitte's Bayreuth visit (1876) was for the opening of the Semper-Wagner theater and the first performance of the *Ring*. For more on Sitte and Wagner see p. 15.

15. Only two others of Sitte's earlier writings seem to touch upon matters of city building: Bibl. 51 and 52. There seems to be no basis for Hooker's statement that Franz Sitte had designed a Viennese street layout in the 1850's and thus awakened Camillo's interest.

The article on Semper's planning was 'Gottfried Sempers Ideen über Städteanlagen,' *NWT*, Jan. 22, 1885, apparently done in collaboration with the editor Schembera, who signed it. This formed the nucleus of Sitte's discussions of Semper in his book. Others of his articles about Semper include:

'Gottfried Semper: zum 70. Geburtstage,' *NWT*, Nov. 29, 1873.
'Gottfried Semper: Nachruf,' *SGB*, 1879.
'Eine Handschrift Gottfried Sempers,' *NWT*, Jan. 9, 1885.
'Gottfried Semper und der moderne Theaterbau,' *NWT*, Jan. 17, 1885.

16. Sitte appears to have served as juror on competitions for Munich, Mainz, Hamburg, and Hanover.

17. The following is a list of city-planning projects with which Sitte was involved. They are listed in alphabetical order of location; not much is known about the dates. See also Note 19.

Brünn (Brno), Moravia. Sitte was approached on this as early as 1889–90. We do not know if it was carried out.

Constantinople, Turkey. He worked out a land-parcelling for the Mechitarists.

Laibach (Ljubljana), Slovenia. Project for the layout and expansion of the city after the earthquake of April 1895. It appears that the plans of the Viennese Fabiani were used in preference to Sitte's. See *ZOV*, XLVIII, 1896, pp. 73–74; and *Zbornik Za Umetnostno Zgodovino* (Ljubljana), IV, 1957, pp. 211–220.

Linz, Upper Austria. Same situation as Brünn.

Marienberg, Silesia. This plan for a city expansion was often illustrated and much discussed. It is the classic Sitte plan; it was dealt with by Stübben, *Handbuch*, 1907, Figs. 480, 508, 619, and by Peets, Bibl. 363. See Bibl. 90 for Sitte's own presentation of it and his church design there. Plan shown at the 1910 Berlin exhibition. Our Pls. II, III.

Marienthal, Lower Austria. This was Sitte's favorite plan, and must have been drawn up in his last years. It was for a summer resort around a water reservoir high in the mountains. Shown at the 1910 Berlin exhibition. See *StB*, 1910, Pl. 38, and our Pls. XII, XIII.

Nuremberg, Germany. He is supposed to have advised on the modernization of the Königstrasse in the old town.

Oderfurt (Přivoz), Silesia. He did the church square and layout of a city extension, as at Olmütz and at the Ostraus. This was described and illustrated by Sitte himself in Bibl. 74. Always cited as his most important work, the architectural construction was supervised by his son Siegfried. Our Pl. V.

Olmütz (Olomouc), Moravia. Requested along with Brünn and Linz, it was carried out by 1896. A subdivision of land around the old city. Shown at the 1910 Berlin exhibition. See Stübben, *Handbuch*, 1907, Fig. 589, and Hegemann & Peets, *Civic Art*, Fig. 150. He also designed a civic ensemble here consisting of town hall, church, parish house, and a monument. See *Sitte*, p. 182.

Ostrau (Ostrava), the twin-cities of Mährisch-Ostrau (Moravia) and Polnisch-Ostrau (Silesia). Sitte seems to have made layouts for both. We have seen no illustrations. At Polnisch-Ostrau he is supposed to have erected a civic group similar to Olmütz. Mährisch-Ostrau plan was underway in 1900 (see *Sitte*, p. 182).

Reichenberg (Liberec), Bohemia. City-expansion plan for his father's birthplace, designed during a visit at Whitsuntide 1901.

Temesvar, Hungary. Small subdivision. We have seen no description or illustrations. He also designed parish-church in the old town.

Teplitz (Teplice), Bohemia. Subdivision of a large sloping area near the city. Shown at the 1910 Berlin exhibition. See Hegemann & Peets, *Civic Art*, Fig. 151.

Teschen (Cieszyn), Silesia. A city-expansion of before 1900 that was often mentioned (e.g. *Sitte*, p. 182) but no details or illustrations are available.

Venice, Italy. Sitte is supposed to have been consulted on the plan to run a street railway into the city. We presume that his reaction was negative!

Some idea of how he would lay out a subdivision, in comparison with Stübben or Baumeister, is gained from the illustrations in *StB*, I, 1904, pp. 5–8, 17–19, 35–39, and our Pl. IV.

18. 'Der Städtebau nach wissenschaftlichen und sozialen Grundsätzen.' This was reported in most of his obituaries.

19. The following is a list of architectural projects with which Sitte was associated. They are listed in alphabetical order of location. Exact dates are not known for most of them. See also Note 17.

Graz, Styria. He is reported to have been building a sanatorium there during the last five years of his life.

Klein-München, Upper Austria. Project for a parish church.

Marienberg, Silesia. Church and town hall as part of his city-expansion project. Church and plaza are illustrated in Bibl. 90. Our Pl. III a-b.

Oderfurt (Přivoz), Silesia. Church and its plaza, work being supervised by his son Siegfried. See his own description and illustrations in Bibl. 74 and our Pls. VI–VII. This was apparently for the Kaiser's Jubilee competition, which he won.

Olmütz (Olomouc), Moravia. Civic center consisting of town hall, church, and parish house. Also the base of a monument to the Emperor (by Brenek). Probably all completed by 1896. See Bibl. 75 for the monument.

Polnisch-Ostrau (Ostrava), Silesia. Civic center similar to that of Olmütz.

Sierndorf, near Korneuberg in Lower Austria. Alterations to the castle and construction of a chapel in the woods. This was done sometime after 1883 for Count Hans Wilczek, one of his later patrons, and owner of the nearby Burg Kreuzenstein (see Note 13). One source reports a parish church there by Sitte, too.

Temesvar, Hungary. Parish church in the inner town. Various dates are given: 1873–74, 1883–84. In the German Renaissance style and considered important by his biographers.

Vienna, Mechitaristen church, 1873–74. Paintings 1898–1900. See p. 10, Note 10, and Pl. I.

Vienna, Competition project for Kaiser's Jubilee Church.

Vienna, Design for a second State school of applied arts.

Near Zbirow, Bohemia. A hunting lodge (after 1883) for the Prince Colloredo-Mansfield, another of his later patrons.

——, Project for a double-villa. Published in Bibl. 115.

20. The Sittegasse in District XV. Described in *StB*, X, 1913, p. 60. Stübben was particularly laudatory of Sitte's 'invention' of the turbine-plaza and added a new paragraph (p. 146) and two illustrations (Figs. 476, 357) to his 1907 edition explaining its merits. Compare in *Sitte*: Figs. 22, 24, 25, 43, 107, 108, and p. 34. The modern Greek planner Constantine Doxiadis employs turbine-plazas in the community superblocks with which he is attempting to preserve human scale in the great cities of today: 'Camillo Sitte,' remarks Doxiadis, 'was my first master.'

21. For a biography of Siegfried Sitte see Bibl. 158. Eight of his town-plans and projects were exhibited at Berlin in 1910; a number of them were also published in *Der Städtebau*. His successful project for Göteborg was printed in 1901 (by the Mechitarists!). His Garden City plan for Dzieditz (Silesia), carried out between 1912–20, is illustrated in Schwarzl *op. cit.* He became active in the Zentralstelle für Wohnungsreform and later in the Bund Österreichischer Bodenreformer. Characteristic publications include:

'Entwurf für ein Städtebau-Gesetz,' *StB*, XIV, 1917, pp. 7–9, 14–18.

Hauszinssteuer oder Bodenwertabgabe, Vienna, Bund Östr. Bodenreformer, 1921.

Wirtschaftsbild und Bodenreform, same publisher, 1924.

Städtebau und Bauordnung, same publisher, 1926.

22. In a letter to Ferdinand von Feldegg reported in the latter's commemorative speech on the occasion of the 80th anniversary of Sitte's birth

in 1923 (Bibl 155). This lecture gives interesting insights into Sitte's personality. Feldegg (1855–1936), an architect and philosopher of art, was a staunch supporter of Sitte and, among other things, editor of *Der Architekt* of Vienna.

The writings of a number of other city planners over the turn of the century do, indeed, reveal a conscious search for 'true German' city forms. This goes a long way to explain their veneration for the old picturesque medieval towns of Germany as over against the classical traditions of Italy and France. Stübben ridiculed it in Henrici's writings (Note 97). One also detects this Germanic spirit in Baumeister and others.

The tradition probably goes back to Goethe's youthful essay *Von Deutscher Baukunst* (1773) and to Johann Gottlieb Fichte's image of Germany's medieval Golden Age, as described, for instance, in his sixth address to the German Nation (1808):

> 'Amongst these [the Germans who remained in their fatherland] arose cities built by members of the people. In these cities every ramification of cultural life developed rapidly to fairest bloom. Civic institutions and organizations evolved, and, although on a small scale, these were excellent in their way; and from these cities a picture of order and a love of it spread over the rest of the land. Their extensive commerce helped discover the world. Their league was feared by kings. The monuments of their building arts still stand, defying the destruction of centuries and admired by a posterity which recognizes its own impotence.'

Sitte's reputed German nationalism hardly ever shows through in his own writing. But the smallish medieval New Towns that were to become the ideal of Nazi planners seem to have been an outgrowth of the search for a *Heimatstil* which his followers set in motion. The roots of German totalitarian city planning have apparently been little studied, viz., the extent to which it relied on Baroque vistas, Schinkelesque civic groups, or medieval street patterns. Interesting comments on the way in which the Nazis corrupted the investigation of German national town-forms that Sitte had helped initiate are to be found in the recent Czech history of city planning by Grushka (Bibl. 221).

Notes to Chapter 2

THE STATE OF CITY PLANNING IN GERMANY AND AUSTRIA

23. Among useful historical and interpretive summaries of the development of German city planning are the following:

Gurlitt, Bibl. 314; Horsfall, Bibl. 467; Muthesius, Bibl. 198; Brix, Bibl. 177; Lichtwark, Bibl. 350; Baumeister, Bibl. 264; Stübben, Bibl. 416; Brinckmann, Bibl. 276.

24. Alfred Lichtwark (1852–1914), writer on all things artistic including the city, was an admirer of Sitte. He was as concerned with his native Hamburg as was Sitte with Vienna, and he may have been responsible for Sitte's professional connections with Hamburg. (See p. 12.) Hamburg had

been one of the first cities to undergo and then to react against the 'Cult of the Engineers' in planning. As Sitte did not discuss Hamburg, it is not clear whether he owed anything to its example, but certain of its city-planning experiences are pertinent enough to our story to merit a brief summary here.

The chronicle begins with William Lindley (1808–1900), a British-born engineer who devoted his life to large-scale civic improvements on the Continent—notably in Hamburg. He had been active there at first in rail-road construction and land-drainage, but his real opportunity came with the destructive Hamburg fire of 1842, which he fought with such dramatic measures as blowing up the town hall. He then seems to have been largely responsible for the plan of reconstruction of the city. From the key municipal positions that he occupied (like Haussmann), he proceeded to carry out sweeping reforms: sewage systems, waterworks, gas works, port construction, and land surveys. His sewage system was copied in Frankfurt a.M. and in American cities. His waterworks were largely resisted (until after Hamburg's 1892–93 cholera epidemic), which may explain his abandoning the city about 1860 to work out similar projects for a dozen other major European cities. His was a classic instance of the engineer-technician at the controls.

Resistance to the dictatorship of Lindley in particular and engineers in general came from Carl Friedrich Reichardt (1803–71), a Hamburg architect and Schinkel student who seems to have served with Lindley on the technical commission to draw up the new city plan. Between 1842 and 1863, when he was not voyaging to the Americas, Reichardt composed a series of pamphlets on city-planning questions in which he rejected the preocupation with engineering and called for more attention to aesthetic considerations (Bibl. 366–371). In his writings he anticipated a number of Sitte's favorite precepts about city building. For instance, he pointed out the ugliness and boredom of long straight streets and of too regularly shaped plazas. He called for variety in the exteriors of buildings by the use of broken frontage lines, balconies, portals, etc., such as Sitte extolled in his Chapter X. Reichardt also stressed the direct beneficial effect that good civic art exerted on the spirit of the populace and the need for all categories of artists to combine in this effort. It seems unlikely, however, that Sitte, who never mentions him, was acquainted with Reichardt's writings since, directed at local problems, they were not listed in even the more extensive bibliographies, like Stübben's.

Lichtwark's criticism of the engineers came later, of course, at a time when one was not so much concerned with the technical dictatorship of the engineers—which Sitte had already begun to overthrow—as with the artistic clichés that the engineers had taken over from romantic planning in England—whence had come the engineering itself (e.g., Lindley). Lichtwark wrote about this in various places, including Bibl. 350. The situation was later described in Schumacher, *Wie das Kunstwerk Hamburg nach dem grossen Brand entstand*, Berlin, K. Curtius, 1920. A recent critique of the matter is Fischer (Bibl. 180), to which we refer in Note 310.

Lichtwark said, 'One wishes to translate into action the artistic interpretation of city planning whose basis we owe to Camillo Sitte and to apply with discretion all the hygenic installations and precautions which facilitate civic administration.' (Bibl. 351, p. 403.) His strictures concerning civic art have several things in common with Sitte. They come mainly somewhat later than Sitte, but are not necessarily derived from him; it *was* in the air. Like Sitte, too, Lichtwark based his analyses of the city on direct visual observation. (He was, incidentally, a founding member of *Der Städtebau.*)

Of particular interest to us with regard to Hamburg is Gottfried Semper's little-known intervention in the replanning of his native city after the 1842 fire. This is dealt with by Schumacher and Fischer. It is illustrative of the pivotal position that Semper occupied in things architectural, urbanistic, and aesthetic throughout Central Europe.

25. Paul Wolf is one who stressed the still-unresolved character of this clash between architects and engineers in planning (Bibl. 217).

26. See his fourth edition (Bibl. 13), pp. 97, 134, 136, 140.

27. Stübben discussed this development in Bibl. 416.

28. Stübben later came around to Sitte's way of thinking about the preservation of old squares from traffic, and in his 1907 *Handbuch* (p. 232) he added an extensive illustrated passage about it as part of his discussion of Buls' work on the Grand' Place of Brussels.

29. In the early years of the German planning movement Stübben had written an important study of the Paris transformation (Bibl. 375), which he later made part of his *Handbuch*.

30. On Pettenkofer see Note 322.

P. Hauser, *Madrid, bajo el punto de vista médico-social,* Madrid, Sucesores de Rivadeneyra, 1902 (dedicated to Pettenkofer), is an example of the type of study to which we refer. It is a model of thoroughness and is noteworthy for its recognition of the contribution of the architect Mariano Belmás to workers' housing and to the heroic efforts of Arturo Soria to introduce Spaniards to the concept of scientific, comprehensive planning for the future. (See Bibl. 453.)

A thorough summary of 'sanitary' city planning and the laws that were in effect when Sitte wrote is to be found in E. Flügge, 'Anlage von Ortschaften,' in Pettenkofer and Ziemsen's *Handbuch der Hygiene und der Gewerbekrankheiten,* Th. 2, Abt. 1, Hälfte 1, Leipzig, Vogel, 1882, pp. 1–72. This includes the text of the sanitary resolutions passed by the Berlin *Verein* in 1874 and much useful bibliography.

31. *Verein für öffentliche Gesundheitspflege.* The state official behind this organization appears to have been Johann von Miquel (1829–1901), onetime radical, who held key positions in the state of Hanover and later in the German Empire. He was active in matters of housing for the poor, reform of the tax system, and agrarian policy. The most significant of the Association's resolutions on urban questions are printed in the Appendix to the various editions of Stübben's *Handbuch.* We list here the subjects and dates of several of the resolutions with the names of their sponsors (usually Baumeister or Stübben):

Hygienic principles for the extension of cities, 1885 (Stübben and Becker);
Recommendations for the sanitation of cities, 1886;
Recommendations about restrictions on industrial building, 1888;
Project for a law to ensure healthy dwellings, 1889 (Miquel and Baumeister);

Suggestions about the different building regulations for inner and outer parts of cities and their surroundings, 1893 (Adickes and Baumeister);
Principles to follow in the spacing of buildings, 1894 (Adickes, Hinckeldyn, and Classen);
Measures to be taken for the adequate and healthy development of cities, 1895 (Stübben and Küchler).

32. See Bibl. 181 (Part VII) and our Note 315.

33. On the development of these English parks in the 19th century see George F. Chadwick, *The Works of Sir Joseph Paxton (1803–1865)*, London, Architectural Press, 1961, Chap. VIII, and Albert Fein, 'Victoria Park: Its Origins and History,' in *East London Papers*, V, Oct., 1962, pp. 73–90.

34. The examples of derogatory remarks about American planning are too numerous to list. Baumeister spread the ugly rumor about ruthless, speculative hexagonal planning in the United States (cf. Note 248), which was picked up by many others and even diagrammed by Stübben (*Handbuch*, Fig. 80). Sitte (p. 126) made scurrilous remarks about the motives of the Americans and allowed that a grid plan was good enough for their wilderness. In his early writings Stübben never lost a chance to castigate us: 'Artistic activity seems to be weakest in North American city building' (*Handbuch*, p. 192). He illustrated Manhattan's checkerboard plan, and his only illustration of Latin American planning is a frightening gridiron system for Montevideo (*Handbuch* 1907, Fig. 625). However, looking back on his own career and that of city planning in a lecture of 1920, Stübben acknowledged many merits to be found in American planning—even some that had not developed under German influence (!). (Bibl. 416).

35. *Sitte*, pp. 182, 194. A later regulation of this type for Posen is quoted in the appendix to Stübben's 1907 *Handbuch*. His 1924 edition contains a law of July 15, 1907, which incorporated Sitte's principles about variable flushlines.

36. *Krumme oder gerade Strassen*. This practico-aesthetic tug-of-war surged back and forth during the entire formative stage of German planning, from the 1870's to the early 20th century. It was already very fashionable to quote historical authority in city-planning debates, and in this case Alberti was available. There is the apparently anomalous remark by Alberti (Book IV, Chap. V) about the beauties of the concave vista of a curved street, in a treatise that is otherwise quite classical in tone. Art historians have seized upon this as being an anachronistic medievalism in an otherwise enlightened text, but it may also be understandable as a desire on Alberti's part to perceive the city in terms of discrete and fathomable units; after all, a straight street is 'undefinable' unless the spectator is so located that its sides lead to a central perspective point. (See also our p. 46.)

During the period with which we are concerned, Baumeister had led off, in his book of 1876 (Bibl. 252), with criticism of the checkerboard plan and appreciation for the visual effect of curvature in streets. The following year Stübben discussed the matter at length in an article in *Deutsche Bauzeitung* (Bibl. 372), that later became a part of his *Handbuch* (Pt. II, Chap. IV), saying that straight streets are natural for traffic and new layouts, but that curved streets have great charm, etc. The matter rested until Henrici reviewed Stübben's *Handbuch* in 1891 and took Stübben to task for emphasizing traffic and the efficiency of straight streets. Stübben replied. Then in 1893, the same periodical featured another set-to by the same men on essentially the same subject; their argument is described on pp. 83–84. By 1906 the Sittesque point of view was pretty much dominant. In the resolution of that year of the Berlin Architects and Engineers' Association (actually proposed by Baumeister) it was recommended that long stretches of street be broken, that streets adapt themselves to irregularities in terrain, that concave sides be sought out, etc., traffic and other considerations allowing. Nearly every book on city building warmed this subject over.

In 1909, replying to an attack on Sitte by Brinckmann in the magazine *Die Raumkunst* (No. 6, 1909), Theodor Goecke pointed out that the aesthetic fad for curved streets came out of the activities of Henrici and Gurlitt, not from Sitte. He insisted that in suggestions for modern planning systems, Sitte had employed only regular layouts, all of them in the tradition of the Baroque. (*StB*, VI, 1909, pp. 164–65.)

37. This association published, from 1899 on, the periodical *Deutsche Kunst- und Denkmalpflege.* One of the key meetings was its fourth, held at Erfurt in 1903, on the subject of building-frontage lines in old cities; this was reported *in extenso* in *DB*, XXXVII, 1903, pp. 578–583, 586–591, 598–603, and in *KC*, XV, 1903–04, pp. 32–43, 48–58. The resolutions of this meeting, drawn up by Stübben, Hofmann, and Gurlitt, are printed in the appendix of Stübben's 1907 *Handbuch.*

The group applied itself especially to an old problem, on which Sitte had taken a strong stand: whether churches should be freed up or built in. Buls gave a paper on the subject (Bibl. 286) at the 1908 meeting in Lübeck, which was translated in full in *StB*, VI, 1909, pp. 29–33. The question is discussed in our Note 165.

The attitude of German architects, planners, and city officials in at first relentlessly carving up their old cities, and then—around the turn of the century—taking protective steps in order to rescue historic buildings is paralleled in at least two other European capitals: Brussels and Rome. One suspects that in both Italy and Belgium each of these successive phases bore, as in Germany, a symbolic relation to their emergence as new nations seeking a national identity (cf. Note 22); in Italy a commission to draw up a *piano regolatore* was appointed ten days after the Italian troops entered Rome in 1870. Down to about 1909 the work was conducted in the Haussmann manner; then the tide turned toward Sittesque principles—perhaps owing to the intervention of Buls, who saved the Piazza Navona from being bisected when he was invited to advise on the planning of the city. On Rome see, for instance, Werner Weisbach, 'Stadtbaukunst und Terza Roma,' *Preussische Jahrbücher*, CLVII, 1914, pp. 70–100; Bibl. 282; Bibl. 220 and 379 *passim.*

38. For instance, von Moltke, the Prussian general and victor over France in 1871, wrote in his letters of the superiority of Vienna's crooked and picturesque streets to the straight new streets of Berlin. His remarks were frequently quoted.

Another example is Wilhelm Heinrich Riehl (1823–97), novelist and one of the founders of sociology in Germany. In his book on *The Family* (third volume of *Die Naturgeschichte des Volkes als Grundlage einer deutschen Social-Politik*) which came out in 1854 and had gone through its ninth revised edition by 1882, Riehl wrote that the natural street has both large and small houses, some protruding, some further back—a lively caucus of human activity. He was opposed to current building regulations in the layout of streets, saying that a picturesque effect could be attained by following the natural path of a stroller's feet. Such a graceful curvilinear trajectory is observable in the villages and is 'an honor' to imitate. (Compare Sitte's snow-men simile on his p. 21.) Riehl's writings on the character of old cities were influential.

These ideas actually went back a century or more. Willebrand, in one of the most venerable writings on the aesthetics of planning (*Grundriss einer schönen Stadt*, Hamburg, 1775) already dealt with the beauties of old towns. An early example outside of Germany is Samuel Huggins, whose 'Remarks on the form, disposition, and treatment of streets,' in *Building News* (London), IV, (Jan. 15, 1858), p. 73, go into the special beauties of European towns, with their variety of effect, etc. Eitelberger's lecture of the same year (Bibl. 290) is another instance. In 1871 a special meeting of the Berlin Architects' Association was devoted to those virtues of old planning that were lacking in new sections of cities. The statement by their companion group in Vienna in 1877 (Bibl. 457) to which Sitte seems to have owed so much, was quite definite about the superiority of planning in the old towns in contrast to the banality of new city extensions.

39. Stübben in Bibl. 399. Gurlitt in Bibl. 317, pp. 255–57. See also our p. 44 and notes.

40. This and other strange real-estate problems are illustrated in Stübben's *Handbuch*, Part IV, Chap. IV (1907).

41. Stübben, Bibl. 407. The argument went, then, Baumeister, Bibl. 259, Sitte, Bibl. 88, Stübben, Bibl. 407. Unwin summarized the matter in his *Town Planning and Practice* of 1909 (Bibl. 215), pp. 111–114, using as illustration Sitte's suggestions for Cologne.

42. Published in *DB*, VIII, 1874, p. 346, and in the Appendix to Stübben's *Handbuch*. (First three principles appear in Sitte's text, p. 121.) The resolution dealt with the following:

1. The primacy of traffic considerations in planning.
2. City plans to concentrate on main arteries, all other aspects to be controlled by local conditions.
3. Importance of flexibility in the layout of new sections, taking terrain into account. Sitte took this as an attack on a-priori planning. (See his p. 121.)
4. Regulations for the protection of tenants, etc.
5. Expropriation and redistribution procedures.
6. Financial matters.
7. Legal problems.

43. The 1906 resolutions are in the Appendix to Stübben's 1924 *Handbuch*. Baumeister's explanation of them is printed in *DB*, XL, 1906, 347–49, 556–58, 568–73, 577–82, 604–05. They can be summarized as follows:

1. General statement of principles.
2. The overall plan: fixing of traffic elements, need for zoning, importance of public buildings and open spaces.

3. Streets: their categories, retention of old trajectories when possible, aesthetic considerations, heights of buildings.
4. Plazas: their number and their aesthetic character.
5. Buildings: their types, their density, zoning, building lines.
6. Expropriation laws.
7. Financing.

44. Among the considerations stemming from Sitte would be: Emphasis at several points on the aesthetic implications of the plan, especially with regard to the siting of public buildings, the treatment of open spaces, and the character of streets (cf. Note 36). The considerable attention to matters of terrain and historical tradition in the layout of both streets and boundary lines. The recommendations about closure of plazas, scale of buildings to their squares, and the advantage of turbine-plazas.

45. See Giedion, Bibl. 181, Part VII, regarding Paris.

Notes to Chapter 3

IMPORTANT CONTEMPORARIES OF SITTE: BAUMEISTER, STÜBBEN, BULS, AND OTHERS

46. Incredible as it may seem, there apparently does not exist on Baumeister a single published book, monograph, thesis, article—or a biographical or bibliographical study of any substance—even in German. This may be because so many of his publications were in the category of handbooks or textbooks, but they are by no means secondary sources, being up-to-date and even prophetic manuals. He was very much interested in education, particularly in the instilling of an artistic point of view into the engineering curriculum. He wrote on the 'Technische Hochschule' in 1886, and on engineering design—especially that of bridges—in 1866, 1878, 1899, and 1904. His *Architektonische Formenlehre für Ingenieure* (Stuttgart, 1866) is a charming period piece. We have listed in Bibliography F only his publications dealing with matters of city planning.

In order to demonstrate the breadth and modernity of his point of view and yet its utter dissimilarity as a book to that by Sitte, we print the chapter headings of his *Stadt-Erweiterungen* of 1876 (Bibl. 252):

Part I. The task in general
- Chap. 1. The problem of increase in urban population
- ,, 2. Housing questions
- ,, 3. City traffic
- ,, 4. Regulations for the community
- ,, 5. How to design plans: city extensions; districting; differences between general and detailed plans

Part II. Basic aspects
- Chap. 6. Streets
- ,, 7. Horse-trams
- ,, 8. Steam-trams
- ,, 9. Water conduits

Chap. 10. Squares and parks: open plazas; planted squares and rows of trees in streets; squares; parks
„ 11. Sanitation

Part III. Ordinances of the building office
Chap. 12. Tasks of the building officer
„ 13. Frontage lines
„ 14. Fire prevention
„ 15. Matters of public health
„ 16. Spacing of buildings

Part IV. Economic aspects
Chap. 17. Expropriation
„ 18. Redistribution of plots
„ 19. Financing the plan
„ 20. Public streets
„ 21. Private streets
„ 22. Actual carrying out of city extensions

Chapters 20 and 21 present his theory that abutters should be responsible financially for certain street and park improvements; his reviewer challenged this (Bibl. 253).

Baumeister was represented in the Berlin exposition of 1910 by his plans for Altona and Mannheim.

47. As with Baumeister, it is also unbelievable that Stübben has never been the subject of any extended published study. Such biographical items as have appeared are listed in Thieme-Becker. Of his obituaries, that in the *R.I.B.A. Journal* is of interest (XLIV, 1937, p. 363). His architectural works are said to be undistinguished; they are listed in Thieme-Becker, where a list of the honors he received is also to be found.

The cities for which he planned extensions, transformations, or original layouts include the following: Aachen, Altona, Antwerp, Basel, Bilbao, Bruges, Brno, Brussels, Chemnitz, Darmstadt, Düren, Düsseldorf, Emden, Flensburg, Funchal, Ghent, Heidelberg, Helsingfors, Kiel, Cologne, Lyons, Liège, Luxembourg, Madrid, Malmö, Posen, Rostock, Schwerin, Torgau, Tournai, Warsaw, Wesel, and Wiesbaden, among others. These plans were frequently illustrated, and most of them can be found in the editions of his *Handbuch.*

His *Handbuch* was extremely influential, and its elements turn up in much subsequent literature in Germany and other countries. Some of its translations and important excerpts or summaries are listed in Bibl. 380–382 and described on p. 88. In 1920 he claimed that a certain Aristide Caccia had pirated it completely in a handbook published in Milan; we have not seen this. That the 1894 précis (Bibl. 382) was not recognized as being his suggests that American architects were not familiar with Durm's series of basic German textbooks, of which Stübben's *Handbuch* formed a part.

A synoptic idea of Stübben's attitude toward city planning is best revealed by the way in which he organized his *Handbuch* and what he discussed under its divisions. What follows is from the original 1890 edition —contemporary with Sitte's book; divisions and subjects were considerably juggled in the later editions.

Part I. Fundamentals of City Building
- Urban housing problems
- Categories of city traffic
- Public buildings and their relation to the city plan

Part II. The Outline of the Plan
- Preparation of the plan
- Grouping of the various elements of the city
- Building blocks
- Streets
- Open spaces and their importance in the plan
- The artistic aspects of open spaces
- Bodies of water
- Categories of railways
- Examples of good city extensions and city plans

Part III. Practical Execution of the Plan
- Responsibilities of states, municipalities, and individuals
- Controls over construction
- Expropriation
- Building lot regulations
- Financing
- Private usage of streets
- Building laws

Part IV. Construction under and over the Streets
- Water, sewage, etc.
- Lighting systems
- Paving
- Signs and advertisements
- Street decoration, placement of monuments, etc.

Part V. Planted Areas in the City
- Streets
- Squares
- Parks

Appendices. Laws, Decrees, local ordinances, and resolutions of societies

By way of conclusion to his handbook, Stübben remarked, 'City planning is the comprehensive activity that provides for physical and mental well-being of the inhabitants [Aristotle!]; guardian of its sanitation and health; cradle, robe and ornament of the city. It embraces all public and private enterprise in a higher unity. City planning is an important and independent art.'

48. For this reason Hermann Jansen reviewed it very critically in *Der Städtebau* when it made its third appearance (Bibl. 384), but Werner Hegemann, then editor of the magazine, intervened and insisted that it was poor taste to attack the patriarch of city planning, many of whose principles still held good.

49. See pp. 96–97 and Note 117.

50. Hermann Eduard Maertens (1823–1898), an architect active in the Rhineland, retired to Bonn in 1870 in order to pursue his effort of making the results of Helmholtz' investigation of physiological optics available for

use in the fine arts. Assuming from Helmholtz' work that the function of the eye is reducible to strictly mathematical laws, he attempted to develop similar set rules for matters of scale in artistic creation of all categories.

That Maertens' results were universally accepted is testified to by the fact that authorities like Buls and Brinckman cited him unquestioningly. Buls in his 1906 paper in London (Bibl. 285); Brinckmann first in his *Platz und Monument,* and then as late as 1920 when a whole chapter in his handbook of city planning was based on this method (Bibl. 267, 276). Also see Hans Schmidkunst, 'Optisches im Städtebau,' *StB*, VI, 1909, pp. 85–87, 104–106.

Maertens merits a study, if only as a curiosity—like phrenology. His publications on our subject are listed in Bibliography F, but they are, unfortunately, hard to come by. However, the reader will find summaries of his theories, with illustrations, in the following: Stübben, *Handbuch* 1907, pp. 520–521; *StBV*, II, No. 1, 1909, pp. 40–43; Hegemann & Peets, *Civic Art*, pp. 42–44. See also 'Scale in Civic Design,' by Hans S. Blumenfeld (a Brinckmann student) in *TPR*, XXIV, 1953, pp. 34–46.

51. Charles F. G. Buls (1837–1914) was trained as a goldsmith and spent much of his life nurturing the arts and crafts in Belgium. He entered political life in 1862, travelled extensively in Europe and published books, such as Bibl. 277, about its cities. In addition to translating Stübben, he also (in 1912) translated a lecture by Gurlitt, a Sitte follower. Buls became increasingly receptive to Sitte's ideas; at the 1906 Congress in London (Bibl. 285) he said that he preferred Sitte's opinion about traffic plazas to that of his friend Stübben who was occupying the platform with him.

The works which we mention here by Buls are listed in Bibliography F along with others of his publications.

Again, the best description of his 1893 book is probably provided by the titles of its sections:

I. The need for this study
II. Technical point of view
III. Aesthetic point of view
IV. Archaeological point of view
V. Public squares
VI. Plantings
VII. Suburbs
VIII. Private buildings
IX. Public buildings
X. Administrative aspects
XI. Conclusion (a project for Brussels)

We have used the American translation of 1899, which condensed slightly the French original.

52. About this see Note 28. A picture illustrating what Buls did at the Grand' Place is to be found in Hegemann & Peets, *Civic Art*, Fig. 47.

Notes to Chapter 4

THE TRANSFORMATION OF VIENNA

53. Among informative accounts of the planning of Vienna are:

Ludwig Förster, 'Der preisgekrönte Konkurrenz-Plan zur Stadterweiterung von Wien, '*ABZ*, XXIV, 1859, pp. 1–13 and pl. 1. Description of the winning plan by the editor of this magazine, who was also the winner.

R. Eitelberger, Bibl. 291, 1859. A discussion of the several ranking plans.

F. R. Farrow, Bibl. 460, 1888.

C. Sitte, Bible. 57 and 73, 1891–94.

A. Shaw, 'The Transformation of Vienna,' Chap. VIII of Bibl. 482, 1895.

H. Goldemund, 'Die bauliche Entwicklung und Stadtregulierung von Wien,' in *Fortschritte der Ingenieurwissenschaften*, s. 2, IX, Leipzig, 1902.

K. Mayreder, 'Stadtentwicklung,' in Bibl. 472, I, 1905, pp. 49–79.

L. P. Abercrombie, Bibl. 172, 1910. Draws heavily on Bibl. 472.

W. Hegemann, 'Wien,' in Bibl. 323, II, 1913, pp. 249–261.

F. L. Hauser, 'The Ecological Pattern of Four European Cities and Two Theories of Urban Expansion,' *JAIP*, XVII, 1951, pp. 111–129.

S. Lang, 'Vienna and the *genius loci*,' *ARev*, CXXIV, 1958, pp. 21–24.

S. Dimitriou, 'Groszstadt Wien—Städtebau der Jahrhundertwende,' *Der Aufbau* (Vienna), XIX, Hefte 4/5, 1964, pp. 188–200. Most recent summary; appeared when our book was in press.

54. Bibl. 458. A good idea of the character of the rampart area before demolition can be obtained from Hegemann & Peets, *Civic Art*, Fig. 137.

55. The Emperor's decree, addressed to the Minister of the Interior, reads as follows:

Dear Freiherr von Bach,—

It is my will that the enlargement of the inner city of Vienna, for the purpose of a suitable connection of the same with the suburbs, should be undertaken as speedily as possible; and also that the improvement and adornment of my residential and capital city should be considered concurrently therewith. For this purpose I decree the abolition of the enclosure and fortifications of the inner city, together with the ditches thereof.

Every part of the area obtained from the abolition of the fortification, ditches, and glacis, which is not designated on the accompanying plan for a particular purpose, is to be sold as building land, and the proceeds thereof are to be devoted to the establishment of a building fund, from which is to be defrayed the cost of carrying out this alteration of the public property, the direction of public buildings, and the provision of the necessary military establishments.

In the preparation of the necessary ground plan, and for my approval thereof, the following points must be attended to in the carrying out of the city enlargement:

The removal of the fortifications and the filling-in of the ditches is to be commenced in the space between the Biber bastion and the enclosure wall of the Volksgarten, so that a broad quay can be formed along the Danube Canal; and the space obtained from the Schotten Gate to the Volksgarten can be partly made use of for the modification of the parade ground.

The enlargement of the inner city is next to be undertaken, in the direction of the Rossau and the Alser suburb, between these two points, following on the one side the Danube Canal, on the other the boundary line of the parade ground, and taking into consideration the suitable enclosure of the Votive Church now in course of erection.

In the arrangement of this new quarter of the city, care is to be taken to include the erection of a fortified barrack building, in which also are to be located the great military bakery and the city prison, and these barracks are to be situated in the axial line of the road to the Augarten Bridge, distant 80 Viennese fathoms therefrom [c. 480 feet].

The square in front of my palace, next to the gardens on both sides, is to remain in its present condition pending further arrangements.

The area outside the palace gate, as far as the imperial stables, is to be left open. Also, that part of the city walls (the Biber bastion) on which the barracks called by my name abut, is to remain.

The further enlargement of the inner city is to be proceeded next with the Kärnthner Gate, and thence on both sides of the same in the direction of the Elizabeth and Mondschein Bridges as far as the Caroline Gate.

Consideration is to be given to the provision of the following public buildings: a new War Office, a City Marshal's Office, an Opera House, Imperial Archives, a Town Hall, and the necessary buildings for Museums and Galleries, and sites for the same are to be allotted, as well as for the following open spaces:

The area from the Caroline Gate to the Danube Canal shall be left open, to be added to the great garrison parade ground in the neighborhood of the Burg Gate.

From the fortified barracks on the Danube Canal to the great parade ground, a space of 100 Viennese fathoms is to be left free from building. Moreover, from the junction with the quay along the Danube Canal a boulevard around the inner city, of at least 40 fathoms in width, is to be arranged on the site of the glacis, including a roadway, with foot and riding ways on both sides, so that this boulevard may include an assemblage of buildings alternately with open spaces laid out as public gardens.

The remaining chief streets, and also the cross streets, are to have a width of at least 8 fathoms.

No less care is to be taken in the arrangement to provide for markets, and for their suitable distribution. Together with the arrangement of the ground plan of the city enlargement, attention is to be given to the arrangement of the inner city in connection with the main arteries of communication with the suburbs, and the provision of the necessary bridges for these lines of communication.

For the purpose of obtaining a ground plan, a competition is to be promoted, and a programme is to be drawn up on the lines of the principles herein indicated, but nevertheless with freedom of conditions, so that the competitors may be allowed free scope for the conception of their designs, consistent with the carrying out of the proposals herein contained.

For the selection of the plans submitted a Commission is to be appointed of representatives of the Ministries of the Interior and of Commerce, of my Central War Department and Chief Police Department, a Member of the Representative House of Lower Austria, and the Burgomaster of Vienna, who are to submit the plans to a Committee of Specialists appointed by the above-mentioned representatives and the Minister of the Interior, and by this Commission three designs are to be selected, and premiums of 2,000, 1,000 and 500 gold ducats awarded.

The three ground plans thus premiated are to be submitted to me for final selection, so that I may arrive at a resolution as to the further details of the carrying out of the premiated designs.

You will arrange forthwith the necessary steps for carrying out this my decree.

Vienna, 20 December 1857. FRANZ JOSEPH.

This text is taken from Farrow, Bibl. 460, who translated it from the *Wiener Zeitung* of Dec. 25, 1857. See next note.

56. Stache's project was presented in an interesting booklet prepared by its author under the device A.E.I.O.U. (an anagram for 'Austria will be the Empress of all Cities'): *Denkschrift zu den Plänen für die Erweiterung und Verschönerung Wiens*, Vienna, Mechitharisten-Buchdruckerei, 1858. Included in the volume are the complete text of the Emperor's decree of Dec. 20, 1857, and the detailed requirements of the competition itself, as announced Jan. 30, 1858.

57. For special discussions of the Ringstrasse buildings as architecture see the following:

R. Eitelberger, Bibl. 292.

Hans Semper, 'Austrian Architecture—Nineteenth Century,' *AA*, XXXI, 1891, pp. 19–20, 35–36, 51–53, 67–69, 83–85, 99–101. This was translated from Planat, *Encyclopedie de Architecture et Construction*, II–1, Paris, c. 1888, pp. 172–198.

H. R. Hitchcock, Bibl. 465, *passim*.

The following is a list of the major architects employed in the area, with some data about them and the buildings that concern us. See plan, Fig. 2.

Heinrich von Ferstel, 1828–83.

See R. Eitelberger, 'Heinrich Ferstel und die Votivkirche' (1873), in Bibl. 292, pp. 271–348.

1856–79, Votive Church (see Note 290).

1868–71, Austrian Museum of Art and Industry.

1872—, Cottage Anlagen in District XVIII (see pp. 20, 95–96).

1873–84, University.

Ludwig Förster, 1797–1863.

1836 on, editor of *Allgemeine Bauzeitung* (Vienna).

1842, Leipzig, preliminary plan and model for Viennese Ringstrasse.

1858, first prize in Ringstrasse competition (see Note 53).

Theophil von Hansen, 1813–91.
1872–76, Academy of Fine Arts.
1872–77, Bourse
1873–83, Parliament Building
Peter von Nobile, 1774–1854
1821–23, Theseus Temple
1821–24, Burgtor (see Note 298).
Friedrich von Schmidt, 1825–91.
1872–83, Rathaus
Schmidt had worked on the completion of Cologne Cathedral, the well-spring of German neo-Gothicism. For Schmidt's medievalism, his 'honesty' as regards materials, and his structural clarity, see C. Sitte, Bibl. 111. See also R. Eitelberger, 'Friedrich Schmidt' (1878), in Bibl. 292, pp. 380–426.
Gottfried Semper, 1803–79, and Karl von Hasenauer, 1833–94.
For the nature of their collaboration see Manfred Semper, 'Hasenauer und Semper, eine Erwiderung und Richtigstellung,' *ABZ*, LIX, 1894, pp. 57–63, 73–82, 85–96, and plates.
Hasenauer was a pupil of van der Nüll and Siccardsburg. For biographical data on Semper see our Note 288.
1869–71, Plan for the new Hofburg court (see Note 261).
1872–81, Imperial Museums of Natural and Art History (see Note 261).
1873–88, Burgtheater
Eduard van der Nüll, 1812–68, and August Siccard von Siccardsburg, 1813–68.
1858, prize in the Ringstrasse Competition.
1861–69, Opera House.
Both were pupils of Sprenger (cf. p. 6). For the rather tragic story of these two fellow-architectural students, see R. Eitelberger's biographies of 1869 in Bibl. 292, pp. 228–270. Adolf Placzek reports the following Viennese jingle about their Opera House:

'Herrn Siccardsburg und van der Nüll
die haben leider keinen Stül (style).
Ob Gothik oder Renaissance,
das ist den Herren alles 'ans (one).'

Alexander von Wielemans, 1843–1911.
1874–81, Palace of Justice.

58. On the Karlskirche setting see Hegemann & Peets, *Civic Art*, pp. 58–61, and *Sitte*, p. 30.

59. Buls, Bibl. 278, 2nd edit., p. 21, and Bibl. 277.

60. On the medieval revival in Austria see Sitte's essay (Bibl. 111), especially pp. 175ff, and R. Eitelberger, 'Die kirchliche Architektur in Oesterreich im Jahre 1852' (1853), in Bibl. 292, pp. 349–379.

61. In an amusing way (pp. 16–17), Eitelberger relates that after classical Greeks like Hippodamus had tried to straighten up and widen the streets of their ancient crowded towns, there were still those who preferred the old ways. He suggests that even in those days (late 5th century B.C.) there must have been a difference of opinion among architects as to whether regular or irregular planning was better. He cites as evidence of this a wry

passage in Aristophanes' *Birds* (994–1010) where Meton says to Peisthetairos:

Meton: 'I want to measure geometrically
Your atmosphere and map it out in acres . . .
A straight rule I apply to measure with
That so your circle may become quadrangular.
Market place in the middle
Straight roads converging to the very center
And thus, as from a star, being circular
Straight rays may flash their light in all directions!'

62. The complicated history of Semper's Hofburg plan is best illustrated in Alphons Lhotsky, *Die Baugeschichte der Museen und der Neuen Burg*, Vienna, Berger, 1941 (vol. I of *Festschrift des Kunsthistorischen Museums* . . . , 1941–45). Semper first submitted his ideas in the form of sketches in 1869, and came to Vienna in 1871 to execute them (with Hasenauer). See Note 288.

63. Sitte, Bibl. 53. The importance of Semper to city planning is a subject that has received little attention in the English-speaking world. (See Schumacher, Bibl. 205, pp. 44–47, and Fischer, Bibl. 180, *passim.*) Unfortunately, many of the basic publications about him are hard to come by in American libraries.

64. Bibl. 457. The passage quoted here is on p. 73.

65. In a letter written from Vienna, April 24, 1897. See Bibl. 352, I, p. 256.

66. Gurlitt, Bibl. 317, pp. 255–257.

67. The encircling roadway had been suggested in Stübben's winning plan in the 1893 competition. The green-belt was the idea of Eugen Fassbender (1854–1923), a Sitte follower who received a second prize in the 1893 competition. It was carried out in 1905 and seems to have become the model for such buffer zones in other world capitals. Fassbender described his project in Bibl. 293–295, but especially in Bibl. 293, which was devoted to the scheme, namely to leave open a 2000-foot-wide area outside the densely built-up section of the city. This belt would have no buildings in it, but instead would be planted so as to serve as a large 'air reservoir' and 'people's ring' for recreation and relaxation. Although Fassbender was a great admirer of Sitte's ideas, they seem to have played no part in this particular proposal. Sitte expressed enthusiasm about Fassbender's *Volksring*, but felt that the majority of the other competition entries were most unoriginal, especially Stübben's! (Bibl. 73).

The official plan for the green belt was worked out by the planning office under H. Goldemund: 'Wald- und Wiesengürtel Wien,' *ZOV*, LVII, 1905, pp. 465–470, 681, pl. XXII, and in *DB*, XXXIX, 1905, p. 361.

68. The results of the competition were reported in *ZOV*, XLVI, No. 9, 1894. Stübben himself was asked by *Deutsche Bauzeitung* to discuss the merits of the various competition entries which he did in Bibl. 395. He expressed great praise for Otto Wagner's plan.

The planning bureau was under the general direction of H. Goldemund (Note 67). A plan of his printed in *StB*, VII, 1910, pl. 52, suggests that Goldemund had become a Sittesque planner by that time.

The definitive overall plan for Vienna was published and discussed at length by Karl Mayreder in *WBZ*, XII, 1895, pp. 545–548, 567–570. Karl, the eldest of the brothers who had won the competition, was an architect and taught at the Hochschule; the younger brothers were an architect (Jules) and an engineer (Rudolph).

69. Bibl. 428. The format of this booklet makes one think of Frank Lloyd Wright's later pamphlets and broadsides. We have listed some of Wagner's major writings on city planning in Bibliography F.

His competition project had been published in 1893 (Bibl. 425) under the motto: 'Artis sola domina necessitas (Necessity is the sole mistress of art),' a slogan which he suggests he took from Semper, but ultimately is out of Aeschylus (*Prometheus Bound*). Wagner's early precepts on planning are to be found in his revolutionary book *Moderne Architektur* of 1894 (Bibl. 426). Although Sitte respected Wagner and later commented that it was a shame to lose him to the Sezession (*StB*, VI, 1909, p. 51), their criteria for a good city plan were far apart.

70. The important publications on this controversy are the following:

K. Mayreder's report on his final plan for the inner city in *WBZ*, XIII, 1896, pp. 251–256, 268–274, pl. 33.

Report on the public exhibition of the plan in *ZOV*, XLVIII, No. 7, 1896, pp. 87–89, pl. V.

Discussions of the freeing-up of old St. Stephen's in *ZOV*, XLVIII, Nos. 15, 18, 19, 1896, pp. 231–238, 281–284, 296–297.

Mayreder's public defense of the plan, *ZOV*, XLVIII, No. 26, 1896, pp. 389–394.

The five days of public discussion, in *ZOV*, XLVIII, Nos. 27–31, 1896, pp. 406–410, 419–424, 433–443, 447–455, 466–471. Sitte's contribution is reported on p. 410.

Stübben then summed the matter up in *DB* for October 1896. (See Bibl. 399.)

Notes to Chapter 5

SOME OTHER SOURCES OF SITTE'S IDEAS

71. See, for instance, Leixner, in Note 1. Sitte started quite a fad for this sort of thing. A good example is the article by Friedrich Kittner, 'Vitruvius und der Städtebau,' in *StB*, IV, 1907, pp. 31–36, which uses as its theme Sitte's admonition 'to go to school with the ancients.'

72. On Alberti as city planner, see W. E. Eden, Bibl. 178, and Etta Arntzen, *Alberti on City Planning*, unpublished M. A. essay, N.Y.C., Columbia University, Department of Art History and Archaeology, 1959. For text and pagination we have used Leone Battista Alberti, *Ten Books on Architecture* (Leoni trans.), London, Tiranti, 1955.

Notes to Chapter 6

SITTE'S POINT OF VIEW AND ANALYTICAL PROCEDURES

73. *Die Alten:* the word Sitte used, was a favorite expression of his which we have translated variously: 'our elders,' 'our predecessors,' 'the ancients,' 'the old masters,' etc.

74. F. Hoeber, in *StBK*, I, 1920, p. 233. This was not always used in a complimentary fashion. As Brinckmann saw it, Sitte's planning consisted of nothing but pictorial arrangements (Bibl. 267).

This taste for architectural closure of a scene which Sitte seems to share with Impressionist painting may owe something to the character of travel-book illustration. Compare Pissarro (Pl. VIII) with the view of a Florentine street that was done earlier by Bauernfeind (Pl. VI in the *Sitte* volume).

75. Walter Gropius, 'Tradition and the Center,' *Harvard Alumni Bulletin*, LIII, 1950, pp. 68–71.

76. It is hardly necessary to point out that the *Stadtbilder* tradition to which Sitte contributed so importantly had its origin, in part, among Venetian painters—Canaletto and Guardi—, and that the late Impressionists shared Sitte's enthusiasm for Venice. It is probably owing to Sitte's ecstatic description of it that the Piazza San Marco received so much attention in subsequent books on city planning.

77. Schumacher considered Sitte's emphasis on rhythmic spatial relationships instead of the customary solid building blocks to be a basic contribution of his book (Bibl. 205). Also see Goecke's remarks in Bibl. 14.

78. On this subject there already existed a sizable bibliography (witness Flügge in Note 30) and much lore, as we know from Sitte's Appendix I. See also Notes 322, 323. The British were unquestionably the pioneers in these matters, led by men like Sir Edwin Chadwick (1800–1890). They seem inevitably to have assumed a moral point of view on issues of city planning; Horsfall in his report (see our p. 19 and Note 100) was obsessed with the idea that owing to their more healthy environment the Germans drank and gambled less than the British (Bibl. 467, p. 161).

One only has to compare Stübben's long section on planted areas in his *Handbuch* to see how refreshing is Sitte's analysis of the same subject.

79. An account of how these ideas of Sitte's began to exert an effect in Germany by about 1910 is to be found in Hugo Koch, 'Neue Gartenkunst,' *StB*, IX, 1912, pp. 25–31. Henrici's republication of Sitte's article in 1901 (Bibl. 343) may have helped.

The article (*Sitte*, Appendix I) was omitted from the American edition of his book in 1945. Oddly enough Hegemann & Peets did not include any reference to it in their *Civic Art*, although Peets himself was much interested in theories about landscape architecture (e.g., Bibl. 361, 362).

80. For example, Chap. XI pp. 128–129. The most concise and faithful summary of Sitte's book which we know is one that exists unfortunately only in manuscript—a brief article prepared by Elbert Peets some years ago but never published (Bibl. 365).

Notes to Chapter 7

THE SUCCESSIVE EDITIONS AND TRANSLATIONS OF THE BOOK

81. For an exact description of each edition, see Bibliography A.

We have been unable to secure absolute figures of printing runs, sales, etc., of the various editions. It appears that each printing, German or

French, had been out of stock for some years before republication. Certainly the first German edition is rare, although most of the others are obtainable second-hand. The Spanish edition of 1926 was a small one and is still available; unfortunately, Spanish-speaking countries know Sitte mainly through the French translation, which seems to have had a very large distribution abroad.

82. This would include the Russian edition of 1925 and the perennial plans for an English edition. A Japanese translation was started a number of years ago by Professor Minoru Ohta of Hokkaido University (translator of Giedion—Bibl. 181), but it remains unfinished.

82a. We are indebted to Arthur R. Sprague for locating the Russian edition for us in Moscow and providing the translation of its Foreword which we print here.

83. Camille Martin, 1877–1928, was a Swiss architect and archaeologist, educated in Zürich, Munich, Karlsruhe, and Fribourg (Switz.). Attracted to city planning as a profession as a result of his work on Sitte's book, at the time of its translation he was still largely concerned with the restoration of medieval buildings. His schoolmate Hans Bernouilli tells us that while the translation was in progress they were both absorbed in Ruskin's *Seven Lamps of Architecture*. Ruskin does not talk much about the city-planning aspects of medieval life, but his general spirit can account for some of the liberties Martin took with Sitte. Incidentally, Ruskin, in discussing medieval asymmetries as purposeful creations, was a prototype for the ideas of Sitte on that subject which we have discussed on p. 57:

> 'I imagine I have given instances enough, though I could multiply them indefinitely, to prove that these variations are not mere blunders, nor carelessnesses, but the result of a fixed scorn, if not dislike, of accuracy in measurements; and, in most cases, I believe, of a determined resolution to work out an effective symmetry by variations as subtle as those of Nature.' *Seven Lamps*, Chap. V, para. XVIII.

Martin travelled extensively, was a teacher and editor, and ended up in the city-planning administration of Geneva. He laid out extensions for Chaux-de-Fonds and Nyon, drew up Geneva's zoning law, and was responsible for the Zürich city-planning exhibition during the year he died. He wrote standard French handbooks on the Romanesque art of France and Italy, the Gothic and Renaissance art of France. See his obituary by Bernouilli and Hoechel in *Das Werk* (Zürich), XV, 1928, pp. 366–367.

Martin was assisted in his work on the Sitte book by Bernouilli, Friedrich Puetzer, and H. Hindermann. Hans Bernouilli (1876 1959), a compatriot, friend, and frequent collaborator of Martin, became a city planner of note in Switzerland. His works were exhibited at Berlin in 1910, and he wrote a number of books and articles on planning problems, including contributions to *Der Städtebau* in its early years. Friedrich Puetzer (1871–1922), a Sittesque planner and student of Henrici whom we have mentioned elsewhere, was active mainly in Darmstadt where he was professor at the Hochschule. His city extension projects for Wiesbaden, Darmstadt, and Mainz were frequently illustrated (including at Berlin in 1910) and were commented upon favorably by Stübben, Unwin, and others. That for Darmstadt is discussed and illustrated in our Note 295. About Hindermann nothing further is known.

84. Georges Rohault de Fleury, Bibl. 479, 480; Stübben, *Handbuch.* In those cases where we have employed Martin's plans instead of Sitte's, we have usually indicated the source Martin used.

85. Michel A. E. A. Clerc of Marseille, professor at its University and École des Beaux-Arts, director of its archaeological museum, and president of its civic society, appeared on the masthead of the first issue of *Der Städtebau,* so he must have been in fairly close touch with the Sitte group.

86. George Ellsworth Hooker (1861–1939), a graduate of Amherst College and Yale Law School, attended Union Theological Seminary and Yale Divinity School. He was a member of the New York Bar and a pastor in the State of Washington before becoming a writer for Chicago newspapers. He travelled abroad a great deal in his study of city problems, and he became a representative at the League of Nations on such matters. He was Civic Secretary of the Chicago City Club and was active in the National Conference on City Planning. In addition to articles of immediate interest to us (Bibl. 156, 466), he wrote about traffic and the city plan (1908), congestion in Chicago (1910), street-railways in Chicago (1898), and the need for a union station in Chicago (1914). His project to translate Sitte is mentioned in many of the latter's obituary notices, although not in the article by Hooker himself.

87. Nils Hammarstrand, Swedish scholar, wrote a number of basic historical articles about city planning that appeared in the *Journal of the American Institute of Architects* between c. 1917 and 1926. He was later professor of architecture at the University of Virginia.

Notes to Chapter 8

SITTE'S IMPACT ON GERMAN CITY PLANNING

88. Among informative discussions of the first effects of Sitte's book are the following:

Necker (Bibl. 5); T. Fischer (Bibl. 297); Brix (Bibl. 177); Muthesius (Bibl. 198); Stübben (Bibl. 416).

89. The prize-winning Munich plan was published many times and was exhibited in Berlin in 1910. See pp. 83–84 and Note 98. He also won a prize for his Hanover plan, illustrated in Bibl. 337. Henrici's most pertinent publications are listed in Bibliography F.

90. Theodor Fischer (1862–1938) is another individual who merits a thorough study in English, because of the wide range of his influence on the modern movement. He was associated with the Jugendstil artists Eckmann, Endell, and Obrist in the Munich Secession. His humanistic interests are evidenced by his preoccupation with matters of proportion, perhaps inherited from his teacher, Thiersch. See Bibl. 296–300.

91. Theodor Goecke (1850–1919), in addition to his duties as editor of *Der Städtebau* from 1904 until his death, was professor at the Technische Hochschule of Berlin and protector of artistic properties in the province of Brandenburg (Berlin). Because of the number of books on Brandenburg

monuments edited under his name and the great deal of writing, signed and unsigned, that he did for the periodical, his bibliography is immense; we list in Bibliography F those titles that are significant to our study. Despite his many activities, he managed to carry out a number of planning projects, three of which were displayed in the Berlin exhibition of 1910. See his obituary in *Der Städtebau*, XVI (1919), pp. 1–3.

92. Fassbender: see Note 67.

Felix Genzmer, 1856–1929, partner with Joseph Brix in both architectural practice and sponsorship of the Berlin-Charlottenburg city-planning seminar (see p. 93). He taught at the Technische Hochschule in that city, was also active in Hagen and Wiesbaden. See Bibl. 301–304.

Karl Hocheder, 1854–1917, a colleague of Theodor Fischer at Munich, wrote unusual and perceptive aesthetic analyses of architectural problems. He has apparently never been the subject of a study in English.

Hermann Jansen, 1869–1945, editor of *Der Baumeister* and winner of the Greater-Berlin competition of 1910. See p. 58, and *StB*, XXIV, 1929, pp. 269–84.

Otto Lasne, 1854–1935, active in Munich. His plans were frequently published.

Friedrich Puetzer: see Note 83.

Others were Heinrich Goldemund (Note 68), Georg Metzendorf (Note 114), Friedrich Ostendorf, Robert Riedel, Richard Riemerschmid (Note 114), and Paul Schultze-Naumburg (Note 98). The magnitude of the commitment of these and others to Sitte would be a study in itself. The number of writers on cities and city history affected by Sitte is extremely large. Also the impact of Sitte on Scandinavia during this period is said to be profound: Eliel Saarinen is a case in point (see pp. 91–92).

93. On this see the extremely informative articles by Paul Klopfer on architectural developments (pp. 1555–1575) and Baumeister on city planning in Bibl. 264.

94. The contributions of the Tauts, Adolf Behne, Hermann Finsterlin, Paul Gösch and others to the 'Frühlicht' section of Gurlitt's magazine are as deliciously zany and Scheerbartian as one can find anywhere. Unfortunately, the early issues of *Stadtbaukunst* are now very rare, but some of this material has been described, excerpted, and illustrated in a recent book *The Architecture of Fantasy* (Bibl. 456). The statement with which Gurlitt was finally to read them out of the magazine is printed on p. 219 of volume I of *Stadtbaukunst*; it has just been reprinted with a collection of the Frühlicht articles (see Bibl. 421).

95. It would seem that prior to Sitte there existed very few studies of the architectural character of cities in history. Whether he was responsible for the rash that then broke out or he was merely part of that tendency is hard to say. There had, of course, long existed treatises in various languages on the city as a cultural or social phenomenon and as a legal entity—few of these are of concern to us. The successive editions of Stübben's *Handbuch* form a good barometer of this new taste in scholarship throughout the world. There is a marked increase in historical material in his later printings and a tremendous rise in bibliographical listings. Two serial publications, *Der Städtebau* (1904–) and *Städtebauliche Vorträge* of the Berlin city-planning seminar (1908–) include much research of this

type. An early effort was Fritz's *Deutsche Stadtanlage* of 1894 (Bibl. 461) which concentrated on the question of whether medieval layouts in Germany were primarily regular or irregular in plan—a dominating professional concern of the moment. Stübben reviewed the book and, as one might expect, Sitte, Buls, and Henrici were all mentioned (Bibl. 394).

These studies tended to search for answers to several questions that we have discussed elsewhere, among them: (1) was the picturesque character of the medieval town planned or accidental? (2) did the Middle Ages actually prefer irregularity or regularity? and (3) were churches and public buildings built in or left free by preference? Almost immediately it was pointed out that many new towns and new streets of the later Middle Ages had been laid out with compass and ruler, as in the bastides; this has been reiterated since by Hegemann & Peets (*Civic Art*, p. 228), Braunfels (Bibl. 452, p. 101), and others. In his *Handbuch* Stübben went to considerable length to demonstrate that the narrowing down of the corner openings of market places in such regularly planned towns had nothing to do with any aesthetic desire for closure, but was only to obtain longer and more profitable building frontages at those points. (1907, Fig. 484.) It would appear to be Brinckmann who led the most active assault on Sitte's concept of the medieval town. Brinckmann assumes a characteristic Wölfflinian position as regards the history of styles. The acknowledged leader of Renaissance planning theorists, he considered that the urban spaces in medieval towns were inert, unintegrated entities (Wölfflin's 'primitive') until virtually Renaissance times. According to his evolutionary scheme, plazas then improved qualitatively from the Renaissance to the Baroque, to be followed by a period of artistic degeneracy (because of lack of articulation) in the early 19th century; Sitte then reestablished formal relationships, but he was a hopeless romantic, etc.

Actually, Sitte's importance in the development of Baroque studies deserves attention. If, as those who have explored the matter suggest, the first art-historical writings that really discussed the Baroque in terms of its own qualities instead of treating it pejoratively were Gurlitt's *Geschichte des Barockstiles in Italien* of 1887 and Wölfflin's *Renaissance und Barock* of 1888, then Sitte, writing in 1889, should share honors with them for dignifying the style. His seventh chapter dwells on the peculiar virtues of Baroque planning so insistently that it is difficult to comprehend how later generations in Germany could have taken him to be purely a medievalist. For Sitte the Baroque and the pre-Baroque were simply two different methods of viewing a townscape (*Stadtbild*)—a manner of visual confrontation of styles that was not as systematic but yet not dissimilar to Wölfflin's. For background to such a study see O. Kurz, 'Barocco: storia di una parola,' in *Lettere Italiane*, XII, 1960, pp. 414–444, and R. Wittkower, 'Il Barocco in Italia,' Accademia Nazionale dei Lincei, *Problemi attuali di scienza e di cultura*, Quaderno 52, 1962, pp. 319–327.

96. This argument in *Deutsche Bauzeitung*, vol. XXV, 1891, proceeded as follows: Henrici, pp. 81–83, 86–91; Stübben, pp. 122–128, 150–155; Henrici, pp. 295–298, 301–302, 320–322; Stübben, pp. 368–370. Bibl. 336, 385, 337, 386.

97. The second exchange in *Deutsche Bauzeitung*, XXVII, 1893, was as follows: Henrici, pp. 271–274; Stübben, pp. 294–296; Henrici, p. 326; Stübben, pp. 349–350, 373–374, 415–418. There was a postscript in

XXVIII, 1894: Henrici, pp. 501–502, 506–509, 524; Stübben, pp. 608–610; Henrici, p. 628. See Bibl. 339, 388, 340, 389, 341, 394.

98. See Stübben's criticism of Henrici's Munich plan in *DB*, XXVII, 1893, pp. 193–194. A description of the whole competition is contained in the same volume, pp. 305ff., 329ff., 341ff., 389ff., 397ff., 401ff.

Henrici's renderings have been often reproduced: *DB*, XXVII, 1893, p. 273 and XXVIII, 1894, pp. 503, 509; and in Bibl. 323.

A very characteristic book of Sittesque sketches by an architect of the day is Otto Bünz, *Städtebau Studien*, Darmstadt, Zedler & Vogel, 1909. We note elsewhere Unwin's use of such pictures (p. 79 and Note 103). Schultze-Naumburg's book on city planning was entirely based on this system of *Stadtbilder*, relating photographs of city views to plans that have lines-of-sight drawn in; it is a sort of how-to-do-it handbook of Sittesque principles: *Städtebau* (Kulturarbeiten IV), Munich, Callwey, 1906; 2nd edit. 1909. This method of presentation has been revived in recent years by Gibberd (Bibl. 464), Logie (Bibl. 470), and Rauda (Bibl. 475–477). Some of those who are trying to incorporate the modern freeway more aesthetically into the city through which it slashes are using the *Stadtbilder* technique of analysis (*AF*, CXIX, October 1963, pp. 75–77, 'The View from the Road'). There have been attempts to evolve a symbolic notational system to indicate the *stadtbildlich* aspects of a town: P. Thiel, in *TPR*, XXXII, April 1961, pp. 33–52, and in *AR*, CXXXI, May 1962, pp. 320ff. A recent, very intricate example of this type of visual analysis in terms of *Stadtbilder* is *The Italian Townscape* by the de Wolfes and Kenneth Browne (Architectural Press, 1963).

The German literature on *Stadtbilder* is very extensive.

Notes to Chapter 9

THE INFLUENCE OF SITTE AND GERMAN PLANNING ABROAD

99. Theodor Goecke reported, on the occasion of Henrici's 75th birthday celebration, that the controversy that had greeted Henrici's Dessau and Munich plans subsided in time. Sitte had told Goecke that he liked both the plans very much. *StB*, XIV, 1917, p. 56.

100. In England an early example was James Pollard, who published *A Study in Municipal Government: The Corporation of Berlin*, Edinburgh and London, Blackwood, 1893 (2nd edit. 1894). Of greater influence on planners was, however, Thomas C. Horsfall (1841–1931) whose first visits to Germany led to his preparing a study on the city government of Manchester in 1895 and to an extended German study-tour in 1897. From the latter experience derived a quantity of lectures and newspaper articles, culminating in 1904 with the first book in English that reveals any first-hand contact with the personalities and ideas of Baumeister, Sitte, and Stübben: his *Example of Germany* (Bibl. 467). Unwin intimates that it was the reading of Horsfall's book that got him started, thus setting off the whole chain-reaction in Great Britain. On the influence of Horsfall see Bibl. 478.

Among similar individuals in the United States was Albert Shaw (1857–1947), an extremely influential figure who travelled on the Continent in 1889 and again in the 1890's, gathering materials for his *Municipal Government in Continental Europe* of 1895 (Bibl. 482). Shaw's public lectures on this subject, which included the Transformation of Vienna, received much publicity, and the American *Review of Reviews,* which he edited for many years, was full of reports about European developments. Also early was Sylvester Baxter (1850–1927), a Boston journalist who had been educated in Leipzig in the 1870's. Baxter is best known to art historians for his Latin American activities and his publication on Mexican Baroque architecture (1902). However, he also travelled in Europe and lectured and published from 1889 on about Germany's handling of municipal problems. He was a leading force in the development of Boston's famous municipal park system. While Secretary of the Metropolitan Improvements Commission of Boston, he translated Sittesque writings into English (Bibl. 298, 315), and he also wrote on civic art. Apparently a close friend of Edward Bellamy (1850–98), Baxter contributed the biographical introduction to the often-reprinted memorial edition of Bellamy's utopian novel, *Looking Backward.* Also see Bibl. 176.

Another figure of influence was Robert C. Brooks (1874–1941), a travelling-fellow in German universities during 1898–99, whose work with the magazine *Municipal Affairs* is discussed in our text. More interested in artistic matters was Charles Mulford Robinson (1869–1917) who was in Europe in 1891 and made a special study-trip for *Harpers Magazine* in 1899. George Ellsworth Hooker (see Note 86) is one who holds special interest for us because of his direct contact with the Sitte group whom he apparently met while in Germany during 1894–95. Hooker's newspaper article of 1904 on the German municipal reform movement is an admirable summary of that subject (Bibl. 466).

101. Regarding Baxter, see previous Note. For Fischer's lecture see Bibl. 298.

102. John W. Simpson (1858–1933), later president of the R.I.B.A. and secretary-general of its 1910 town-planning conference. His was a faithful, well-illustrated summary of the entire book, including Martin's chapter on streets. He also added a bit of his own on the controversy over traffic intersections (see Note 234). He mentioned in his lecture that he had on hand the translation of the 1893 Stübben paper by Buls, whom he knew. His presentation was enthusiastically received by the meeting, provoked much discussion, and was referred to in later years.

103. (1) Raymond Unwin (1863–1940). His *Town Planning in Practice* was most influential both in transmitting the Garden City idea, for which purpose it was composed, and Sitte's planning, on which it was based. It was much read, being reprinted in 1910, revised in 1911, reprinted again in 1919 and 1932; it was translated into German (1922), French (1924), and Russian. Not only did Unwin express unqualified praise for Sitte, Stübben, and other German planners, but the book is more thoroughly permeated with Sittesque images and ideas than even its author realized. In fact, its first six chapters might be said to be pure Sitte-artistry, its last six, pure Garden-City economics, law, and sociology. It is obvious that Unwin employed the French edition instead of the German, although he apparently could have read the latter quite easily. As we have noted elsewhere,

there is no better corpus of *Sittesche-Stil* plans and *Stadtbilder* to be found anywhere. He employed 'good' vs. 'bad' city vistas to drive home his points, a device that had been practiced on the Continent by Gurlitt, Schultze-Naumburg, and the periodical *Der Städtebau*, of which he made great use. He regretted (p. 225) that he and Parker had laid out the town square of Letchworth before he discovered Sitte's book, but made up for this in his later work—witness the turbine-plazas at Hampstead Garden Suburb. His study of German planning had been rapid and thorough. He claimed to have first heard about it in 1904, yet his 1906 paper at the London architects' congress showed him to be already well acquainted with the intricacies of its theories. (See also *JAIP*, Nov. 1964.)

(2) H. Inigo Triggs (1876–1923) seems to have been, after Unwin, the most effective exponent of German planning theories in Great Britain. Both his R.I.B.A. paper on public spaces and his book, *Town Planning, Past, Present, and Possible* (Bibl. 211) drew heavily on Sitte, Stübben, and Brinckmann for concept and illustration. Triggs considered the 1906 London congress to have been the turning point in the development of town planning in Great Britain.

(3) Patrick Geddes (1854–1932) was so strongly impressed by a tour of German cities undertaken in 1909 with S. D. Adshead and others that he devoted nearly three chapters to it in a general treatise on city planning which he was composing at that time (published in 1915 as Bibl. 222).

His comments about Sitte and Stübben are interesting:

> 'Dr. Stübben, the great authority on town planning, to whom Cologne and now Berlin owes the direction and general design of its contemporary expansion, is, despite all his unquestionable merits, too much of a Haussmann *redivivus* . . . His successor in Cologne realises this, and is modifying his designs in detail as fast as may be in harmony with the later and freer taste. Gently curved streets now tend to replace straight ones. . . .
>
> After the influence of Haussmann and Stübben there has also come in that of Camillo Sitte, that admirable architect of Vienna, who has done for the appreciation of the medieval city as a whole what the romantic revival did for its cathedral or town house. Since then we have come to forget that these were once regarded as chaotic and barbarous, and that the very name of "Gothic" was given to pointed architecture as a term of contempt and abuse. . . . But while we in British cities are still for the most part cheerfully proceeding with the removal of such characteristic minor features of the past as are necessary to isolate our monuments, and set them in the midst of the incongruous and transient ugliness of the present, it has been the great achievement of Camillo Sitte's memorable book to convince architects and art lovers generally that the antique city planners knew what they were doing better than we had ever realised, that their crowding up of the cathedral was no mere concession to the exigencies of space within a populous and small walled city, but was also the very condition of its towering sublimity, the artistic enhancement of its effect.' (Bibl. 222, pp. 200–202.)

Geddes was finding in the principles of Sitte a vindication of the techniques of 'conservative surgery' for urban troubles that he had arrived at through his quite different methods of analyzing man's environment. It is interesting to note that Geddes' prescription for the laying out of trees in the public squares of India was quite the same as Sitte specified in his 'Greenery within the City.'

104. While the 1910 Berlin-Düsseldorf exhibition was concerned with a variety of things, Sitte and his school received great emphasis. Both Otto March, who was in charge, and his student Werner Hegemann, who actually ran the exhibit, were admirers of Sitte. (See March on Sitte in Bibl. 192, p. 29. March, like Sitte, had been a student of Ferstel, and in turn was a considerable influence on Hermann Muthesius.) Numerous plans by Fischer, Goecke, Henrici, Puetzer, Siegfried Sitte, and other members of the school were displayed. Sitte's plans for Marienthal, Teplitz, Marienberg, and Olmütz were shown as well as a bronze portrait relief of him. That of Marienthal, the favorite of his last years, we illustrate in Pls. XII, XIII; Marienberg, Pl. II. See Goecke's review of the exhibition (Bibl. 311) and also the guides to the Berlin and Düsseldorf exhibitions (Bibl. 462, 463). Jansen, Goecke, and Stübben were members of the organizing committee for the exhibition.

105. Werner Hegemann (1881–1936) is another of the pivotal figures in the development of modern architecture and city planning who have gone unchronicled and virtually unnoticed. He is undoubtedly the most underrated member of the German intellectual diaspora of the 1930's, perhaps because he died, tragically, before the real impact of his tremendous knowledge could be felt in America. For nearly three decades he had reported from one side of the Atlantic the architectural progress of the other, publishing as much informative data of this type as did Berlage, Mendelsohn, Neutra, Le Corbusier and Frank Lloyd Wright put together. His education had been extensive, including studies at the technical institutes of Charlottenburg and Munich, the École des Beaux-Arts of Paris, and universities in London and Philadelphia. By 1905 he was conducting housing studies for the city of Philadelphia. In 1909 he organized a city-planning exhibition in Boston, in 1910 that of Berlin-Düsseldorf in Germany. In 1912 he was prosecuted for the publicity he gave (with Käthe Kollwitz) to wretched housing conditions in Berlin. The following year he was invited by the People's Institute to give a nationwide lecture tour and advice to municipalities in America. The war caught him on the high seas, visiting China, Japan and Australia. During 1913–16 he had been engaged in planning the East Bay community of San Francisco. From 1916–21 he was in partnership with Elbert Peets and Joseph Hudnut in the layout of communities in Wisconsin and Pennsylvania (some of these plans are shown in their *Civic Art*, pp. 198, 213, 216–217, 223, 280–283). After more travel in Western Europe and the Near East, he was called to Berlin to edit the two Wasmuth publications, *Der Städtebau* and the *Monatshefte*, which were amalgamated in 1930 under his direction. He lectured and consulted in Argentina in 1931. Hegemann was personally brave and intellectually scrupulous; no enthusiast for the contemporary styles, he provided them an open forum and wrote countless articles and monographs on even the most eccentric of his contemporaries. In 1931, on the occasion of his 50th birthday he was accorded felicitations from the most oddly-assorted artists (*Wasmuths Monatshefte*, XV, July 1931, pp. 335–336). A student of economics and political science, he wrote a number of outspoken political books and essays. He attacked hero-worship in particular—Napoleon and Frederick the Great. He had called the latter 'as great a scoundrel as

Hitler' and, when his last such book—*History Unmasked*—was on the presses in 1933, he felt constrained to leave for the United States! Here he taught at Columbia University and at the New School for Social Research until his untimely death. For his publications on city planning see Bibliography F.

Elbert Peets, born 1886, received his master's degree in landscape architecture from Harvard in 1915, and was awarded a Charles Eliot travelling fellowship. Following his partnership with Hegemann, he was active in governmental planning and housing and as a lecturer at Yale and Harvard. He has been one of our most discerning historians of city planning, especially regarding Washington, where he now resides. For a selection of publications by him, see Bibliography F.

106. Professional reaction to *Civic Art* was mixed in the U.S.A. and U.K. which were both in the grip of informal planning at that time (Bibl. 327–330). Peets shortly afterwards attacked heatedly in the *American Mercury* the picturesque school of landscape architecture as it was taught at Harvard University and elsewhere (see Bibl. 361–362).

107. The magazine *Der Städtebau* can claim, in 1904, to be the first city-planning periodical devoted exclusively to that subject. Before its time city planning had been treated in architectural and engineering magazines, and in periodicals devoted to housing, house-and-garden, and municipal affairs. There had been considerable reportage and discussion of planning in these other types of magazines, but it had never received more than a section, a supplement, or a special issue. Actually there had been one predecessor to *Der Städtebau*—the magazine *La Ciudad Lineal* of Madrid (1897–1932). However, this was not internationally known at that time, it doubled in function as a community news sheet, and it pushed one particular scheme of planning as was the case with *Garden Cities and Town Planning* of London, which was started late in 1904. *La Ciudad Lineal*, originally called the 'official organ of the Compañia Madrileña de Urbanización,' had in 1902 revised its masthead to read, 'Revista de urbanización, ingeniería, higiene, y agricultura'; so that before 1904 it was appearing as a predominantly city-planning periodical (see Bibl. 453).

Some idea of the enormous range of serial publications that have to be consulted for early information on planning and civic affairs can be obtained from the magazines listed in *Municipal Affairs* for 1899. By the time of World War I, such sources were much more numerous; see *Municipal Reference Library Notes* of the New York Public Library, III, March 9, 1917, pp. 190–195. Important early serials devoted purely to city planning, listed in the order of their emergence, were:

1897	*La Ciudad Lineal* (Madrid)
Jan. 1904	*Der Städtebau* (Berlin & Vienna)
Oct. 1904	*Garden Cities and Town Planning* (London)
1908–	*Städtebauliche Vorträge* (Berlin)
1909–	*The American City* (NYC)
	Proceedings of the National Conference on City Planning (Boston)
1910–	*Town Planning Review* (Liverpool)
1912–14	*La Cité-jardin* (Paris)
1914–	*Journal* [Papers and Discussions] *of the Town Planning Institute* (London)

1915–18	*The City Plan* (Boston)
1919–	*La Cité* (Brussels)
	La Vie urbaine (Paris)
1920–	*Stadtbaukunst* (Berlin)
	Tijdschrift voor Volkshuisvesting en Stedebouw (Amsterdam)
	Civitas (Barcelona)

Der Städtebau, as one might surmise from its title, put emphasis from the start on Sitte's principle of overall building plans of a three-dimensional character, artistically devised with city vistas (*Stadtbilder*) in mind. This, as opposed to the simple two-dimensional engineering survey. Incidentally, it retained an elaborate Jugendstil and Viennese-Sezession format down to the time of its change in editors in 1919.

Founded by Sitte and Goecke, *Der Städtebau* first appeared in January of 1904, published by Ernst Wasmuth Verlag in Berlin and Vienna, edited by Goecke (Sitte died before the first issue appeared). Upon Goecke's death in 1919, the architect H. de Fries became editor. Publication was suspended 1923–24, resumed in 1925 under the editorship of Werner Hegemann, who also edited *Wasmuths Monatshefte* (founded 1914). In January 1930 the *Monatshefte* absorbed *Der Städtebau* which then appeared as a quarterly supplement until 1939; the *Monatshefte* ceased publication in 1942. Hegemann had left Germany in 1933. During its publication the complete title of *Der Städtebau* changed slightly, and for a time it came out only bi-monthly.

108. This photograph, now in the files of the Harvard University city-planning library, was taken at the 1910 Berlin exhibition by George B. Ford, the Harvard planner. See Note 17.

109. Bibl. 198. The contributions of Hermann Muthesius (1861–1927) to the modern movement in architecture and design are well known. He was undoubtedly one of the avenues by which the Prussian government, of which he was a part, insinuated itself into the city-planning movement. After all, the building of cities was only one of the several activities in which organized groups in Germany were at this time seeking to attain beauty and efficiency of design. The way in which the improvement of cities had become a basic ingredient of Imperial political policy before World War I is made clear in the writings of Frederick C. Howe (1867–1940) one of the later students of municipal affairs in Europe: 'City Building in Germany,' *Scribner's Magazine*, XLVII, 1910, pp. 601–614; *European Cities at Work*, NYC, Scribner's, 1913, *passim*. Compare Note 22. Patrick Geddes, too, showed himself to be acutely aware of this in his discussion of German planning (Bibl. 222).

As founder of the Werkbund, Muthesius' endorsement of Sitte must have been very influential on the younger generation in Germany, as was his espousal of the Garden-City idea: the two converged in the designing of Riemerschmid's Hellerau suburb. The points Muthesius emphasized in his 1910 testimonial to Sitte should be of interest to students of modern theory. Muthesius was an original associate of *Städtebau* magazine and was probably responsible for the 1914 Werkbund Exhibition being laid out as an exemplar of Sittesque city building.

110. For an account of the Canberra competition, descriptions of the ranking projects in the competition, and the work of the winner, Walter Burley Griffin (1876–1937), see Peisch, Bibl. 473.

111. For the London and Vienna congresses see Bibl. 487 and 451. For description of the ceremony in Vienna: *StB*, V, 1908, p. 97.

112. Regarding the Vienna Ring, see Note 67. The Berlin scheme had been advanced by the Countess Adelheid Dohna (pseud. 'Arminius'), in *Die Grossstädte in ihrer Wohnungsnoth: und die Grundlagen einer durchgreifenden Abhilfe*, Leipzig, Duncker & Humblot, 1874.

113. Theodor Fritsch, *Die Stadt der Zukunft*, Leipzig, 1896. The 2nd edit. of 1912 had 'Gartenstadt' added to the title. Fritsch's project shared several things with Howard's. Complete control over growth, in this case by zones laid out in harmony with an expanding spiral emanating from the center of the city where there was to be a central plaza with monumental buildings, free of traffic. Land was to be held in common, with a house and garden for everyone. Greenery was used lavishly within the city, and the whole was to be isolated at its periphery by agricultural lands. The city itself was to be much larger in size than Howard's, however, with multilevel streets.

114. Good examples are Richard Riemerschmid's model town of Hellerau near Dresden, and the work of Georg Metzendorf at the Krupp colonies in the Ruhr. On these and others see P. Abercrombie, in *TPR*, I, 1910, pp. 246–250, and H. Muthesius, *Kleinhaus und Kleinsiedlung*, Munich, Bruckmann, 1918 and 1920.

115. Hans E. von Berlepsch-Walenda (1849–1921), a Swiss Garden-City exponent, active in Germany and Austria.

116. A. R. Sennett, *Garden Cities in Theory and Practice*, 2 vols., London, Bemrose, 1905.

117. Ildefonso Cerdá, *Teoría general de la Urbanización, y aplicaciones de sus principios y doctrinas a la reforma y ensanche de Barcelona*, 2 vols., Madrid, Imprenta Española, 1867.

Oskar Jürgens, *Spanische Städte, ihre bauliche Entwicklung und Ausgestaltung* (*Abhandlungen aus dem Gebiet der Auslandskunde*, XXIII), Hamburg, Friedrichsen, 1926.

In Spain, the inventors of Linear Planning recognized very early the affinity of the Garden City with their own intention to urbanize rural life and ruralize urban life. It provided them with an entree into the worldwide city-planning movement by the time of World War I. Benoit-Lévy found himself promoting two types of Garden City, the British satellite one and the Spanish linear one. See Bibl. 453.

118. (1) The City Beautiful in England:

H. H. Stratham, 'Street Architecture,' *Architect* (London), LVI, Dec. 11, 1896, pp. 380ff.

Arts and Crafts Exhibition Society, *Art and Life and the Building and Decoration of Cities*, London, Rivington, Percival & Co., 1897. See especially Chap. II: W. R. Lethaby, 'Beautiful Cities.'

Halsey Ricardo, 'Ideal City,' *Builder* (London), LXXVIII, 1900, pp. 613–618. Partly reprinted in *AA*, XXIX, 1900, pp. 29–30.

T. C. Horsfall, et al., *Papers of the City Beautiful Conference, Liverpool, 1907*, Liverpool, Young, 1907.

Patrick Geddes, 'The City Beautiful in theory and practice,' *GCTP*, n.s. III, 1913, pp. 196–200.

(2) *The Town Planning Review:*

Patrick Abercrombie, 'German Garden Cities,' in I, 1910–11, pp. 246–250, and 'Vienna,' Bibl. 172; 'Berlin, its Growth and Present State,' in IV, 1913–14, pp. 222–230; 'The Era of Architectural Town Planning [Renaissance Principles],' in V. 1914–15, pp. 195–213.

S. D. Adshead, 'Decoration and Furnishing of the City,' in II–V, 1911–1915, *passim* (16 parts!).

119. Rewritten as 'Architecture, Nature and Magic,' *The Builder*, CXXXIV–CXXXV, 1928, *passim*; in book form 1956, London, Duckworth.

120. A. Mathieu, *Projet d'une capitale modèle*, Paris, Baudry, 1880. This ingenious utopian, obsessed with the idea that non-maritime nations are an obstruction to world progress, worked out a siting for his ideal capital that would allow it to be serviced by canals (Le Corbusier's 'route d'eau') as well as by a system of highways and railways. It is essentially a transportation-plan, and interesting to us today are the facts that he segregated his dwellings by height and that the capital has an appendage at the side for its docks and industrial complexes, causing it to resemble markedly Le Corbusier's Plan for a City for 3,000,000 (1921–1922).

121. A good example of this is an article on endless railways and moving platforms, 'Endlose Eisenbahn,' that appeared in *CBB*, IX, 1889, pp. 152–153, summarizing the latest English, American, and French inventions of the day.

122. August Scherl, *Ein neues Schnellbahnsystem: Vorschläge zur Verbesserung des Personenverkehrs*, Berlin, 1909. This was picked up by *Deutsche Bauzeitung* (magazine of the Berlin *Verein*) and by the *Scientific American* that same year.

123. For the traditions that lay behind Garnier's project, see Dora Wiebenson, 'Utopian Aspects of Tony Garnier's Cité Industrielle,' in *Journal of the Society of Architectural Historians*, XIX, 1960, pp. 16–24. More details will be found in her master's essay on the same subject (Bibl. 216), in which there are also perceptive comments on the place of Sitte in the planning traditions of the time, although she assumes him to have been motivated primarily by medieval principles.

124. Bruno Taut, 1880–1938. About his utopian projects see *Architecture of Fantasy: Utopian Building and Planning in Modern Times* (Bibl. 456). See also p. 80 and his publications on planning, Bibl. 418–424.

Taut had certain reservations about Sitte—considering him to be a romantic, looking backwards—but at the same time he felt that Sitte, with the aid of Goecke, had revolutionized city planning. His *Stadtkrone* took its cue from the same remarks in Aristotle about security, health, and happiness that Sitte had cited (see Note 135). His debt to Sitte has been noted by others: R. Banham, *Theory and Design in the First Machine Age*, NYC, Praeger, 1960, p. 255.

125. Some characteristic articles of this nature, usually extolling the European capitals and the buildings of McKim, Mead and White, include:

Barr Ferree, 'Value of Good Architecture in Cities,' *Engineering Magazine*, X, 1895, pp. 671–689;

Charles R. Lamb, 'Civic Architecture from its Constructive Side,' *Municipal Affairs*, II, March, 1898, pp., 46–72;

George Kriehn, 'The City Beautiful,' *Municipal Affairs*, III, December, 1899, pp. 594–601;

Jane L. Boulden, 'Development of Aesthetics in Cities,' *Arena Quarterly*, I, June 1900, pp. 108ff.

126. Le Corbusier's major onslaughts on Sitte occurred in his *Urbanisme* of 1925 (Bibl. 187, pp. iii, 5–6, 9–10) and in *Quand les cathédrales étaient blanches* of 1937 (Bibl. 188, p. 68). The passages are eloquent and clever (see the English translations), but are sinister, leading as they do in his second book to the conclusion that for Sitte, 'confusion is beautiful, and rectitude is base . . .,' an obvious absurdity. These indictments are the more grave since, as has been pointed out, Le Corbusier himself owes a considerable amount to Sitte—as would any planner of the 1920's who was so well acquainted with the history of architecture. The Le Corbusier-Sitte confrontation has been the subject of much writing, of which notable examples are Adshead's 'Sitte and Le Corbusier' (Bibl. 152), the Goodmans' *Communitas* (Bibl. 182, *passim*), and Wittkower's review (Bibl. 22).

127. Besides Bibl. 205 and 206, Schumacher published a fine anthology of writings (mainly German) on city planning (Bibl. 207). This contains selections from some 75 writers, including the following who are of interest to us: Vitruvius, Alberti, Semper, Lichtwark, Riehl, Fritsch, Unwin, Sitte (Chap. X), Gurlitt, T. Fischer, Brinckmann, Otto Wagner.

Incidentally, Schumacher considered that the technical advances in 19th-century planning had not been as satisfactory as Sitte suggested, because sufficient account had not been taken of the social side of the problems which the technicians were trying to ameliorate.

128. Boyarsky, Bibl. 154; the author was handicapped by his inability to read German. Maksimović, in Serbian (Bibl. 162).

NOTES TO CONCLUSION

129. To say, however, as some modern critics have, that Sitte was hampered by not yet possessing the resource of the 'air view,' and that he therefore saw only part of the picture, is unjustified. The bird's-eye-view drawing had been a convention in the study of the form of cities for a couple of centuries before him (witness the large 24-sheet engraving from which our Pl. XI is taken), and one of our best documentations as to the appearance of Vienna in the middle of the nineteenth century is a series of superb old panoramic photographs taken from the tower of St. Stephen's in the center of the inner city. (Photo series is reproduced in Eisler, Bibl. 458, and in Eduard Castle, *Panorama von Wien im Jahre 1860*, Vienna, Staatsdruckerei, 1929.) We know that looking down on a town from above was fundamental to Sitte's own process of analysis (cf. p. 47).

130. Peets (Bibl. 365, p. 10).

CRITICAL AND EXPLANATORY NOTES TO SITTE'S "CITY PLANNING ACCORDING TO ARTISTIC PRINCIPLES"

The following notes refer to the companion volume, *City Planning according to Artistic Principles* by Camillo Sitte, translated by George R. Collins and Christiane Crasemann Collins. That volume contains no numbered references, but the page numbers and catchwords preceding each note below will identify the passage to which it refers.

TRANSLATORS' PREFACE

page XI

131. 'CITY PLANNING': Previous research (Bibl. 478, *Oxford English Dictionary*) has suggested that the years 1906–07 saw the first recorded usage of the word 'town planning' in English. We find, however, that Raymond Unwin employed it so casually in his address at the London Congress of 1906 that it must have been in circulation before that time; the American planner Warren H. Manning spoke about 'city and town planning' in an article in *The Craftsman* (Eastwood, N.Y.), V, February, 1904, p. 425. About 'city planning,' the American equivalent of 'town planning' and a term not recognized by the Oxford dictionary, we have no reliable information; a cursory check suggests that both 'city planning' and 'city plan' (in the sense of professional activity) were used fairly early in the United States. The American translator of Stübben's 1893 paper (Bibl. 390) employed 'city plan,' but talked of the 'laying out of cities' instead of 'city planning.'

As regards the various German terms: *Stadtplan* and *Stadtbau* were used by W. H. Riehl and others before 1860. Eitelberger in 1858 (Bibl. 290) used *Stadtanlage*; Baumeister tended to emphasize *Stadterweiterung* in his early writings, later substituting *Städtebau* in the twentieth century. The Austrians favored *Stadtplan* in 1877 (Bibl. 457), and Sitte seemed to use *Stadtplan* and *Stadtanlage* interchangeably, not always pressing the distinction between them and *Städtebau* or *Stadtbau*, both of which he used.

page XIII

132. WINGED SNAIL: This is very likely by Sitte. He was an accomplished draftsman (see above, p. 9), and his friend Albert Ilg was an expert in nineteenth-century emblem-making: Martin Gerlach and Albert Ilg, *Allegorieen und Embleme*, 2 vols., Vienna, Gerlach & Schenk, 1882–85.

133. OLD PRINTS: A good example is Gustav Bauernfeind (1848–1904), architect and painter of romantic townscapes who collaborated with the

wood-engraver Adolf Closs (1840–1894) in many of the illustrations for Kaden's *Italien* (Bibl. 469), a travel book. For the fanciful restorations of Greece and Rome Sitte drew on *Hellas und Rom* by Jakob von Falke (1825–1897), writer of a number of books on art, styles, costumes, etc. (Bibl. 459). It may be that the character of these illustrations contributed to Sitte's own image of what an old town was and should be. That is to say, the very books from which he drew his illustrations may have been a visual source for his theoretical ideas. The way in which he starts his Conclusion (p. 160) would appear to confirm this.

AUTHOR'S PREFACES

page XVII

134. FOURTH EDITION: Actually none of the changes or additions that were made in the French edition ever appeared in subsequent German ones, except for the inclusion of the Greenery essay, printed in full and not condensed or rearranged as in the French.

Other than the ancient plans mentioned, the only such redrawing seems to have been the plan of Salzburg (Sitte's Fig. 73). See Note 213.

On the occasion of this edition the text was completely re-set for the first time, modernizing the spelling, eliminating some typographical errors, and carrying out minor changes in expression and vocabulary. Some of this modernization of spelling had already been done for the previous edition of 1901.

INTRODUCTION

page 3

135. SECURE AND HAPPY: This appears to be adapted from Aristotle's *Politics*, Book VII, and is a statement that gained certain currency in German city-planning circles, perhaps through the influence of its use here. For instance, Bruno Taut in his *Stadtkrone* (Bibl. 419, pp. 54–55) repeats it after some comments about Sitte and Goecke, and it carried over into Rosa Schapiro's review of *Stadtkrone* in Bibl. 420. See also above, p. 75.

page 5

136. VITRUVIUS: Kindred subjects, Book V, Introduction, paragraph 5; public buildings, Book I, Chapter VII; healthy locations, Book I, Chapter IV; street plotting, Book I, Chapter VI; Dinocrates, Book II, Introduction, paragraphs 1–4; basilica, Book V, Chapter I.

page 6

137. VITRUVIUS ON THE FORUM: Book V, Chapter I, paragraphs 1–2. We have used here: Vitruvius, *The Ten Books on Architecture,* trans. by M. H. Morgan, New York, Dover, 1960, p. 131. In this publication Marcus Vitruvius Pollio is identified as a Roman architect and engineer of the Augustan period. English readers might be interested to know that the translator of the Spanish edition of Sitte in 1926 referred his readers at this point to Bulwer Lytton's *Last Days of Pompeii* [Book III, Chapter 1] for a 'vivid description of this.'

pages 6–7

138. POMPEIIAN FORUM: This plan was drawn for the 4th edition by Siegfried Sitte, replacing an earlier, less correct one that seems to have been based on Overbeck. See Note following.

139. CITY LARES: There is a confusion here. The texts of the German editions, and that of the Spanish one which was based on them, persist in referring to this structure as the Meeting Hall of the Decurions—as it had been represented on the plan that Sitte used in his first three editions (see previous Note). However, in the fourth edition of 1909 his son's new plan identified the building as the Sanctuary of the City Lares, a correction that had already been made in text and plan of the 1902 French edition (and in the 1945 English translation which here followed the French).

Sitte's older plan had also shown more clearly how he thought the building intruded on and replaced the colonnade effect at this point. Actually, there is observable in architectural reconstructions of this period considerable question about the uniformity and character of the surrounding colonnade, which was perhaps less homogeneous in appearance than either of the Sitte plans would suggest.

page 8

140. FORUM ROMANUM: This romantic restoration by Gustav Bauernfeind was engraved by Adolf Closs and H. J. Dignus for Bibl. 459, p. 278, from which Sitte took it for his earlier editions. It was replaced in the fourth German edition by the plan (Fig. 2) drawn by Siegfried Sitte.

141. ARISTOTLE: *Politics,* VII, 12.

142. PAUSANIAS: *Description of Greece,* Book X, Chapter 4, paragraph 1.

143. MARKET PLACE IN ATHENS: This very formally arranged reconstruction of the Athenian Agora, by J. Bühlmann, had appeared in Falke, Bibl. 459, p. 108. It was used only in the first three German editions.

Little was known of the actual disposition of the buildings in the Agora until the American excavations of the 1930's. Baedeker, an ultimate authority on Greek matters in Sitte's day, says as late as 1894 in a second, revised edition:

> 'The visitor, however, must rely entirely on his imagination, assisted by a few historical and topographical notices in Pausanias, if he wishes to form an idea of the former condition of this focus of ancient Athenian life. No traces now remain of the *Metroon* or temple of the Mother of the Gods, the *Bouleuterion* or senate-house, the *Prytaneion,* the King's hall, and the other large and important buildings which once stood here . . .' (p. 86).

page 10

144. OLYMPIA: This was drawn by Siegfried Sitte for the 4th edition.

pages 11–12

145. ATHENIAN ACROPOLIS: The first three editions had employed Thiersch's restoration of 1878. This was replaced in the fourth edition by a photograph and a plan drawn by Siegfried Sitte.

As regards the lower gate and monumental staircase that Sitte mentions and that had figured in Thiersch's restoration, Sitte seems to have been unaware that these elements, whose remains are now removed, had been Roman additions; the Greeks used a zigzag ramp for access, as is clear from any modern restoration and, in fact, from his son's later plan.

It is unfortunate that Camillo Sitte did not possess our contemporary knowledge of the disposition of the Acropolis buildings within their separate precinct walls (which do not appear on the plan) because it would have reinforced considerably his opinions about the closed character and internal arrangement of public spaces. See, for example, R. Stillwell, 'The Siting of Classical Greek Temples,' *JSAH*, XIII, No. 4, December 1954, pp. 3ff.

Notes on Chapter I

THE RELATIONSHIP BETWEEN BUILDINGS, MONUMENTS, AND THEIR PLAZAS

page 14

146. FLORENCE, THE SIGNORIA: This print, used in the first four German editions, was replaced by a photograph in the fifth. It had been designed by G. Bauernfeind and engraved by A. Closs for the travel book, *Italien; eine Wanderung von den Alpen bis zum Aetna* (Bibl. 469) where it appeared on p. 145.

147. LOGGIA DEI LANZI: Although all the German editions used photographs of the Loggia dei Lanzi, we have substituted a print from the same book that Sitte employed so often: Kaden's *Italien* (p. 157). See previous note. The view was drawn by G. Bauernfeind, engraved by A. Closs.

148. FOUNTAINS: Sitte had already written a piece in 1879 about his own restoration of a market fountain in Salzburg, and his periodical *Der Städtebau* was to carry an illustrated series on monumental fountains during its first year (1904, Hefte 10–11).

149. PISA: The illustrations are from the French edition; none of Pisa was included in the German ones. The view of the piazza was drawn for the French edition by H. Hindermann. The plan is after Rohault de Fleury (Bibl. 479, atlas, pl. VIII).

page 16

150. BRESLAU: These remarks about Breslau and the North were omitted from the French edition. The print, by Slapnicka, was replaced by a photograph in the fifth German edition.

page 17

151. VIENNA: On the artistic renaissance that came about in Vienna in connection with the Votive Church and the Ringstrasse development, see Collins pp. 36ff. See also Sitte's own proposals in his Chapter XII. Data on the buildings Sitte mentions in this paragraph will be found in Note 57.

152. GOOSEGIRL: *Das schöne Gänsemädchen* by Ant. Wagner, 1866, was placed in the corner of a small plaza.

page 18

153. MICHELANGELO'S DAVID: We have added this view of the piazza in order to illustrate Sitte's point. It did not appear in the German or other editions of the book. We have selected a photograph that approximates as closely as possible the 'large Alinari photograph' that Sitte mentions but is not suitable for reproduction. He probably saw the statue in its original position, since he traveled in Italy both before and after it was removed. The marble replica was placed there in 1910.

Notes on Chapter II

THAT THE CENTER OF PLAZAS BE KEPT FREE

page 20

154. CENTRAL PLACEMENT: The historical development is not as simple as Sitte suggests. Central placement, in the Imperial Roman and Baroque periods at least, seemed to carry with it certain symbolic images of autocratic power. It was a preferred form in later Roman planning and then appears to have lapsed somewhat during the Middle Ages, so its history was more one of ups and downs than Sitte implies here. In this connection see Hegemann & Peets, *Civic Art*, p. 54, and illustrations 251–264.

Joseph Stübben did not entirely agree with Sitte about the virtues of open centers in public squares. In his review of Sitte's book (Bibl. 4) this was one of the major exceptions which he took to Sitte's ideas; in his *Handbuch* he argued several of Sitte's points about plaza design and cited many examples of what he considered to be fine central placement, although few of them were actually drawn from the Greek, early Roman, or medieval periods.

pages 22–23

155. NUREMBERG: We have used the plan from the French edition as it is more exact than Sitte's. It is after Stübben's *Handbuch*, Fig. 712. Hegemann & Peets point out that the large market place was cleared in the 14th century as part of a reclamation scheme that razed the old ghetto (p. 14).

page 24

156. FOUNTAIN PLACEMENT: The French edition inserts after the Piazza Farnese:

> 'Likewise in France, the Fountain of St. Lazare in Autun (Fig. 3) and the Fountain of the Innocents in Paris. Before 1786 the latter occupied the angle formed by the Rue aux Fers and the Rue Saint Denis, instead of standing in the middle of a *place*."

The final comment of the previous paragraph, about the German custom, was omitted from the French edition, as were numerous other asides throughout this chapter.

157. PADUA, PIAZZA DEL SANTO: This plan is from the French edition; it was not illustrated in the German editions. About this placement, see also Hegemann & Peets, *Civic Art*, Fig. 31, caption.

page 25

158. PADUA, PIAZZA PETRARCA: This is also from the French edition, not being illustrated in the German.

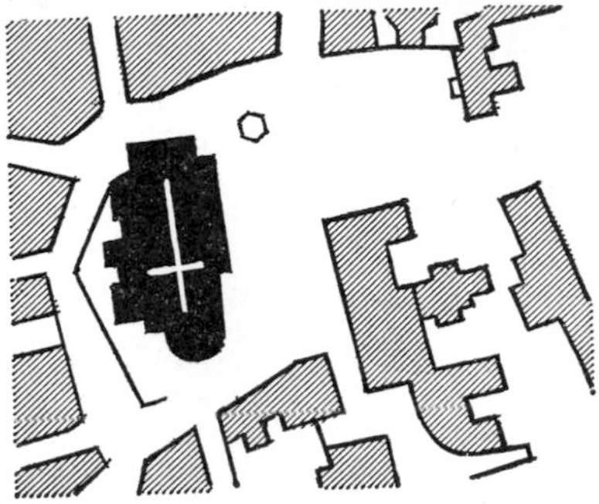

Fig. 3. Autun: Place Saint Louis and the Fountain of Saint Lazare

page 26

159. PIACENZA: This paragraph about Piacenza and its illustrations were omitted from the French edition.

page 27

160. LUCCA, S. MICHELE: We have used the plan from the French edition as it is more exact than Sitte's. It is after Rohault de Fleury, Bibl. 480, atlas II, pl. LI.

161. VICENZA: We have used the plan from the French edition as it is more exact than Sitte's.

162. OLDER FREESTANDING CHURCHES: The French edition also illustrates Pisa (*Collins*, Fig. 4) as an example of this. The Pisa plan, which did not appear in the German editions, is after Rohault de Fleury, Bibl. 480, atlas II, pl. XXXVIII.

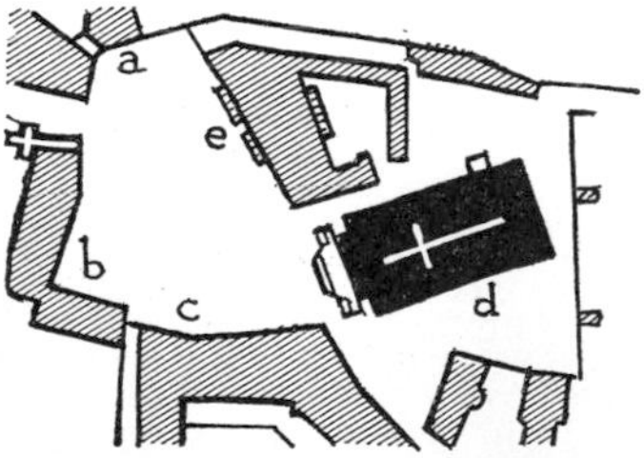

Fig. 4. Pisa. a. Torre della Fame.—b. Palazzo Vecchio.—c. Palazzo del Podestà.—d. S. Stefano.—e. Palazzo degli Anziani

page 28

163. PERSPECTIVE AND STAGE EFFECTS: Sitte's mode of describing and criticizing the formal elements of towns reveals in many ways his preoccupation with the science of visual perception in his day.

Both he and his followers (cf. Camille Martin's remarks in Chapter VIIA) often speak in terms of the principles of linear perspective. In this connection it should be remembered that Sitte was himself a painter as well as a student of the history of perspective. He had written a history of perspective drawing, a study of the perspective of Piero della Francesca, and a handbook on new methods of perspective construction (Note 8). See his other urban analyses of this type: *Sitte*, pp. 39, 44, 79ff., 99, 129.

He relies frequently on such terms as 'line of sight' or 'line of vision' (*Visurlinie*) to make his points or to support his aesthetic judgments. He parallels, in this sense, the Hildebrand-Fiedler-Wölfflin ideas that both an aesthetics and a history of aesthetics can be based on the artist's or spectator's visual habits or patterns. For Sitte the ultimate in beauty was apparently a panorama of somewhat kaleidoscopic pieces in a closed but asymmetrical pictorial arrangement, hanging like a tapestry in front of the eye of the passing, savoring spectator—essentially a late Impressionist mode of vision. He speaks in terms of controlled or unobstructed, *but closed off*, lines of sight: *Sitte*, pp. 24, 33, 34, 97, 101–102. Or in terms of what the spectator can take in at one glance: *Sitte*, pp. 29, 34, 40, 49, 91, 149. Or, here, as though we were looking at a stage-set—certainly a Renaissance or Baroque conceit. Note also *Sitte*, pp. 79, 81, 109.

He by no means limited himself, however, to simple physical or geometrical aspects of vision, but tackled the formal problems of city building from the most advanced psychological points of view, which verged on the intuitive and were characteristic of the new anti-rational orientation that marked the Art Nouveau period. This is especially observable in his comments about space perception in his Chapter IV (pp. 41–42) and V (pp. 48–49).

With regard to the matters of proportion that are inevitably involved in this, he was interested in the Golden Section and its practical usage (Bibl. 106). See his Chapter V, pp. 51–52, for his discussion of Proportion and Symmetry.

All of this is treated above pp. 50ff.

page 29

164. VIENNA, KAROLINENPLATZ: This plan (which Sitte did not illustrate) is taken from Stübben's *Handbuch*, Fig. 63. Stübben also cited it as a bad example, although for rather different reasons.

165. SITING OF CHURCHES: Sitte, as an architect and archaeologist, was interested throughout his life in the construction, placement, and preservation of church buildings. He wrote on the history and restoration of St. Wolfgang's in Kirchberg a.W. in 1886, on the new church architecture of Austria-Hungary in 1887, on the restorations in the cathedral at Gurk (Kärnten) in 1892, and on his own design for a neo-Gothic church in Oderfurt-Přivoz in 1895.— See Note 13 and Bible. 74.

Whether, in history, churches had actually been built-in or designed free-standing proved to be a moot point that came in for considerable discussion after Sitte had touched off the argument among historians of city planning. The bibliography is too long to cite here because it was, naturally, involved with medieval archaeology and with emotional issues in the profession of restoration and conservation of historic buildings. An interesting discussion is that of Fritz Hoeber (*StBK*, I, 1920, pp. 215–217, 230–233) who attributes the freeing up of churches in the North to the Reformation's concept of the purity of the free-standing temple in its cemetery yard, liberated from the shops and pent-houses of tradesmen. Hoeber also stressed Renaissance ideas of symmetry as being responsible for free-standing churches within the Catholic orbit. (Alberti, *De re aedificatoria*, Book VII.) See Note 37.

page 30 and Plate VI

166. FLORENCE, VIA DEGLI STROZZI: This print, used in the first three German editions, was replaced by a photograph in the fourth. It had been designed by G. Bauernfeind and engraved by A. Closs for p. 148 of Kaden's *Italien* (Bibl. 469).

page 30

167. KARLSKIRCHE: The discussion of the Karlskirche (S. Carlo Borromeo) is omitted from the French edition. The desire of later planners to isolate Fischer von Erlach's church, precisely what Sitte warned against, is clearly demonstrated in the various projects illustrated in Hegemann & Peets, *Civic Art*, pp. 60–61.

168. BAUMEISTER, *Stadt-Erweiterung* (Bibl. 252), p. 183.

page 31

169. CITY GATES: Sitte actually cited a 'Porta Pia' in Regensburg, but apparently meant the Porta Praetoria, a Roman gate that had been discovered in 1885 and cleared in 1887, only two years before his book was printed.

The French edition does not mention any of these German examples, but concludes the chapter instead with the following:

> 'The example of the portals of Bern (Fig. 5) shows us how the needs of circulation can be satisfied without suppressing completely the purpose of the old monuments of the past.'

The view of Bern was drawn for the French edition by H. Hindermann. Hegemann & Peets wrote of it:

> 'The tower, formerly the entrance gate to the city, but now standing in its heart, closes the view down the main street (Kramgasse) so completely that the arcaded avenue gains the character of a well framed plaza' (p. 11).

Many examples of the freeing-up of city gates that so horrified Sitte are to be found illustrated in Stübben's *Handbuch*, especially pp. 179ff. He was not as upset as Sitte with this process.

Fig. 5. Bern: the Clock Tower

Notes on Chapter III

THAT PUBLIC SQUARES SHOULD BE ENCLOSED ENTITIES

page 34

170. CABINET-MAKING: Such a comparison as this may seem far-fetched (in fact the French translator omitted the final sentence), but it reminds us that Sitte was something of a Viennese William Morris, involved during the greater part of his career in the Arts and Crafts—their practice, teaching, adminstration and reform. See above, pp. 10–11 and Notes.

171. PISTOIA: This plan is taken from the French edition; it was not illustrated in the German editions. It is after Rohault de Fleury, Bibl. 480, atlas II, pl. LVI.

page 35

172. PARMA: Sitte illustrated Parma but did not refer to it in his text. The French text did, however, (instead of S. Clemente at Brescia) so we have included the plan at this point.

173. FLORENCE, THE SIGNORIA: The plan in the French edition (which was adapted from Rohault de Fleury, Bibl. 480, atlas I, pl. I) is used here in place of Sitte's plan.

page 36

174. VIENNA, NEUER MARKT: The French edition stops at this point, omit-

ting the Austrian examples and illustrations. The print of the Neuer Markt in Vienna, used in the first four German editions, was replaced in the fifth by a photograph.

175. FLORENCE, UFFIZI: This illustration of the Uffizi, showing its original condition without the added fourth story, is after C. Gurlitt's pioneer study of the Baroque, *Geschichte des Barockstiles in Italien*, Stuttgart, 1887, p. 7. It was drawn by André Lambert and E. Stahl. In the fourth and fifth German editions it was replaced by a photograph.

176. VAULTED PASSAGEWAYS: The French edition omits the German and Austrian examples following Nijmegen and reads instead:

> '. . . the belfry tower at Rouen, the monumental gates of Nancy, the *guichets* of the Louvre, etc. Fig. 6 represents the Piazza dei Signori at Verona whose outline is completed by monumental archways of simple, but grandiose effect.'

The view of the Piazza dei Signori was drawn for the French edition by Hans Bernouilli.

177. VIENNA, JOSEFSPLATZ: For an illustration of this point in both plan and elevation, see Hegemann & Peets, *Civic Art*, Figs. 118–119. For an up-to-date and extended analysis of the Josefsplatz, the reader is referred to Eduard F. Sekler et al., *Historic Urban Spaces*, Harvard University, 1962.

Fig. 6. Verona: Piazza dei Signori

page 37

178. POMPEII: This print, used in the first three German editions, was replaced by a photograph in the fourth. It had been designed by Karl Lindemann-Frommel and engraved by A. Closs for p. 352 of Kaden's *Italien* (Bibl. 469).

179. COLONNADES: Here the French edition adds after St. Peter's:
'. . . ; on a more modest scale in the hemicycle of the Place Carrière at Nancy [Figs. 26, 27].'

Notes on Chapter IV

THE SIZE AND SHAPE OF PLAZAS

page 39

180. SPACE AND PROPORTION: The matters of spatial proportion and psychological perception of spatial effects in town planning which are discussed in this chapter have received considerable attention since Sitte's day, particularly among German scholars—undoubtedly inspired by Sitte's interest in psycho-aesthetic phenomena. For a brief, well-illustrated effort in this direction see Wolfgang Rauda, Bibl. 475. It contains a basic bibliography of the subject.

181. FLORENCE, S. CROCE: We have used the plan from the French edition as it is more exact than Sitte's. It is after Stübben, *Handbuch*, Fig. 388.

page 40 and Plate XI

182. VICENZA: This print, used in the first four German editions, was replaced in the fifth by a photograph. It was designed by G. Bauernfeind and engraved by A. Closs and J. Niedermann for p. 52 of Kaden's *Italien* (Bibl. 469).

pages 41–42

183. DRILL GROUNDS: Elimination of drill and parade grounds from the categories of squares which he discusses caused Sitte to ignore the Latin-American tradition of the *Plaza de Armas*, which is usually exactly rectangular, frequently huge and often very handsome. As late as 1920 Stübben admitted that the Germans knew very little about Spanish city planning (Bibl. 416).

page 43

184. PROPORTIONAL SIZE OF PLAZAS AND BUILDINGS: The problem of the proportional size of a building in relation to its square has been discussed by many writers since the time of Alberti. Stübben devoted considerable attention to it in his *Handbuch* (part II, chap. IX, section c). An example of a writer who thought that such proportions *could* be determined by precise rule was Hermann Maertens who is discussed above, pp. 30–32 and Notes.

Regarding the Maria Theresa Monument see *Sitte*, p. 120.

page 44

185. SQUARE PLAZAS: Sitte's observation is not entirely true for, as we have said, it overlooks a venerable tradition current in Spain and its colonies. See Note 183.

page 45

186. AGORAPHOBIA: The fear of squares and open places. Sitte shows himself to be particularly timely in citing this malady, which he calls *Platzscheu* and is also known as *Platzangst*. Its study had been initiated only a few years before, and its earliest cases were examples of a strictly urban malaise resulting from the experience of being on vast squares. The first account of it appears to be by Carl F. O. Westphal in the *Archiv für Psychiatrie* (Berlin), III, 1871. This led at once to a quantity of publications in other countries, the earliest of which are summarized in the *Journal of Mental Science* (London), XIX, 1873–74, pp. 456–458. We have been informed by Dr. Félix Martí-Ibáñez, historian of medicine, that by 1889 when Sitte was writing, both claustrophobia and agoraphobia 'were very much in the interests and on the minds of physicians, writers, and artists.' It is ironic that the physicians had termed the disorder 'fear of the *agora*,' an agora being precisely the sort of public square that, as Sitte was to demonstrate, did *not* possess such a terrifying openness.

page 46

187. BAUMEISTER, *Stadt-Erweiterungen* (Bibl. 252).

Notes on Chapter V

THE IRREGULARITIES OF OLD PLAZAS

page 47

188. IRREGULAR PLAZAS: The French edition omits the cathedral squares of Padua and Syracuse and supplies as examples instead Pisa (Fig. 4) and S. Gimignano (Fig. 7), the latter after Rohault de Fleury, Bibl. 480, atlas II, pl. XXIV.

189. PADUA, PIAZZA DEGLI EREMETANI: This plan is taken from the French edition; it was not illustrated in the German ones.

pages 48–49

190. VERONA, PIAZZA ERBE: The drawing was made for the French edition by H. Hindermann. The square was illustrated in the German editions only by its plan.

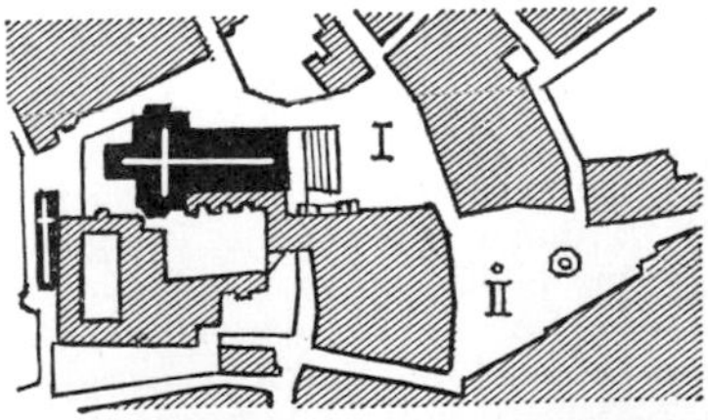

Fig. 7. S. Gimignano. I. Piazza del Duomo.—II. Piazza della Cisterna

Notes on Chapter VI

PLAZA GROUPINGS

page 54

191. MODENA: We have used the plan from the French edition as it is more exact than Sitte's.

pages 55–56

192. LUCCA: We have used a plan of our own making in order to correct an error in the French editions. Sitte did not illustrate his point about Lucca. The French edition did, but employed a portion of Rohault de Fleury's plan of the medieval town which did not include either the Piazza Grande (actually of Napoleonic origin), the Piazza del Giglio, or the Piazza Antelminelli. Although Martin labelled his plan 'Piazza Grande' it was of only the Piazza S. Giovanni, the Cathedral plazas, and the connecting Via del Duomo.

Rohault de Fleury's plan (Bibl. 480, atlas II, pl. LI) was based on Matrajas' reconstruction of the layout of the town in the twelfth century. About this matter see above, p. 66.

page 57

193. PERUGIA: We have used the plan from the French edition since Sitte's did not indicate the position of the famous fountain referred to in an earlier reference to Perugia on his p. 23.

194. VICENZA: The plan from the French edition has been used here as it illustrates Sitte's point more clearly. There was a curious error in the German plan: a cross, by which Sitte generally indicated a church and its orientation, was inscribed upon Palladio's Basilica. It would appear that either a draftsman or the printer had taken the word *Basilika* for its common German meaning of 'Church.'

page 59 and Plate X

195. VENICE, THE PIAZZETTA: This print, used in the first three German editions, was replaced by a photograph in the fourth.

Notes on Chapter VIIA

STREETS

page 60

196. AUTHORSHIP OF CHAPTER VIIA: Sitte seems to have had little or nothing to do with the writing of this chapter. It appeared first in the 1902 French translation of the book, but was not added to the subsequent editions in German or Spanish, which were edited under the direction of his sons. There seems to be no doubt that it was composed by the translator Camille Martin, whose deviations from Sitte's ideas we have described at length above (pp. 63–72 and Notes). The idea of extending Sitte's analysis

to cover the artistic problems of the street he probably owed to Karl Henrici who had already done just that himself. Werner Hegemann, who should know, wrote, 'the translator with the cooperation of Sitte's disciples added a special chapter on street design.' *Civic Art*, p. 18.

Ironically enough, in the composing of the chapter, Martin seems to have drawn more on Stübben—who did not agree with Henrici or Sitte on the designing of streets—than on the Sitte followers. Specifically, Martin appears to have relied on the following:

(1) Stübben's *Handbuch*, especially part II, chaps. 4–7, dealing with streets. Stübben emphasizes the beauty of concave street-sides and discusses how to treat streets that run over ridges (pp. 78–81)—subjects that he had already discussed in his 1877 article on streets (Bibl. 372).

(2) The dispute between Henrici and Stübben over *krumme oder gerade Strassen* that went on in *Deutsche Bauzeitung* intermittently from 1891–1894. See above, pp. 83–84 and Note 36.

(3) Stübben's paper (in French) on streets and squares at the 1898 Brussels Congress (Bibl. 402).

The type of drawings that Martin's friends made for him had been popularized by Henrici in his 1893 Munich project. See Note 98.

In spite of our doubts about Sitte's part in this chapter, we have included it with his text rather than in these critical notes where most of the other French additions are to be found. It is a classic example of Sittesque methodology; it is characteristic of his followers everywhere in their preoccupation with the closed effect of curving streets; and it is appropriately situated as the 7th chapter in the development of basic principles that underlie the aesthetic effects of the town. Furthermore, it has, rightly or wrongly, been very frequently cited in later discussions of Sitte's ideas about city building.

page 64

197. STRAIGHT STREETS AND WINDS: The idea of avoiding an excessive straightness of streets not only comes from a study of old city plans but also out of the writings of previous authorities on the subject. Aristotle, Vitruvius, and Alberti all agree on this for practical, military or, in the case of Alberti, also aesthetic reasons. Vitruvius was obsessed with preventing strong winds from sweeping up streets, and he devoted the whole of his discussion of street layout (Book I, Chapter VI) to the matter. (See Note 278.) In the Baroque period, however, these considerations of comfort were overshadowed by an enthusiasm for the formal beauty of broad straight streets, and we find Descartes criticizing the 'crookedness and irregularity of streets' in ancient towns, attributing them to chance (*Discours de la Méthode* of 1667).

The 19th century put a new twist on this matter, ultimately vindicating Vitruvius in terms of hygiene as well as comfort. Pioneer hygienic research had brought about the idea of broad plazas, wide straight streets, and well-separated houses being necessary as the 'lungs of the city.' However, subsequent investigators disputed the value of such openness, pointing out that the germ-laden dust resulting from the drafts and winds of open streets was deposited everywhere, boulevards and gardens included. For this see Sitte's later writings, such as his Appendix to his book (*Sitte*, pp. 167ff.) and his Foreword to the first issue of the *Städtebau* periodical (*Sitte*, Appendix II).

page 64 and Plate XVI

198. BRUGES, RUE DES PIERRES: This drawing was made for the French edition by F. Puetzer.

page 66

199. BRUSSELS, MARCHÉ AUX POULETS: It might be of interest to note that when Hegemann & Peets reprinted this illustration in their *Civic Art*, they entitled it: 'Example of the type of sinuous medieval streets advocated by many self-styled followers of Camillo Sitte,' (Fig. 153). This drawing was made for the French edition by F. Puetzer.

200. LÜBECK: This drawing was made for the French edition by Hans Bernouilli.

Notes on Chapter VIIB

THE LAYOUT OF PUBLIC SQUARES IN THE NORTH OF EUROPE

page 69

201. OLDER FREE-STANDING CHURCHES: Here the French edition differs; instead of Ulm, Stettin, and Vienna, it cites the Church of St. Stephen at Beauvais, the Cathedral of Saint Sauveur at Bruges (Fig. 8), and the church of Notre Dame at Bruges.

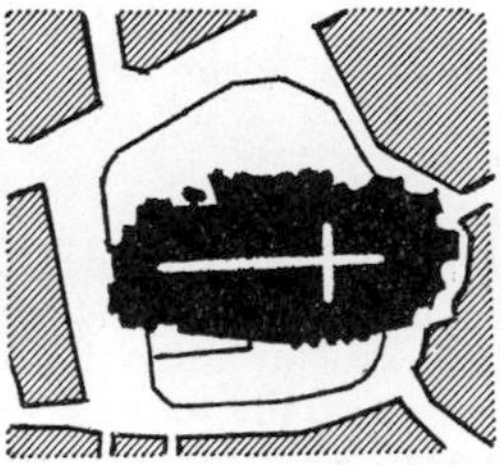

Fig. 8. Bruges: Cathedral of Saint Sauveur

202. FREIBURG: We have used the plan from the French edition as it is more exact than Sitte's. It is after Stübben, *Handbuch*, Fig. 395.

203. ISOLATED GOTHIC CHURCHES: The French text varies so greatly from the German original here that we print the French passage in its entirety; it contradicts Sitte somewhat about the opening of streets toward church façades:

> 'The buildings which in Northern countries are isolated, are only half so and then quite differently from our modern fashion. The typical situation with regard to the Gothic cathedral is as follows: behind the choir and along the side aisles stand neighboring houses, separated from the sanctuary by a narrow little street. In front of the main portal a certain expanse is necessary to improve the effect of the façade and its two symmetrical towers. But one is mistaken in believing, as we do today, that a cathedral gains by having a very extended parvis. The

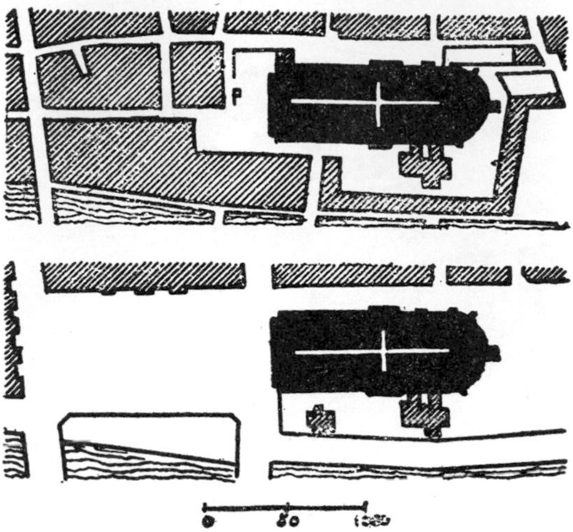

Fig. 9. Paris: Cathedral of Notre Dame—Original situation (above)—
Present state of surroundings (below)

example of Notre Dame of Paris (Fig. 9) is a good one to demonstrate the error of those who sustain such an opinion. The effect of its imposing façade is now much less than it must have been when the neighboring structures had not yet been removed and its parvis had much less area than today. Often a street opens in the direction of the main portal so as to contrive a perspective view of this impressive motif. What a majestic effect many cathedrals produce if this street is neither too long nor too broad! The view of the Cathedral of Strasbourg taken from the Rue Mercière is evidence of this (*Sitte*, pl. XII). Similar perspectives have been arranged bearing on the transept portals of Amiens (Fig. 10)

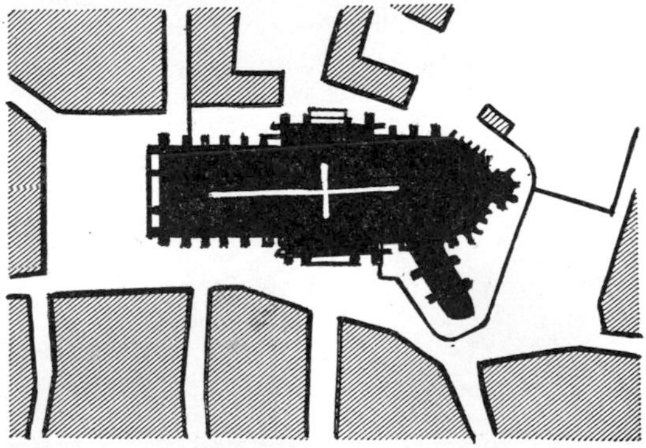

Fig. 10. Amiens: Cathedral

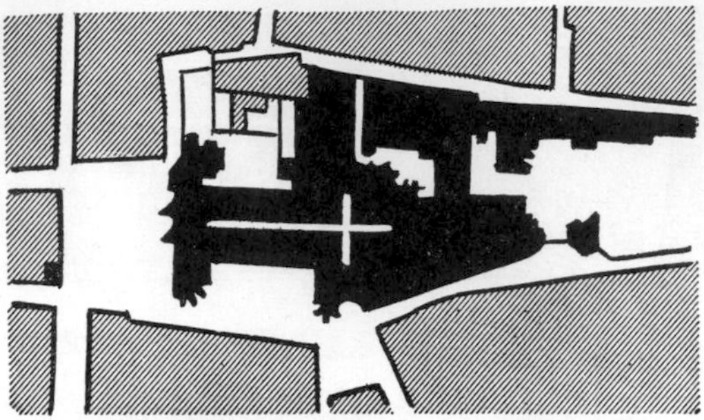

Fig. 11. Rouen: Cathedral

and at Rouen (Fig. 11). One tried to do the same in Nuremberg, at St. Sebaldus and St. Lorenz, so far as the narrow and winding character of the streets would allow.'

page 70

204. CATHEDRAL OF STRASBOURG: Pl. XII, used in the first three German editions, was replaced by a photograph in the fourth. It is from Fig. 669 of Vol. II of W. Lübke's *Geschichte der Architektur*; the artist, Mezgers, had adapted it from the frontispiece of P. Chapuy's *Vues pittoresques de la Cathédral de Strasbourg*, 1827.

Hegemann & Peets comment about the situation at Strasbourg:

'The Rue Mercière leads right to the central entrance of the cathedral. The effect is good because the street is narrow and short and the houses lining it are not too high. The appearance of the highly symmetrical central features of the western façade can thus dominate the view. If the street were longer and wider, the unsymmetrical tower development and perspective diminution would become disturbing factors.' (*Civic Art*. p. 13.)

205. SIDE VIEWS OF CHURCHES: Peets in his essay on Sitte (Bibl. 363) took exception to this opinion. Speaking of Sitte's proposal for the Vienna Votive Church (see *Sitte* pp. 143ff.), Peets observed,

'Sitte cut off complete sidewise views of the church because it was asymmetrical lengthwise . . . [but] visual symmetry is not essential at

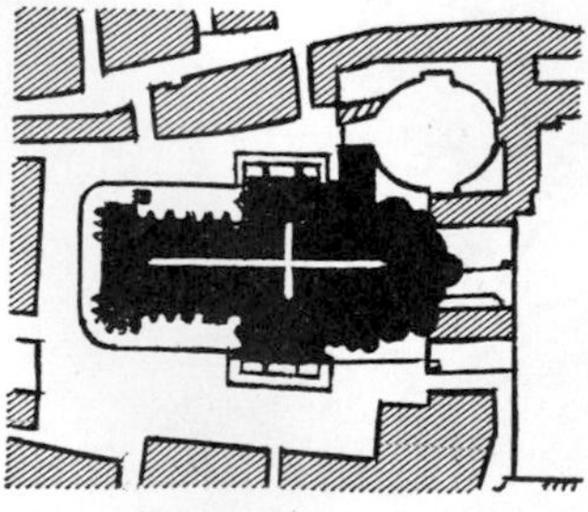

Fig. 12. Chartres: Cathedral

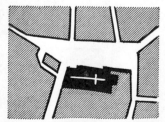

Fig. 13. Strasbourg: St. Thomas

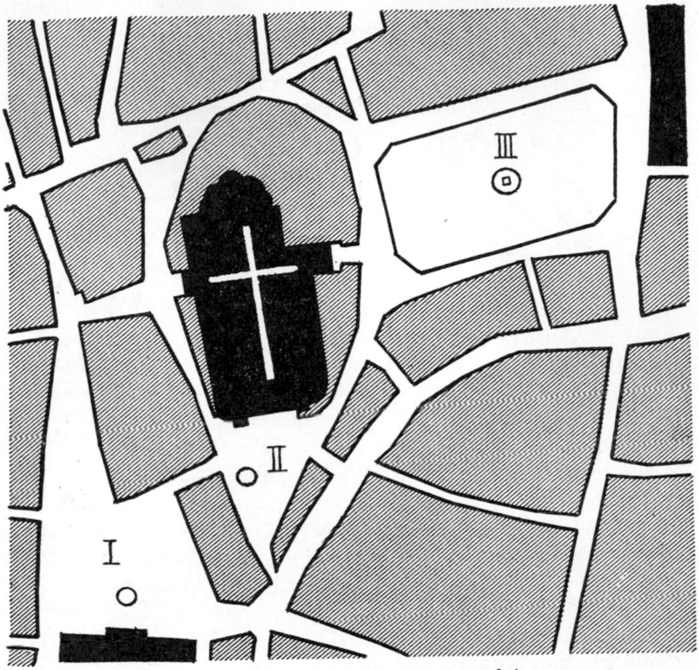

Fig. 14. Antwerp. I. Grand'Place.—II. Marché aux gants.—
III. Place Verte

the side or rear of a building provided one has a sense of order and definite orientation. The side view of a horse is asymmetrical' (p. 258).

page 71

206. BUILT-IN BUILDINGS IN THE NORTH: The French edition inserts before the remark about Strasbourg's churches:

'In Paris the following churches can be cited that actually remain built against other structures despite frequent breaking through of streets: St. Germain de Prés, Saint Séverin, the Sainte Chapelle, Saint Merri, Saint Eustache, the churches of the Val de Grâce, of the Sorbonne, and of Saint Gervais, etc. At Rouen, the Cathedral (Fig. 11) and Saint Maclou. At Chartres, the Cathedral (Fig. 12), Saint Aignan and Saint Pierre. At Antwerp, the Cathedral (Fig. 14).'

To Sitte's following sentence the French edition then adds an illustration of St. Thomas in Strasbourg (Fig. 13). Hegemann & Peets reprinted the French plan of Antwerp, saying of it:

'A typical example of a medieval cathedral surrounded by plazas without giving a full view of its elevation except the façade. The irregular side elevations are screened, full views from the plazas being given only to the transepts' (p. 15).

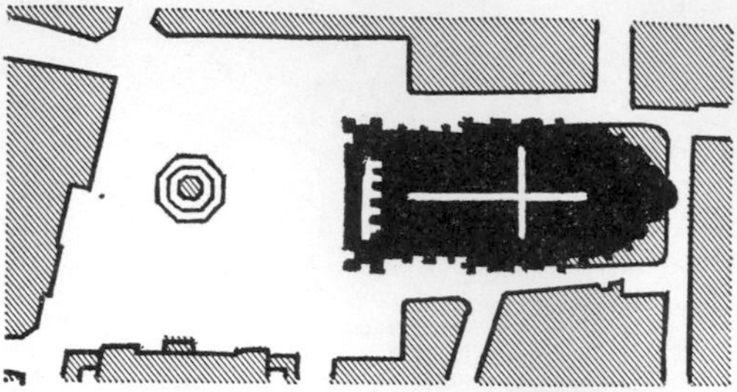

Fig. 15. Paris: Place Saint Sulpice

The plan of Chartres employed by Martin (Fig. 12) would appear to be either an old one or another of his attempts at medieval reconstruction. By Martin's day the building in front of the cathedral had been removed and there existed in its place a square about the size of the cathedral itself.

page 72

207. OFF-CENTER PLACEMENT: The French edition omits the description of St. Stephen's in Constance, saying instead:

> 'The church of Saint Sulpice in Paris (Fig. 15) is surrounded on three sides by streets, but their width is quite small in comparison with that of the *place* that is laid out in front of the principal façade.'

Hegemann & Peets reprinted the plan of St. Sulpice, remarking:

> 'The plaza in front of St. Sulpice was built by the first Napoleon as a setting for the Renaissance church. The design is interesting for the way in which the short lengths of wall at each side of the church are kept well back from the plane of the façade in order to give good views of the two towers.' (*Civic Art*, p. 22.)

208. REGENSBURG: We have used the plan from the French edition as it is more exact than Sitte's. It is after Stübben, *Handbuch*, Fig. 451. The

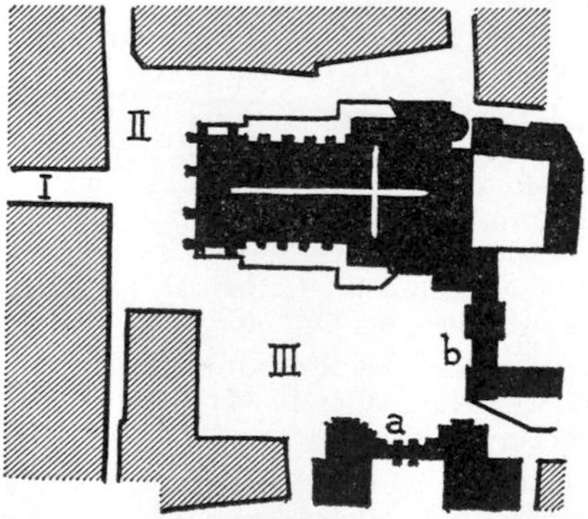

Fig. 16. Strasbourg. I. Rue Mercière.—II. Cathedral square.—III. Palace square.—a. Château de Rohan.—b. School

Fig. 17. Rouen: Place de la Pucelle

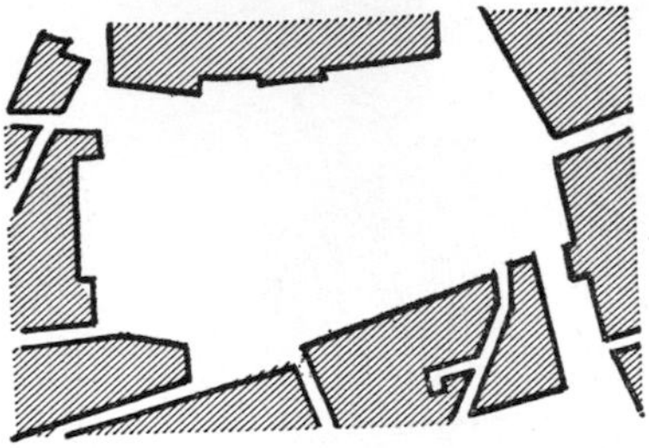

Fig. 18. Strasbourg: Place Kleber

difference is so great in this case between the French plan (labelled 'Ratisbonne') and the German one (labelled 'Regensburg'), that Hegemann & Peets printed them both, apparently not noticing that these are two different names for the same place.

209. PLACEMENTS IN THE ITALIAN MANNER IN THE NORTH: The French edition mentions only the example of the Minster at Constance and adds the plan of the Strasbourg Cathedral squares (Fig. 16). It is entirely different from the German down to the discussion of Brunswick (*Sitte*, Fig. 66) in the next paragraph. All German examples are omitted. The French substitution reads as follows:

> 'The city plans that we have reproduced up to this point are sufficient proof that the old squares of northern Europe do not differ at all from those of Italy as far as their form and dimensions are concerned, and that they exhibit the same irregularities (Fig. 17).
>
> The principles that we have studied are even more obvious in market places or large public squares, generally closed off as they are on one side by the town hall. Numerous public buildings are united around such centers of community life, which are often of considerable size.
>
> The Grand'Place at Bruges (Fig. 19) has an expanse of more than two acres; its present states gives only a faint idea of what it was during the former prosperity of the town. Today there remains only the market-hall building with its belfry and some houses that have been more or less restored. The Place du Bourg, which connects with it, has also lost much of its former splendor. One still sees there the Chapel du Saint-Sang, the town hall and the Palais de Justice. We have reproduced an important part of the plan of Bruges (Fig. 19) in order to illustrate what a variety of squares it includes on a little bit of terrain. After leaving the Place du Bourg, one passes in succession through five squares of different form and aspect before arriving at the canal.
>
> It was the markets which governed the formation of public squares in most towns. Often each commodity had a different place of sale, to which the names of many plazas in Brussels or Strasbourg still testify today; aside from the Grand'Place or the town-hall square, as in Beauvais or Brussels, one often finds markets dedicated to special purposes, such as the sale of eggs, herbs or fish. Unfortunately, many of the market places of former times are today encumbered with iron market halls—as that at Rouen—which have disfigured them forever.

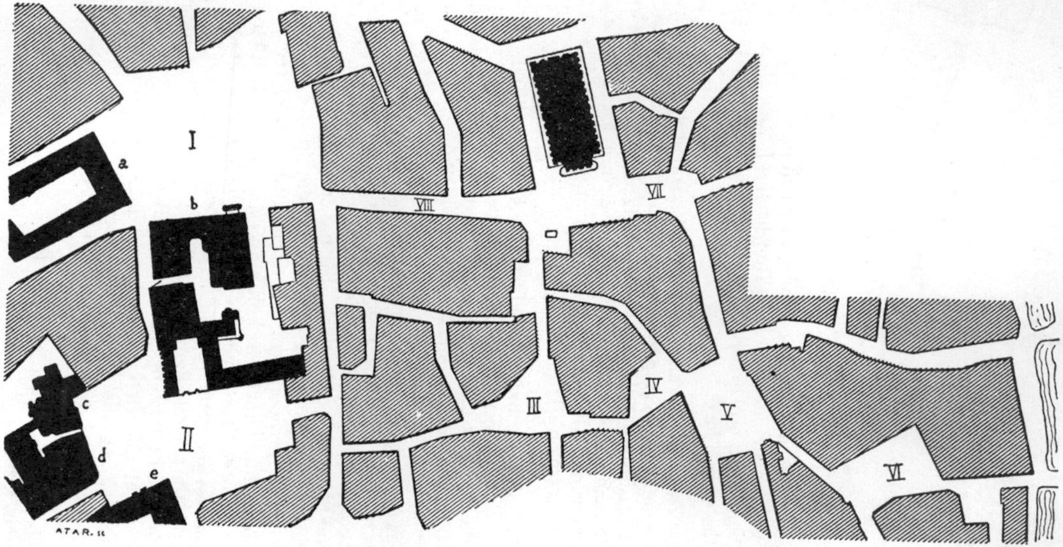

Fig. 19. Bruges. I. Grand'Place.—II. Place du Bourg.—III. Place Saint-Jean.—IV. Place des Biscayens.—V. Place Jean van Eyck.—VI. Marché du Mercredi.—VII. Place de la Vieille Bourse.—VIII. Rue Flamande.—a. Market halls.—b. Hôtel provincial.—c. Chapelle du Saint Sang.—d. Hôtel de Ville.—e. Palais de Justice

[Compare Sitte's remark on p. 14.] Besides market places one should mention parade grounds, which we encounter especially in later times. The Place Kleber at Strasbourg (Fig. 18) formerly served as a drill ground. Although devoid of important monuments, it certainly has a special character owing to its fine proportions and its uninterrupted enclosure by houses.'

The French edition then changes the end of the paragraph dealing with Brunswick.

page 75

210. COLOGNE: We have used the plan from the French edition as it is more exact than Sitte's.

211. LÜBECK: We have used the plan from the French edition as it is more exact than Sitte's. It is after Stübben, *Handbuch*, Fig. 403.

page 77

212. BREMEN: We have used the plan from the French edition as it is more exact than Sitte's. It is after Stübben, *Handbuch*, Fig. 407.

213. SALZBURG: The Salzburg plan (Fig. 73) underwent more changes in successive editions than any other in the book, some of them so drastic as to suggest that there may have been rearrangements in the circuit of buildings itself between c. 1890 and c. 1900. The plan used in Sitte's first editions is identical with that of Baedeker guidebooks of the 1880's, although one would expect Sitte to have drawn the familiar site himself. The first French edition of 1902 employed Stübben's *Handbuch* plan (Fig. 457) upside down. We have used here the version that was completely redrawn for the 1909 German edition in a new special scale; four trees were added to this plan to illustrate a point in the new Appendix (*Sitte*, p. 174). The description of Salzburg in the French text was considerably condensed.

page 78

214. ERACLIUS: Sitte is here quoting from a medieval document published by his friends Albert Ilg and Rudolf Eitelberger: Heraklius [pseud], *Von den Farben und Künsten der Römer* [On the Colors and Arts of the Romans], in *Quellenschriften für Kunstgeschichte und Kunsttechnik des Mittelalters und der Renaissance*, IV, Vienna, 1873. 'Eraclius' is thought to be an Italian of Beneventum who lived sometime during the 8th to 10th centuries and who actually wrote only the earlier two of the three sections of the treatise that is attributed to him. The Spanish translator of Sitte, in one of his rare lapses, took him to be Heraclitos of Ephesos. We have used the translation of Mary Philadelphia Merrifield (1849).

The entire paragraph about Hildesheim and Eraclius was omitted from the French edition, as was the reference to Trento and Trier in the preceding paragraph.

215. THE MODEL OF ANCIENT ROME: On this point, Martin's French text reads as follows (compare it with Sitte's!):

> 'Just as Roman art yielded to the styles of the Middle Ages, so the latter, after having flourished for several centuries, arrived at their decline when they began anew to imitate ancient models.'

This altogether different and essentially anti-Renaissance interpretation of the history of style by Camille Martin certainly did much to make Sitte out to be a romantic medievalist. Wittkower, in his review of the American translation of Sitte (Bibl. 22) took the translator to task for the following version (which had apparently been derived from the French):

> 'Ancient splendor gave way to the world of medieval art, which, having attained its heights of greatness, went to its decline in a sterile imitation of the ancient forms that had preceded it' (p. 49 of American edition).

page 79

216. THREE-SIDED FORECOURTS: The French edition simplifies this idea somewhat, saying, 'The horse-shoe plan became characteristic of building in this epoque.'

217. BAROQUE MASTERS: Here, with a nice Gallic twist, Martin said: 'The reigns of Louis XIV and Louis XV have marked the apogee of the new art of building cities.'

page 80

218. THE CAPITOL IN ROME: Here the French edition adds the following sentence and then skips the rest of Sitte's paragraph about Vienna, as well as omitting the succeeding paragraph that deals with palaces and monasteries:

> 'Its [the Capitol's] disposition admirably exploits the accidental configuration of the terrain; its restricted dimensions and its contraction toward the rear make a limited space perfectly proportioned to the statue of Marcus Aurelius.'

This statement is illustrated by the addition of a plan (Fig. 20) which did not appear in the German editions; it is based on Stübben, *Handbuch,*

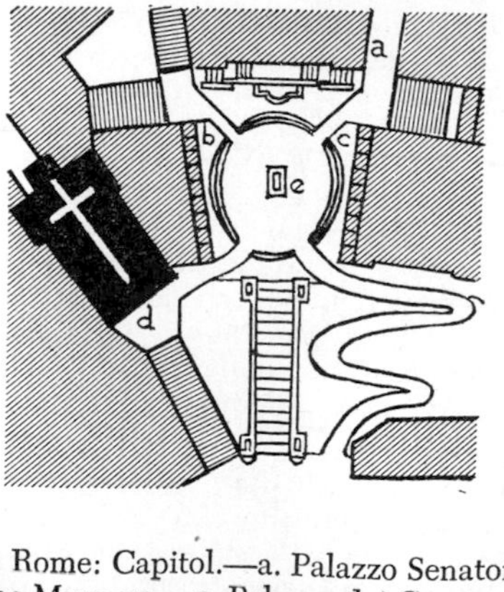

Fig. 20. Rome: Capitol.—a. Palazzo Senatorio.—
b. Capitoline Museum.—c. Palazzo dei Conservatori.—
d. S. Maria d'Aracoeli.—e. Statue of Marcus Aurelius

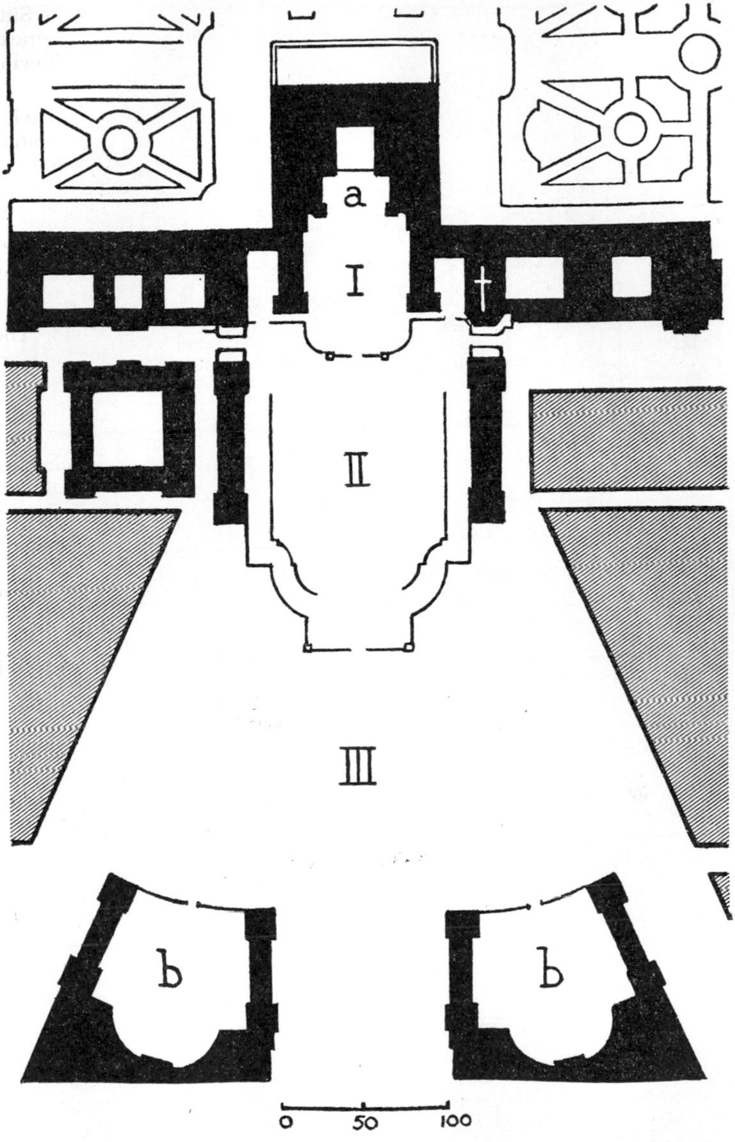

Fig. 21. Versailles. I. Cour Royale. II. Court of the Ministers.—
III. Place d'Armes.—a. Palace.—b. Stables

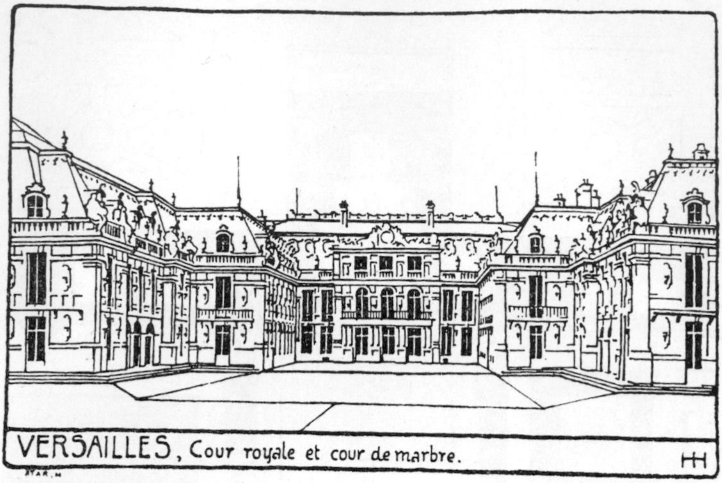

Fig. 22. Versailles: Cour Royale & Cour de Marbre

Fig. 406. Hegemann & Peets commented as follows on the old engraving from Blaeu that they used and we have added as Sitte's Pl. XXIII–a:

> 'It is interesting to learn from this engraving that in the old days carriages discharged their passengers at the foot of the ramped Cordonnata, instead of meandering up a steep drive and entering the plaza at one corner, as carriages do now. The old stately approach on axis and the banishment of carriages from the floor of the plaza display much the keener sense of the dignified place of architecture in the drama of civic life' (p. 17).

219. SCHÖNBRUNN PALACE: A print used in the first three German editions was replaced in the fourth by a photograph similar to ours showing the River Wien bridge to which Sitte alludes.

page 81

220. THEATRICAL PERSPECTIVE: The French edition adds the example of the Palace of Versailles (its Cour d'Honneur and Place d'Armes). See Figs. 21 and 22. The view of the palace was drawn for the French edition by H. Hindermann.

221. BUILDINGS WITH INTERIOR COURTS: The French edition omits all discussion of Viennese examples down to the last sentence of Sitte's chapter. Nor does the French chapter stop there, but instead continues with Martin's version of the first part of Sitte's Chapter XI, 'Improved Modern Systems' (cf. Table above, p. 70). The variations introduced in that material by the French translator are discussed in the critical notes to Sitte's Chapter XI (Nos. 255 to 285).

Notes on Chapter VIII

THE MEAGER AND UNIMAGINATIVE CHARACTER OF MODERN CITY PLANS

page 84

222. BAUMEISTER: *Stadt-Erweiterungen* (Bibl. 252), p. 97. Baumeister's importance as one of the founders of German city planning is discussed above, pp. 26–27.

page 85

223. PHIDIAS AND MICHELANGELO: Up to this point the French edition (in its Chapter IX, 'Modern Systems') follows the German Chapter VIII, with certain rearrangements in the order of the paragraphs, but then it continues with about two-thirds of German Chapter IX (also called 'Modern Systems'). Martin made minor changes, most significant being the avoidance of the word 'Baroque,' employing 'modern' or 'eighteenth-century' instead. He also substituted the word 'signoria' for 'acropolis' in the first paragraph.

224. BAUMEISTER: *op. cit.*, pp. 97 and 98.

225. MARSHAL MACMAHON: Baumeister quoted this in a footnote on p. 10 in the same book. For a similar opinion by MacMahon's opponent von Moltke, see Note 38.

page 86

226. OLD ARCADES: The rest of this paragraph dealing with arcades and with Vienna was omitted from the French edition, and Martin again deleted the word 'Baroque' at its beginning.

page 87

227. STREET PATTERNS & HOUSE PLANS: Baumeister, *op. cit.*, p. 96. We have quoted one more sentence here than Sitte did.

page 89

228. IRREGULARITIES IN MEDIEVAL GROUND PLANS: Compare Ruskin in Note 83.

229. PROJECTIONS AND RECESSIONS: The French edition omits the ending of this chapter, substituting a slightly condensed version of the termination of German Chapter IX. See table, p. 70 above.

Notes on Chapter IX

MODERN SYSTEMS

page 91

230. THE THREE MAJOR METHODS: This mode of categorizing city-plan types seems to be based directly on Baumeister, who employed it in his book *Stadt-Erweiterungen* (Bibl. 252) and in his brochure on the same subject, Bibl. 255.

What Sitte said from his fourth sentence down to p. 100 is to be found in Chapter IX of the French translation where it follows a portion of German Chapter VIII. (See above, p. 70.) It is introduced slightly differently in the French and is expressed with certain modifications.

page 93

231. LYONS: Sitte had called this 'Place Louis XVI,' perhaps an older name for the Place Morand.

232. MANNHEIM: Mannheim was not illustrated in any of the editions of Sitte. We have taken this plan from Friedrich Walter, *Mannheim in Vergangenheit und Gegenwart*, 1907, II, p. 887. It was drawn by P. Dewarat. See *Der Städtebau*, XIII, 1916, pp. 40–44 and plates 23–28.

233. BAUMEISTER: In *Stadt-Erweiterungen* (Bibl. 252). This reference to Baumeister was omitted from the French translation.

page 94

234. TRAFFIC INTERSECTIONS: Fig. 83 is one of the few plans to have been changed in the course of successive German editions; we employ it as it appeared in the 4th. In earlier editions the description of the trajectory of the vehicles did not correspond to the diagram, so the plan was later rotated counter-clockwise 90° with respect to the letters. Actually, there still remained a discrepancy in the text description, which we have corrected. The French translation followed the early, erroneous system.

The earlier editions also read, '12 cases of intersecting traffic' instead of 16 and 'four times as many' instead of five times—errors in arithmetic which were corrected in the 4th German edition, but not in the French ones. These totals would be easier to visualize if Sitte had included in his plan the two other straight paths A to C and B to D; his own error had resulted from neglecting the four intersections of the straight paths with each other.

Stübben corrected these errors in the diagrams in his articles on streets (Bibl. 385, pp. 150–155) and in the second edition of his *Handbuch* (Fig. 303). He claimed that any scheme of offset intersections using a pair of junctures like Sitte's Fig. 82 would actually increase the vehicular encounters (to 18) and would cut down visibility. We do not print his illustration of this here (Fig. 304) because he padded his figures by including tangential meetings of vehicles as well as head-on and side-on encounters.

The subject was further discussed by Simpson (Bibl. 159) who corrected Stübben and by Unwin who presented both sides of the argument and noted that the invention of the rotary intersection by Hénard had solved the problem (Bibl. 215, pp. 237–241). For a final technical treatment of the whole matter see E. Schachenmeier, 'Über Strassenkreuzungen (Mathematische Festlegung der Fahrlinien),' *StB*, X, 1913, pp. 67–71, 77–82.

235. PROMENADERS: The French editions omit the Viennese examples cited by Sitte, remarking only: 'Each one of us can observe this in his own city.'

page 96

236. LONDON: This plan is from the French edition. It was not cited or illustrated in the German editions because Sitte had not visited England. It is after Stübben, *Handbuch*, Fig. 286.

page 98

237. LOSS OF BEARINGS: These rather curious criticisms of plazas that are circles or regular polygons would seem to represent an instance of Sitte's concern, in cityscapes, with a type of aesthetic experience that is also found in late 19th-century painting and that we have ascribed to him in Note 163, and p. 50 above. The orientation (*Orientierung*) that Sitte is seeking and has emphasized in this passage does not correspond to the meaning of that word either as a compass-bearing or as the state of being in harmony with one's cosmos, but refers instead to his private search for ever-unique, highly-characteristic civic tableaux that evoke responses he will later remember. He is on the one hand very pragmatic and on the other quite epicurean but is never platonic or cosmological as far as his planning theory is concerned.

Regarding the matter of finding one's bearings on these *rond points* (such as l'Étoile in Paris), Sitte's remarks are the more paradoxical since the *rond point* type of plaza is presumed to have been inserted into cities for just that purpose, having been taken over from the large French gardens and hunting parks of the Baroque age where, as elevated center-points of radiating paths, they served the purpose of orienting hunters and strollers in heavily wooded areas.

That Sitte's opinion about *rond-point* squares, although posed in such convincing terms, actually represents a highly personal taste, is demonstrated by comparing Stübben's description of the same type of plan:

> 'An engaging aspect of the star-plaza is that from its center one can enjoy a perspective vista of one after another of the streets which diverge more or less like rays, so that a sequence of city street-views, like a panorama, unrolls before the spectator. Especially excellent in this respect is the energetic and exemplary renovation of Paris. The splendid views in all directions from the Place de l'Étoile, the Place d'Italie, the Place d'Eylau, the Rond Point, and other plazas are unforgettable to the visitor to Paris; the impressive street perspectives, usually embellished by greenery and enhanced by artistic terminations, do recall to many the pettiness of the conditions at home. Also Antwerp, Brussels, Berlin, Dresden, and other cities owe their effective embellishment to the radial grouping of streets around certain traffic squares.' *Handbuch*, p. 147.

For Camille Martin's comments on *rond points* see Note 239 below.

238. PARIS: L'Etoile, as in the French edition, is based on Stübben's *Handbuch*, Fig. 345. It was not illustrated in the German editions. We have also added Pl. XVIII.

page 99

239. PARIS AS AN EXEMPLAR FOR FRANCE: The sentence that is complimentary to the Baroque tradition was omitted from the French translation. The French translator added the following paragraph, not in the German editions:

'It would, nevertheless, be an error to believe that the procedures employed in Paris, usually through necessity, are good to imitate everywhere. The enormous volume of traffic and a fear of riots have forced the technician to use radical measures that are not always satisfactory from an aesthetic point of view. It is to pre-occupations of a rather political character that we owe the creation in the Second Empire of the famous *rond points* and streets that were too wide and too long but easy to watch over. In taking these for models in cities of lesser importance one has sought more to imitate a great capital than to satisfy the actual local needs.'

240. BRUSSELS: Plate XV-a was drawn for the French translation by F. Puetzer. The point was not illustrated in the German editions.

241. MARSEILLES: This plan appeared in the German editions inverted and labelled 'Nîmes.' The error was corrected in the French, Spanish and Italian editions but not in the American one of 1945.

Hegemann & Peets point out that the faults in the architectural frame of this square had been remedied by the planting of dense rows of trees as a frame for the inner area (*Civic Art,* p. 13).

page 100

242. THE AVENUE MOTIF: German and Austrian examples were largely omitted from the French edition, as was the comment about the spirit of the Baroque.

243. ART AND THE TEACHINGS OF HISTORY: The French Chapter IX omits this paragraph and inserts a large part of German Chapter VIII (see above p. 70).

244. TREE-LINED AVENUES AND GARDENS: Certain of the ideas that follow were later employed in Sitte's articles on City Vegetation, included as an Appendix in the 4th German edition. The French translator used a number of the pages of this chapter as an important part of his own Appendix on Greenery that purported to be a summary of Sitte's article, but actually bears very little relation to it (see above, p. 70).

page 101

245. BAROQUE PARK: Martin called it 'the French park' (!) On the popularity of English parks in Germany see Note 310.

page 102

246. RETURN TO BAROQUE MODELS: Instead of 'Baroque models' the French translation reads 'gardens of the XVIII century.'

247. DEMAND FOR OUTSIDE APARTMENTS: The remainder of this paragraph, the following one, and the first sentence in the next paragraph after that appear nowhere in the French edition.

The sentence itself, however, calls for comment. It is hard in our day to visualize why a housing project consisting only of outside apartments (witness the Marina City in Chicago) would be considered a 'detriment' for that reason alone. But we must realize that Sitte's ideal for a contemporary urban settlement was related to that which he valued in old European towns, namely a rational alternation of building masses and enclosed spaces. He seems to have considered city blocks to be best when perforated with court-spaces as aerators. Compare *Sitte*, pp. 181ff. His preference for intermittent groups or islands of vegetation instead of long, shaded streets, as described in his Chapter IX and Appendix I, is another example of this taste.

page 104

248. HEXAGONAL BLOCKS AND THE CHICAGO PLAN: Sitte's reasoning here about the economic advantage of polygonal or circular blocks seems to be faulty. From a purely geometric point of view a circular city block would have the *smallest* perimeter for a given area, not the largest. Disregarding the matter of equality of area, however, a square bulged into the shape of its circumscribed circle would, of course, increase in 'frontage.' This is not really a 'geometric' argument, but a characteristic Sitte-judgment based on the idea of a spectator viewing a building block from a determined point; as he later suggests on p. 133, a convex façade occupies more 'frontage line' than its chord would. There may also be some German surveyors' theory involved here; lots regularly laid out with radial boundaries in circular or polygonal blocks would perhaps have a generally more profitable frontage for their area than would the usual subdivisions of rectangular blocks.

The theory that hexagonal city blocks are productive of greater frontage is commonly held; whether it goes back to this passage in Sitte or derives from someone before him is not clear.

The matter of the hexagonal, honeycomb block system said to have been employed in Chicago is a mystery. Sitte apparently picked up this bit of information from Baumeister, who said:

> '. . . in the new Chicago it is said that right angles are not used, instead the house-blocks are laid out as hexagons that join each other like the cells of a honeycomb.' *Stadt-Erweiterungen* (Bibl. 252), p. 96.

Baumeister, in turn, seems to have obtained the idea from a pioneer city-planning study in *Deutsche Bauzeitung* for 1870 on which he had based that portion of his book: E. Bruch, 'Berlin's bauliche Zukunft und der Bebauungsplan,' *DB*, IV, 1870, pp. 151–154. Bruch wrote:

> 'And is then the hexagon, the instinctive building plan of the honeycomb, so completely unsuitable an example to be followed? In any case, I can report that this very device has been seriously considered for use in Chicago where most thorough discussion took place about the basic forms for a new city district.' (p. 152.)

We have been unable to discover the Chicago plan referred to. There is some possibility that it was a project of Olmsted's, lost or abandoned after the fire of 1871. The 1945 American edition of Sitte comments, in a footnote on this matter:

> 'In August 1943 a search of the records of the Chicago Plan Commission was undertaken to determine the extent of this type of plotting. E. Evart Kincaid, Executive Director of the Commission, advised that the search disclosed no evidence of hexagonal planning.' (p. 68.)

It may be that Bruch had in mind the Woodward hexagonal plan that was designed for Detroit after its fire of 1805. If so, he had not seen the plan in question, because, although it was based on a hexagonal street network, the actual city blocks were all rectangular, trapezoidal, or triangular.

Most curious of all is the fact that Stübben also picked up this item about a Chicago hexagonal plan and actually made up a plan to illustrate it: *Handbuch*, p. 61.

We are indebted to Miss Rosemarie Haag and Mrs. Jean McClintock for investigating these matters.

Notes on Chapter X

ARTISTIC LIMITATIONS OF MODERN CITY PLANNING

page 107

249. STREET PANORAMAS: In the French translation the end of this paragraph was condensed, most of the German examples being suppressed.

250. FEAR OF OPEN SPACES: Regarding this malady, see Note 186.

page 108

251. HANDSOME STAIRS: Most of these German examples were omitted from the French editions.

252. LOGGIA, STAIRWAY, ETC.: All these examples were omitted from the French editions.

page 109

253. IMAGINATIVE STAGE SETS: The French translation omitted this entire paragraph.

page 112

254. ADMINISTRATORS: The French translation reads instead:

> 'It is hoped that public authorities will pay to the *aesthetic of streets* [italics ours] all the importance it deserves.'

Notes on Chapter XI

IMPROVEMENTS IN THE MODERN SYSTEM

page 113

255. BLOCK SYSTEMS: The French translation opens this chapter with Sitte's second sentence and then skips to *Sitte,* p. 120, using much of the intervening material in its Chapter VIII, as is observable in the table above on p. 70.

In his Chapter VIII (p. 116 of his 2nd edition), Martin rendered these sentences somewhat differently, e.g., substituting for 'the spirit of the

Baroque': 'ancient traditions' and 'great principles of the better periods.' The remark about the Baroque at the end of Sitte's second paragraph is simply omitted, and the following is substituted:

> 'However, the history of architecture is rich enough in examples of this type which it would have been preferable to mention. The church of the Trinité in Paris (Fig. 23) is erected at the edge of a square, and its three sides are surrounded by relatively narrow streets. One sees there a remembrance of examples from the past, but unfortunately the square is a bit too vast, and, in particular, is too much interrupted to serve as a worthy vestibule to a religious building.
>
> The plans we have studied have made us see that in all times and in all countries, plazas and streets have been constructed according to certain rules that are too little followed today. The fact that these artistic principles were observed wittingly by our predecessors and that they applied them without hesitation, guided by their own good taste, should lead us to recognize the excellent results they obtained. It is only in studying their works that we shall be able to reform the banal arrangements of our modern cities.' [End of French Chapter VIII.]

page 114

256. PARIS. Compare Sitte's remarks in his Chapter IX, pp. 98–99.

The French translation omits this paragraph as well as any suggestion that the 19th-century planning of Paris could have had anything good in it! The French text (now p. 109 of Chapter VIII in the 2nd edition) reads instead, curiously:

> 'Castles have often been the nucleus around which an important city developed. Moreover, it has often been at the inspiration of a prince that good plazas have been laid out in modern times.'

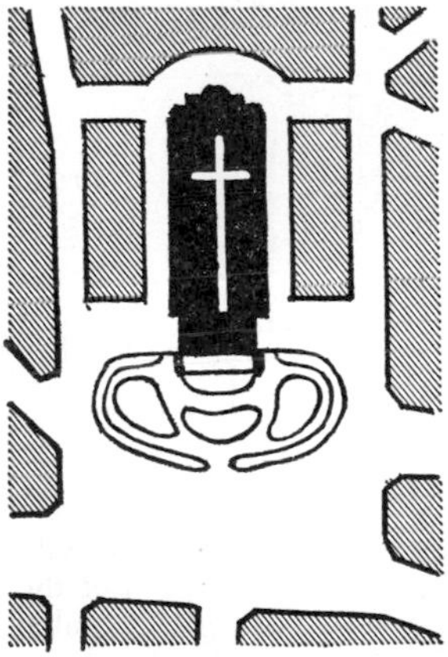

Fig. 23. Paris: Place de la Trinité (after Stübben)

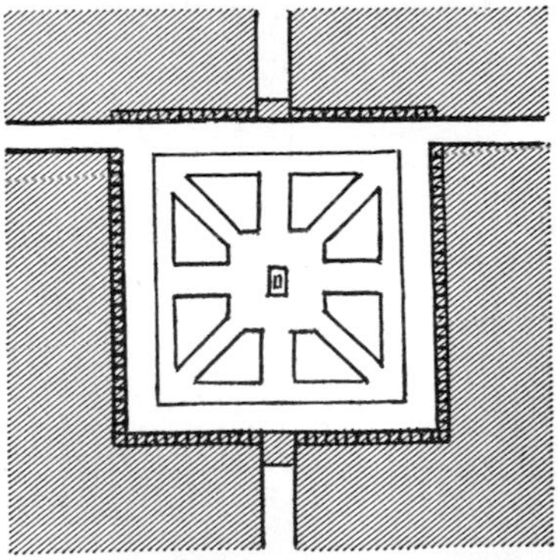

Fig. 24. Paris: Place des Vosges (after Stübben)

257. ST. PETER'S IN ROME: We have taken this plan from the same source that Sitte used: Paul Letarouilly, *Le Vatican et la Basilique de Saint-Pierre de Rome*, Paris, Morel, 1882, II, pl. 2. The engraved view is from J. Blaeu, *Nouveau Theatre d'Italie*, Amsterdam, 1704, IV, plate LXVI.

page 115

258. PIAZZA DEL POPOLO: This piazza was not illustrated by Sitte. We use the plan from the French translation (after Stübben, *Handbuch*, Fig. 341) which went on to say:

> 'We recall also the circular form of the gigantic Piazza del Popolo, a real modern *rond point*, but one which is a great work of art owing to the importance given to the two principal means of access.'

page 116

259. GROUP PLANS: The French editions inserted (after Catania) the following discussion of French examples:

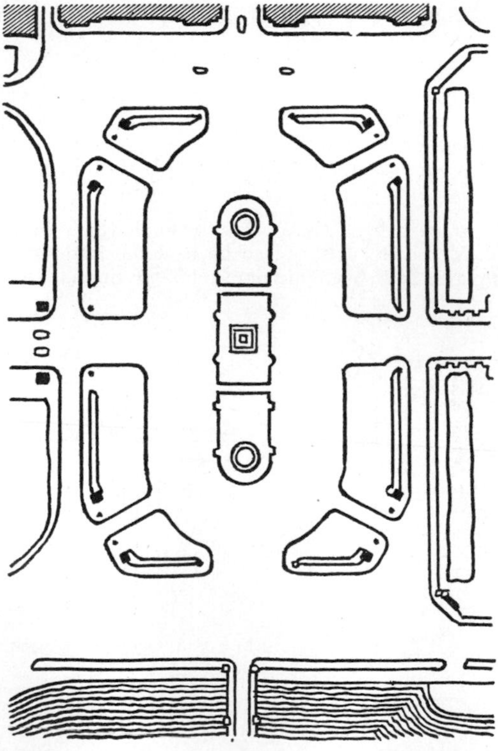

Fig. 25. Paris: Place de la Concorde (after Stübben)

'In Paris one of the oldest public squares created at one stroke is the Place de Vosges, formerly the Place Royale (Fig. 24), which is surrounded with arcaded residences that are all in the same style. Our illustration represents the original state of the square before it became a peaceful retreat and when it still served as a setting for the statue of Louis XIII.

The epoch of Louis XIV saw the construction of the Place des Victoires and the Place Vendôme (formerly Louis-le-Grand), both designed by J. Hardouin Mansart. Their plans do not offer great interest; they rather lend themselves to criticism, and it is more for their decoration that they are worthy of attention.

The Place de la Concorde (Fig. 25) did not at first possess its present form. J. A. Gabriel had already made a complete ensemble of it in 1765, but it was not until 1836–38 that it was finished in the way we now see it. This square, 820 feet in width, is bordered with buildings only on one side. It is bounded on the others, to be sure, by the trees of the Champs Élysées and by the enclosure of the Tuileries gardens, but as a square it differs from the majority of those which we have studied so far in being more open. On all sides grandiose perspectives are offered to our view, and the monumental balustrade with its charming angle-pavilions erected to the glory of French cities does not suffice to enclose it completely. Nevertheless, because of its site, its decoration, and the richness of its embellishment, it passes rightly for one of the most beautiful squares in the world. It is of almost the same date as the Place Stanislas in Nancy (Figs. 26, 27) built between 1752 and 1756 after the plans of Heré. This is in the form of a rectangle with chamfered corners, closed on three sides by the town hall and palaces in identical style, and on the fourth by lower residences which, joined by an arch of triumph, form a transition between the Place

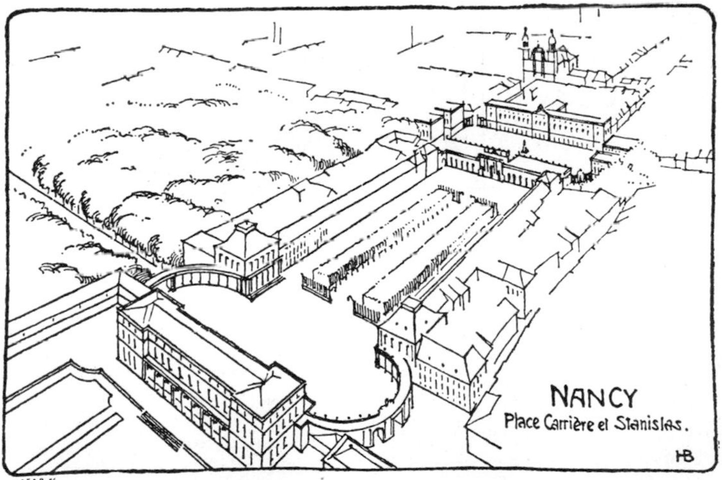

Fig. 26. Nancy: Place Carrière & Stanislas (Hans Bernouilli)

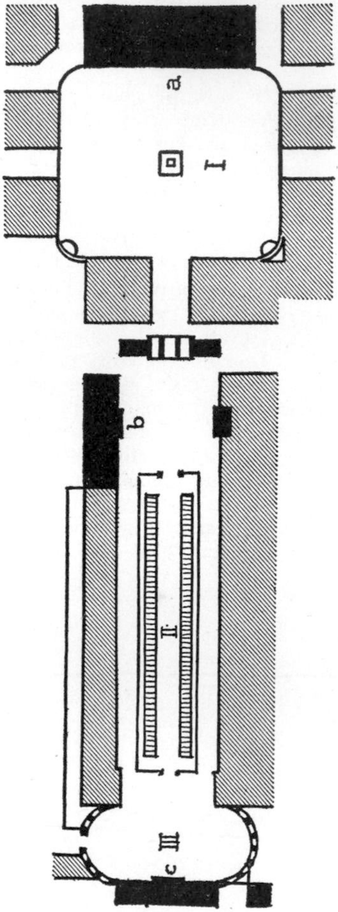

Fig. 27. Nancy (after Stübben). I. Place Stanislas.—II. Place de la Carrière.—III. Hemicycle.—a. Hôtel de Ville.—b. Palais de Justice.—c. Palais du Gouvernement

Stanislas and the Place de la Carrière. The latter, contrasting with the former because of its elongated shape, already existed from the 16th century but was brought to its present state much later. This ensemble of plazas is completed by the hemicycle of the Carrière which is dominated by the government building and surrounded by colonnades. Note the role played by the grilles of wrought iron in enclosing the Place Stanislas. They close off its four canted corners as well as the streets Stanislas and Sainte Catherine, thus making an admirable enframement for its space.'

260. THE ZWINGER: The Zwinger had been built by Daniel Pöppelmann (1662–1736) for Augustus the Strong between 1711–1722, leaving one side open for a new palace building which was never erected. Semper's museum, which served as the picture gallery, was constructed from 1847–1854, closing off that side. The royal theater had been built in 1838–41, but burned in 1869 and was replaced in 1871–78 by an opera house, designed by Semper and carried out by his son Manfred. This description of the Dresden incident is almost identical with Bibl. 53.

page 118

261. COMPLETION OF THE HOFBURG: Unfortunately it did not turn out as Sitte hoped, although the parts that were eventually omitted would probably not have disturbed him as much as did the closure of the Zwinger. Missing today are elements A, C, and D of Semper's plan as well as the two triumphal arches over the Ringstrasse. The Burgtheater (F) was put up elsewhere on the Ringstrasse. See Fig. 115 in *Sitte.*

The new Hofburg was erected from 1871 on after the plans of Semper and his Viennese collaborator K. von Hasenauer. Semper died in 1879; the second wing remained unfinished with the death of Hasenauer in 1894. The two museums had been constructed by Hasenauer from 1872–1881 after Semper's plans.

The plan is taken from Hans Semper (Note 57, p. 84), the bird's-eye view was supplied by the Vienna Kunsthistorisches Museum.

262. GREAT MONUMENTS IN VIENNA: The French translation omitted the Viennese examples down to *Sitte,* p. 120.

263. SCHUBERT MONUMENT: Statue by K. Kundmann, 1872.

264. HAYDN MONUMENT: Josef Haydn statue by H. Natter, 1887.

265. TEGETTHOFF MONUMENT: The monument was designed by Hasenauer and Kundmann in 1886. Baron Wilhelm von Tegetthoff (1827–71), Austrian admiral, was victor over the Italian fleet off Lissa in 1866. There is a good plan of the Prater-Stern in Stübben, *Handbuch,* Fig. 707.

page 119

266. RADETZKY MONUMENT: Field Marshal Josef Radetzky (1766–1858), long-time exponent of reforms in the Austrian armed forces and victor over Charles Albert at Novara in 1849. He was affectionately known as 'Father Radetzky' to his soldiers. This statue, by K. Zumbusch (1892), was not finished at the time Sitte originally wrote this book, but was eventually placed in the Platz am Hof which contained a column to the Virgin (of 1668).

The lecture to which Sitte referred in his footnote was entitled, 'On old city plans, with special reference to plazas and monument-placement in Vienna,' and was later published in *WOV,* Bibl. 54. The lecture was a rather general summary of his book (then in press), but it did recommend the placement of the Radetzky statue near the War Ministry (p. 262). He also wrote elsewhere about this (Bibl. 62).

This original placement of the monument is indicated in *Sitte,* Fig. 97. After the new War Ministry was constructed on the Stubenring about 1910, the Radetzky monument was shifted to that location.

267. AM HOF: We have added this plan, which did not appear in any prior editions of the book, in order to make Sitte's point clear.

page 120

268. MARIA THERESA MONUMENT: Sitte did not illustrate this monument. We have used an old photograph of his time to do so. The monument was designed by Hasenauer and K. Zumbusch.

page 121

269. ARCHITECTS' AND ENGINEERS' ASSEMBLY: *DB*, VIII (Oct. 31, 1874), p. 346; there were seven resolutions in all, which were reprinted in the appendix to Stübben's *Handbuch*. See Note 42. The italics are Sitte's.

page 122

270. OPEN COMPETITION: Sitte seems to interpret rather freely the proceedings of the Berlin meeting of 1874; published reports give no such resolution as he cites. He may have been thinking of the resolutions of the Vienna *Verein* of 1877 which stressed the idea of open competitions—quite a Viennese concern. See above, p. 41.

page 123

271. CHANCE PLANNING: It is hardly necessary to point out that this is a fundamental tenet of Sitte's that the 'picturesque' urban effects of olden times were not fortuitous, but were intentional. On this Brinckmann and others considered him to be a romantic, 'reading into' ancient plans. See above p. 54.

272. THE ROMAN 'CASTRUM': We do not think today that Roman city planning evolved in quite so simple a fashion!

page 124

273. BAUMEISTER: Bibl. 252. Figs. 98–102 are taken from pp. 180–181 of this book (Figs. 8, 12, 4, 1, and 7 respectively). Baumeister had actually drafted the Berlin resolutions.

274. SETBACK OF BUILDINGS: Baumeister, *op. cit.*, p. 99.

page 127

275. DONAUSTADT: The remainder of this paragraph about Vienna and the Danube was omitted from the French editions.

276. IRON GATE: The Iron Gate is the last defile of the Danube below Orsova on what is now the Romanian-Yugoslav border. At this point the river was narrow, plagued by rocks and whirlpools and almost impassable until a long and expensive regulation of it was carried out in the late 19th century. This project had been delegated to the abutting powers by the London Treaty of 1871, to Austria-Hungary by the Berlin Treaty of 1878, and was finally carried out by Hungary at great expense, being completed in 1898: A joint project to improve navigation at this point was inaugurated with great fanfare by Romania and Yugoslavia in September 1964.

page 129

277. PUBLIC GARDEN AND PLAZA ARRANGEMENTS: Sitte never quite makes clear why when he prefers buildings and plazas to occur in continuous, related groupings, he likes public gardens or verdured squares to be widely separated. He seems to have considered the latter two to have been merely the 'ventilators' of the city like courts in buildings (compare Note 247) whereas the public plazas had a more social, civic, and aesthetic use, calling for their arrangement in sequences.

page 131

278. VITRUVIUS AND THE WINDS: Sitte is referring here to a passage in Vitruvius (Book I, Chapter VI) wherein the Roman architect, characteristically, appears to confound cosmic considerations with purely practical phases of city planning.

In order to determine the direction of the prevailing winds of any building site Vitruvius does not employ what would seem to us the obvious procedure of checking them empirically with, say, an upheld moistened finger. Instead he uses a rather involved method of determining the cardinal points of the compass (actually the quarters of the heavens, *Himmelsgegenden*) by means of a gnomon and drawing-compasses, which derives them from the orbit of the sun. Vitruvius then assumes that these celestial quarters are precisely the spaces belonging to the various prevailing winds of the locale in question, and he recommends that the radiating streets of the town plan be laid out along the boundary lines between these eight cardinal winds, so as to avoid their force.

This is indeed a cosmological bit of meteorology, quite distinct from the frame of mind of Sitte who is quite willing to ignore the sacred orientation of European cathedrals in order to place their roofs athwart the prevailing winds of their towns. This contrast between the two practical-minded theorists, Vitruvius and Sitte, is the sort of thing to which we were referring in our discussion of self-orientation in city planning (Note 237). On Vitruvius and the winds see also Note 197.

279. BAROQUE MASTERS: Here Martin managed to give Sitte's observation a Gallic flavor by substituting 'XVII and XVIII centuries' for 'Baroque masters' and introducing the adjective 'symmetrical' to describe their system.

page 133

280. CONCAVITY VS. CONVEXITY: Martin again substituted 'XVII and XVIII centuries' for 'Baroque,' but went on to make Sitte's point more explicit, that is to say that the ideal situation in land speculation is that which provides the greatest possible continuous frontage, viz., the circular or hexagonal city block, decidedly convex in form. Sitte had discussed this in Chapter IX, but may have been mistaken: see our Note 248.

page 134

281. PIARISTENPLATZ: We have used the plan employed by Stübben in his 1907 *Handbuch* (Fig. 414) since it is more detailed than Sitte's and it actually resembles more Sitte's own creation of a Baroque church setting

in his Fig. 103. It is significant that Sitte's ideal approximated the Piaristenplatz and it is odd that he used such a schematic plan of it, because it was apparently a favorite square of his. He had many close personal associations with it; his family had lived in the church parish house, at Lederergasse No. 8, which his father had built, and he attended the Piaristen Gymnasium here, from which he was graduated in 1863.

The French again substituted 'XVIII century' for 'Baroque' on p. 134, with some reason in this case: the church of Maria Treu dates from 1716, the Lady Column in the square from 1713. The Piarists (Pauline Congregation of the Mother of God) are a teaching order, founded in the XVII century, especially strong in Austria-Hungary.

page 137

282. THEATERS AND FIRE DANGER: Concern with the danger of fire actually persisted later into the 20th century than the usual histories of architecture suggest; it was by no means laid to rest by the invention of the 'skyscraper' system of construction and fireproofing that followed the Chicago fire of 1871. The dates of publication of Peter B. Wight's *Fireproof Magazine* were, after all, 1902–07; and we find in its extensive reports of the catastrophes in Baltimore (1904) and San Francisco (1906) that all was not well with a number of highly-touted fireproofing methods.

Theaters had been the scene of some of the most horrible tragedies of this sort during the 18th and 19th centuries, and had therefore stimulated our earliest efforts at devising safe flooring, supports, and ceilings. Gottfried Semper had lost his Royal Theater in Dresden to fire in 1869, rebuilding it shortly thereafter with the aid of his son.

The general plan of Sitte's ideal theater is not unlike Semper's although its relation to surrounding buildings is quite dissimilar (compare his Fig. 95). The rounded and forward-jutting auditorium façade is a feature of both and of the Vienna opera house as well.

283. IDEAL THEATER: Hegemann & Peets mistakenly took this plan to be that of a church (*Civic Art,* Fig. 142b).

page 139

284. A BAD PLAZA: The French editions used a slightly different illustration, from Stübben, *Handbuch,* Fig. 277.

285. IMPROVED PLAZAS: The French translator condensed somewhat these

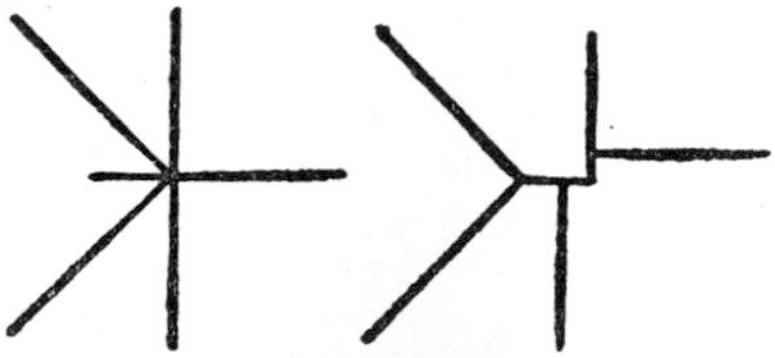

Fig. 28. Schematic diagram of a typical modern traffic intersection (left) and of Martin's suggestion for alleviating it (right)

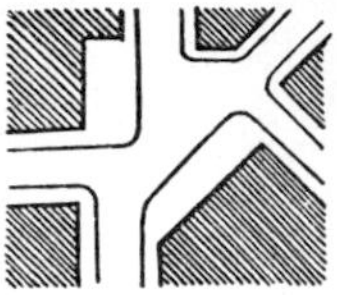

Fig. 29. An actual street intersection based on Fig. 28 (right)

discussions of awkward plazas and intersections. Two special illustrations, Figs. 28 and 29, were inserted to make clear the faults of modern intersections (Fig. 28, left) and their solution both diagramatically and practically (Fig. 28, right, and Fig. 29) by the system of offsets which Martin had described in his special Chapter VIIA (*Sitte,* p. 63). The point became somewhat obscured, however, in the second French edition through the accidental inversion of Fig. 29, so that its relation to the diagrams became unclear.

Notes on Chapter XII

EXAMPLE OF AN URBAN ARRANGEMENT ACCORDING TO ARTISTIC PRINCIPLES

page 141

286. PLANNING ON A MONUMENTAL SCALE: Sitte's first two sentences formed the opening paragraph of the French version of this chapter. The rest of the chapter was organized by Martin as follows:

1. The following heading was inserted:

'PROJECT FOR THE TRANSFORMATION OF A DISTRICT OF THE CITY OF VIENNA worked out by C. SITTE, architect and director of the Imperial and Royal School of Industrial Arts in Vienna.'

2. Then came a short paragraph that summarized our 3rd and 8th paragraphs and mentioned the rapid development of monumental buildings in Vienna, the faults of their surroundings, and the fact that sufficient open space remained to correct the shortcomings of the original plan.

3. The rest of Sitte's chapter is then presented in a curtailed fashion, using only Figs. 112, 113, 115, and ending up with a translation of Sitte's final paragraph. This amounts to compressing about 20 pages of German into about 8 pages of French.

4. The 1902 French edition then continued with three examples of layouts by Sitte followers, which we include in our Note 295 along with their illustrations. These were cut from the 1918 French edition, which ended as Sitte had. See above, p. 70.

287. MUNICH AND VIENNA: Regarding this flourishing building activity in Munich and then in Vienna, see Bibl. 465 and our own text above, *passim.*

page 143

288. GOTTFRIED SEMPER: To help orient the reader somewhat with regard to Semper, who moves in and out of these chapters of Sitte, the following is a rough chronological schema of his life and major works:

1803	Born in Hamburg
1823–25	Studied law and mathematics at Göttingen
c. 1825	Started study and apprenticeship in architecture
1829–33	Travelled in France, Italy, Sicily, Greece
1834	*Vorläufige Bemerkungen über bemalte Architektur und Plastik bei den Alten*, Altona
1834–48	In Dresden as Professor of architecture at the Kunstakademie (at invitation of Schinkel). Designed numerous public buildings there. Also active in Hamburg, especially building residences
1838–41	Dresden, Old Court Theater (burned 1869). See Notes 260, 282
1837	Dresden, plans for the Zwinger Palace. See *Sitte*, pp. 116–118, Fig. 95
c. 1842	Hamburg, plans for rebuilding after fire. See Note 24
1847–54	Dresden, Picture Gallery (Museum). See *Sitte*, pp. 116–117
1849	Fled to Paris
1851–55	In London as a friend of Henry Cole. Active in Department of Practical Art, Marlborough House, and in Exposition of 1851
1852	*Wissenschaft, Industrie, und Kunst*, Brunswick
1855–71	In Zürich as Professor at the Polytechnikum
1860–63	*Der Stil in den technischen und tektonischen Künsten*, Frankfurt and Munich
1864–66	With Richard Wagner worked out plans for the Wagner Festspielhaus in Munich
1869	Submitted his first plan for the new Vienna Hofburg. See *Sitte*, pp. 118, 143, Pls. XX, XXXI, Note 261
1871	Invited to Vienna, primarily to do the Hofburg layout
1871–78	Dresden, designed New Court Opera to replace the destroyed Court Theater (built by son Manfred after his plans). See Notes 260, 282
1872–81	Vienna, Imperial Museums of Natural History and Art History (by von Hasenauer after Semper's plans). See *Sitte*, p. 118, Pl. XXI–a
1873–88	Vienna, Burgtheater (work carried on by von Hasenauer after 1874). See *Sitte*, pp. 151–152.
1879	Died in Rome

For Sitte's own writings about Semper see Note 15. See also Notes 57, 63.

289. HAPPY COMPLETION: Actually never completed. See Note 261.

290. VOTIVE CHURCH: The Votive Church was constructed 1856–79 after the competition plans (1855) of Ferstel. It celebrated the Emperor Franz Joseph's escape from an attempt on his life in 1853. See our p. 36, Pl. IX.

page 145

291. BUILDING PERMITS: It must be remembered that in the Ringstrasse development only the broadest features were laid out by the central authority and most of the lots were sold to individuals for speculative development. See above, p. 35.

page 148

292. CORRECTLY STATED PROBLEMS: This is a characteristic Sittesque variation on the theme of 'Form follows Function,' so universally expounded upon in his day.

page 156

293. MAUSOLEUM OF AUGUSTUS: Sitte was mistaken here. The diameter of his proposed new structure is also less than the Mausoleum of Augustus.

page 158

294. GOETHE MONUMENT: Sitte also dealt with this matter in a lecture which he had delivered at a general meeting of the Goethe Verein on the 22nd of February, 1889 (Bibl. 55). The monument was finally placed in the Opernring.

page 159

295. BLESSINGS OF ART: At this point the chapter also ended in all translations of Sitte except the first French edition of 1902, which added three sample layouts by followers of Sitte. This material, which was cut out of the 2nd French edition in 1918, reads as follows:

'II

'PROJECTED PLAN OF EXTENSION FOR THE CITY OF DESSAU, executed by K. HENRICI, architect and professor of the Polytechnic Institute at Aix-la-Chapelle. [See above, pp. 76–77, 83–84 and enlargement of the plan on our book cover.]

'The terrain to be built up (Pl. XV-a) forms a distinct whole, separated from the city to its SE by the railroad and bounded at the N and NE by a park. Also, the author has surrounded the projected quarter by a belt of boulevards, leaving outside of this circle only some parcels intended to receive villas. The center of gravity of the ensemble has been marked by squares surrounded with public buildings, in accordance with ancient tradition. This center has been connected with other important points, such as the railway crossings and the opening of roads coming in from the country, which in turn are put into communication with each other by means of other arteries. The streets serving these various purposes are either the principal ones of 65-ft. width (*Hauptstrassen*), or the medium ones of 57-ft. width (*Mittelstrassen*). As intersections could only be avoided with difficulty on the main arteries, one has tried to remedy the inconvenience they cause by enlarging the arteries at the points of juncture (crossing of Hauptstr. I and II with Mittelstr. II; that of Ringstr. II and

Hauptstr. III, etc.). The crossings among secondary streets have generally been eliminated. Everywhere that it was possible or necessary the author has broken or curved-in the line of the streets, taking care to set off their concave sides to advantage. It is indicated with crosses on the plan where there are pieces of ground that offer certain advantages of placement. In order to see that the circulation of vehicles in the streets is clearly indicated and well limited, it was necessary that the right-of-way have a uniform width and that the sidewalks be set out in bold lines, not following the ins and outs of the buildings (Westl. Ringstr.). Only in certain places can circumstances permit an enlargement of the street. It is best to anticipate these points on the plan at the very beginning lest each proprietor seek to satisfy his own self-interest as far as possible by covering the entire surface of the land that belongs to him with buildings.

'The market place is oriented north-and-south so as not to be swept by the winds that usually blow here from west to east. It is well framed and is dominated by a public building that is flanked by a bell tower. This belfry would give life to the entire silhouette of the city and would also serve as a point of orientation. Beside the market a little plaza (*Nebenplatz*) absorbs the streets coming from the country, as well as principal street IV, and takes advantage of the public building as its dominating feature. The little plaza planted with trees to the west of the market would naturally become a parking place for the vehicles of farmers coming to market. The church square is not on the route of any large artery; the streets which lead into it are so arranged that one cannot see the church plainly until arriving in the neighborhood. In order to enrich the plaza extending behind the chevet, the author has provided for a Casino whose façade would serve as a sufficient backing for it. The school court has been situated in the interior of a block of houses; it is not too removed from the center of the quarter and yet it lies aside from the noise and dust of the streets. Finally, at the east of the market there is a large court accessible only to pedestrians and surrounded by shops, which would be used for festivals, open-air meetings, concerts, etc.

'The width of its streets assures to this entire quarter an abundance of air and light. Finally, to prevent the inconveniences caused by prevailing winds (here from west to east), the streets running in that direction are not prolonged as far as the countryside, but instead their trajectory is broken or bent. In this way currents of air cannot build up with too great an intensity.

'Gardens in front of the houses and tree-lined avenues have been provided with moderation so as not to incur too much expense and so as not to mar with trees the effect of the streets. The straight tree-lined avenue that bisects the quarter constitutes a sufficient reservoir to renew the atmosphere.

'The terrain situated to the north-east is reserved for a public park.

'This project was one of the first practical applications of the ideas set forth by M. Sitte. Its author, moveover, has not been satisfied with this first attempt, for the plans which he presented for Hanover (*DB*, XXV, 1891, pp. 320–322), Munich (awarded the prize in a public competition and published in Bibl. 338, 1893), for Brünn, Flensburg, etc., are inspired by the same principles. Furthermore, the numerous articles written by M. Henrici in various specialized journals have contributed precision to the theory of this new art of building cities. (See *DB*, Bibl. 336, 337, 339–341; *CBB*, XXI, 1901, pp. 577–580, 590–592; *CBB*, XXII, 1902, pp. 80–82, 85.)'

'III

'DETAILS OF THE PLAN OF EXTENSION OF THE CITY OF MUNICH, carried out under the direction of TH. FISCHER, architect and presently professor of the Polytechnic Institute at Stuttgart. [See above, pp. 76–77.]

'These two examples taken from the plan of Munich (Pl. XV-b) show an effort to restore to our streets the aspect that characterized them in former times, while adjusting their dimensions to the necessities of modern living. (The width of the Arnulfstrasse is at no point less than 90 feet, that of the Prinzregentenstrasse not less than 65 feet.)

'The Arnulfstrasse runs without interruption for nearly a mile. It is notable for its elegant curvature and for the enlargement that it undergoes near one end. This sort of square, lying aside from the stream of vehicles and pedestrians, is ideally suited to receive fountains and a monument.

'The Prinzregentenstrasse is not a continuous public drive. Its course is broken at one point without the traffic being obstructed, because at that place two squares provide the space necessary to facilitate passage. A public building (Theâtre du Régent) is the culminating point of one of the parts of the artery, while a triumphal arch closes off the perspective vista of the other.

'In the two arteries, the opening of lateral streets has been studied so as to form good plans for their corner houses, carefully avoiding acute-angled street intersections.

'The example of Munich can reassure those who doubt the possibility of applying the new principles of city planning to important and populous capitals. The plans illustrated here are not utopian projects; they have been approved by the Bavarian government, and it is along the street alignments indicated in them that the future parts of the city will be erected.'

'IV

'PLAN OF A VILLA SUBURB AT DARMSTADT, designed by F. PUETZER, architect and professor of the Polytechnic Institute at Darmstadt. [See Note 83.]

'This plan (Pl. XVI), less extensive than its predecessors, seems likely to be carried out at this time. The projected neighborhood, being confined only to villas, will never under any circumstances become a place of intense traffic. So it was natural to impose picturesque curves on the lines of the internal streets, while keeping the principal ways clear and continuous in plan. It was especially in the disposition of public squares that the city planner could exercise his art. The author of the Darmstadt plan, taking account of the configurations of the terrain (note the contour lines) has provided for a square in the center of a sort of amphitheater, on the slopes around which the villas will rise up in tiers. The church and the public buildings projected for this spot are not isolated but are related to other parcels, and the villas which bound the plaza on one side are placed at the front edge of their plots so as to complete the enframement better. The street which gives access to the church widens more or less in the form of a plaza. This is the parvis of the sanctuary, on which one can erect a monument or a fountain some day. Thanks to the clever design of the streets one can see the whole church only when one has arrived at a proper distance, and its steeple, rising above the nave and the surrounding villas, will give a picturesque conclusion to more than one street.

'It is not possible to mention all the niceties of detail included in this plan; better to leave to the reader the pleasure of discovering them himself. As each street has its own individuality, it would take too long to describe them one by one. We mention only the fact that in more than one road the alignment of the houses does not follow strictly that of the street, but the latter are instead often disposed according to a concave line so as to present their façades better. It is also interesting to study the division of the terrain into plots and to observe the efforts made by the author of the plan to reserve sound garden areas for the future proprietors of the villas, while taking the best possible advantage of terrain for building.

'We also note that in keeping with the already rustic character of the district, tree-lined walks are not very numerous. They are provided in places where they have the best chance of flourishing and they are planted sufficiently thickly to present compact masses of foliage to the eye and to furnish welcome shade to those passing by.

'The little plan placed below the one that we have just described had been provided originally by the official draftsman for the layout of the same neighbourhood. It is superfluous to make a critique of it. It is a striking example of the principle of least effort and a proof of the complete oblivion into which have sunk the most elementary standards of the aesthetic of cities.'

[Of these three plans, all but Henrici's seem to have been carried out more or less as intended. They are perfect illustrations of the so-called 'Sittesque' school of city planning.]

CONCLUSION

page 160

296. J. G. MÜLLER: Ernst Förster, *Johann Georg Müller; Ein Dichter- und Künstlerleben*, 2nd edit., St. Gall, Scheitlin und Zollikofer, 1854, p. 39. For more about Müller and his relationship to the Sitte family see above, pp. 6–7 and Note 3.

It appears that this project was designed purely for the artist's own purposes and was never published anywhere.

297. BRUSSELS, RUE ROYALE: The story of this ill-fated competition project is related in Förster, *op. cit.*, pp. 161ff. The fact that Müller's plans arrived late was used as an excuse for not reimbursing him, although he received a silver medal for them and certain features of his project were

actually used. The outcome was tragic. Despite long efforts on his part to enforce payment and the return of his plans, the latter arrived only after his premature death from consumption; he was never paid. His designs for what was to be mainly a public market were in the Moorish style and apparently very luxurious. The municipal council of Brussels was enchanted, commenting, 'We asked him for a market, . . . he gave us a palace . . .'

page 161

298. THE OLD BURGTOR: A neo-classical gateway built by Peter von Nobile during 1821–24, never actually dismantled.

Notes on Appendix I

GREENERY WITHIN THE CITY

page 167

299. SOURCE AND SUMMARIES OF APPENDIX I: Apart from some minor typographical changes, the material as printed in the German 4th and 5th editions is identical with its original publication as an article (Bibl. 79).

It is impossible to describe in detail the liberties which the French 'summary' took with the German text; instead, the reader is referred to our chart of correspondences between French edition II and German edition IV on p. 70 above. Martin drastically condensed the material (which in 1902 still existed only in article-form), six pages being reduced in one case to five sentences; he interspersed some fairly exact translations of parts of German Chapter IX where they seemed to apply, instead of summarizing those portions of the German Appendix. German and Austrian examples were omitted, almost without exception.

A free and rather poor translation of the French appendix appeared in *Park International* (Washington, D.C.) I, July & November 1920, pp. 283–285. Boyarsky (Bibl. 154) also included a translation of the French appendix.

300. LICHTWARK, Bibl. 348.

page 170

301. FOLIAGE AND HUMAN RESPIRATION: For examples of extravagant claims of that day about the virtues of foliage as a protector of human life in the O_2-CO_2 cycle, supported by statistical tables and medical testimony, and appearing in presumably reputable peridicals, the reader is referred to:

For England, P. Hinckes Bird, 'On Tree Planting in Towns,' in *The Sanitary Record* (London), IX, July 5, 1878, pp. 1–2.

For France, Dr. Jeannel, 'Des plantations d'arbres dans l'intérieur des villes au point de vue de hygiene publique,' in *Receuil de Memoires de Medecine, de Chirurgie, et de Pharmacie militaires* (Paris), 1872, series, 3, XXVIII, pp. 596–612.

302. PUCHNER: Apparently Heinrich Rupert Puchner (born 1865), German chemist who worked on soils and air content.

303. THE SANITARY WOOLEN SYSTEM: The *Wollregime*, as Sitte called it, was a health cult devised by Gustav Jäger (1832–1916), German naturalist and hygienist—an early follower of Darwin. The tenets of his health regime that concern us here are his insistence that clothes and bedding be made purely of animal fibres rather than vegetable fibres (the famous woolen 'jaegers'), and his advocacy of fresh air attained through room ventilation and by means of his so-called Platinum Lamp. The latter was a device with a spiral platinum filament that generated a substance he called 'ozogen,' which freshened stale air and removed odors. It was apparently an early form of the Nernst lamp which is now used for that purpose. The details of his regimen are set down in his *Die Normalkleidung als Gesundheitsschutz*, Stuttgart, Kohlhammer, 1880: in English as *Health Culture and the Sanitary Woolen System*, New York and London (many edits.).

304. ERNST EBERMAYER, 'Mitteilungen über Kohlensäuregehalt eines bewaldeten und nicht-bewaldeten Bodens,' in *Die landwirtschaftlichen Versuchs-Stationen* (Berlin), XXIII, 1879, pp. 64–66; and *Die Beschaffenheit der Waldluft und die Bedeutung der atmosphärischen Kohlensäure für die Waldvegetation: Zugleich eine übersichtliche Darstellung des gegenwärtigen Standes der Kohlensäurefrage*, Stuttgart, F. Enke, 1885.

page 171

305. ULRICH KREUSLER, 'Über den Sauerstoffgehalt der atmosphärischen Luft,' in *Landwirtschaftliche Jahrbücher* (Berlin) XIV, 1885, pp. 305–378.

306. WALTER HEMPEL, 'Sauerstoffgehalt der atmosphärischen Luft,' in *Berichte der deutschen Chemischen Gesellschaft* (Berlin), XVIII, 1885, p. 1802.

Some tests have actually revealed a minutely higher oxygen concentration in country air than in the city, and in city parks than in city streets. (*Encyclopedia Britannica*, 11th edit., II, p. 860.) The same source (XVIII, p. 266; XXVII, p. 1808) reports that carbon dioxide concentrations are actually less over the sea than over land and that there is a night-day and seasonal variation.

307. FOREST AIR: Alessandro Serafini and J. Arata, 'Intorno all'azione dei boschi sulli microorganismi trasportati dai venti,' in *Bullettino della Reale Accademia Medica di Roma*, XVI, 1889–90, pp. 489–504. Sitte had read this in summary in *Forschungen auf dem Gebiete der Agrikultur-Physik*, XIV, 1891, pp. 176–180, and interpreted it somewhat out of context. The Italian investigators were checking on the popular idea that woods act as a barrier and filter for air-borne malaria germs by means of their foliage. They found that the interior of forests do sometimes contain more microorganisms than their surroundings, but that this was in part due to their physical retention of the matter carried by breezes and winds.

308. MYTHS ABOUT FRESH AIR: Sitte's scoffing at theories about the beneficial effects of forest air is, for the most part, supported by scientific researches conducted since his day. The early idea that forest air was higher in oxygen content and reduced in concentration of carbon dioxide has been disproven. The 'freshness' of forest air is offset by the carbon

dioxide resulting from decomposition of organic matter, but forest air *is* relatively free of the dust and smoke of cities.

However, his comment about the presence of bacteria in forests (p. 171) is perhaps incorrect. It has been found that in forests there are 23 to 28 times less bacteria than elsewhere. The humus of trees is thought to be inimical to pathogenic bacteria; they have not been found in forest soil. In fact, it has even been suggested that forest soil insulates against cholera.

The question of the beneficial effects of ozone still seems to be a puzzling one to scientists. Although Sitte is justified in ridiculing the cults that had sprung up in the mid-19th century, he does not actually refute their hypotheses, and we find there to be a certain viability in some of the old ideas about ozone.

Following the naming of ozone (by Schönbein) and the subsequent investigation into its properties and methods of laboratory and natural generation, there arose many legends about the therapeutic benefits of this isotropic form of oxygen. Practically, it has been used since the 1860's against miasma (the exhalation of putrid matter). Dr. Benjamin W. Richardson described this and other properties of the gas interestingly in *Popular Science Review* (London), V, 1866, pp. 29–40, before it was known precisely what ozone was. It has been used to purify air and to treat materials kept in cold storage. Dr. Richardson later included a central ozone generating plant in his programme for a model town (*Hygeia, a City of Health*, London, MacMillan, 1876).

Schönbein, a pioneer in the investigations of the properties of ozone, recommended it as an oxidizing agent in the treatment of a number of ailments thought to result from poor internal combustion in the body: phthisis, scrofula, diabetes. Others claimed good results in the employment of it against diphtheria and whooping cough. It was thought to possess hypnotic properties. However, the ozone peddled by certain Berlin chemists as a panacea proved to be merely impure oxygen, and the ozone-water of the English druggists was usually a solution of potassium permanganate.

It was noticed that ozone tended to disappear from the atmosphere during epidemics, and special studies were made in Paris around 1870 to determine whether the winds that prevailed during certain epidemical periods were reduced in ozone content.

It also became clear that certain concentrations of ozone were irritating to the mucuous membranes and could be toxic to both human beings and animals. Breathing air with an excess of ozone in it for a brief period will produce the symptoms of nasal catarrh, common cold, or even bronchitis. It is not safe to breathe more than 0.1 part per million for an extended period. Concentration of ozone in the country is usually less than 0.02 to 0.03 parts per million, and city concentrations are even less except under conditions of smog (in which the sun apparently acts on the air in presence of impurities to form ozone). In Los Angeles the concentration of ozone reaches 0.5 parts per million for short periods. The presence of ozone and nitrogen dioxide in such smog is suspected of rendering those who inhale it more susceptible to the bacteria of pneumonia, influenza, etc. (*New York Times*, December 10, 1961).

In an article entitled 'Atmospheric Electricity and Ozone: their Relation to Health and Disease,' Dr. George M. Beard (*The Popular Science*

Monthly, New York, IV, 1873–74, pp. 456–469) summed up our knowledge of ozone to that date, dwelling on its physiological effects, including the fact that the periods of greatest human energy during the day and year correspond to high points in the cycles of atmospheric ozone content.

Attempts to relate the tempo or type of human activity to concentrations of atmospheric ozone still persist. Ellsworth Huntington of Yale suggested, in his investigation of meteorological and other natural cycles, that the seasonal fluctuations in atmospheric ozone may exert profound physiological effects on mankind. Huntington was speaking of minute, virtually undetectable ozone quantities, such as seem to give air its 'fresh' character; he suggests that ozone may be a more important factor in this respect than the ionization of air. In ingenious fashion he relates the annual periods of higher ozone content to drops in mortality statistics, to increases in serious, non-fictional reading (based on library circulation statistics), and to the possibility that children conceived during these periods grow physically more vigorous. ('Climatic Pulsation and an Ozone Hypothesis of Libraries and History,' in University of Pennsylvania Bicentennial Conference, *Conservation of Renewable Natural Resources*, Philadelphia, University of Pennsylvania Press, 1941, pp. 99–147).

The therapeutic properties of ozone continue to be explored. Ozone inhaling machinery is apparently still used. Based on the belief that there is an ozone 'belt' in the earth's atmosphere, respiratory patients are taken up in open airplanes to secure relief from sinusitis, hay fever, and the like.

Sitte was undoubtedly acquainted with Ernst Ebermayer's informative summary of the subject, 'Das atmosphärische Ozon,' in the Viennese periodical *Zeitschrift der Österreichischen Gesellschaft für Meteorologie*, VIII, 1873, pp. 342–345, 369–372. Most writers on city vegetation in his day dealt with the matter. See Flügge in Note 30.

page 172

309. JANISSARIES' PLANE TREE: A huge tree in the outer court of the Seraglio of Constantinople, under which the Janissaries used to meet.

page 173

310. PICTURESQUE TOWN PLANNING: Sitte's contempt for shallow picturesqueness in planning was echoed in the writings of his Hamburg friend, Alfred Lichtwark. As has been made clear by Alice Fischer in her essay on Lichtwark (Bibl. 180), German engineers had not only imposed a rigid gridiron system on the planning of cities, as we would assume to be the case from reading Sitte. Rather, to counter criticism that they were not sufficiently 'artistic,' they had introduced a romantic, anti-geometric style of layout derived from those English principles of planning that Napoleon III had also admired so much. Litchwark lists the three basic and most pernicious ideas of the engineers' romanticism as being: the illusion of unlimited space, the suggestion of 'unspoiled' nature, and the hilly landscape. Thus it would appear that by 1900 the 'old geometric school' was not the only culprit, as Sitte would lead us to believe in the next paragraph.

page 176

311. LUDWIG HERCHER, 'Die Lage der Strassenbahngeleise in breiten Strassen,' *DB*, XXXIII, 1899, pp. 117–118. This particular idea was to

become popular among Sitte's disciples. Martin used it in his inserted chapter on Streets (see *Sitte*, p. 66) and Theodor Fischer stressed it in a lecture on City Building (Bibl. 298).

312. ALLEE: Sitte uses *Allee* in the landscape-gardening sense of a pedestrian and/or vehicular way bordered by long, regular rows of trees or shrubs; it can be a street, a city avenue, a boulevard, a *Ringstrasse*, a country road, a garden vista, or merely a footpath. We have translated the word variously as the circumstances of its use seemed to demand.

He is correct in observing that the *Allee* or 'avenue' (see Webster) arose on the one hand as an approach to a great house and, on the other, as a tree-lined country road. For informative articles about this see *The Garden* (London) LXXXVIII, 1924, pp. 500ff., and *ARev*, CXVI, September 1954, pp. 187ff.

The French translation used 'XVIII century' instead of 'Baroque' at this point.

page 178

313. STÜBBEN, *Handbuch*, Figs. 107–216.

314. EWALD GENZMER, *Über Anpflanzungen auf städtischen Strassen und Plätzen*, Halle, Hendel, 1894.

page 179

315. SQUARE: Sitte's word 'Square,' as employed here, is the *Gartenplatz* —the garden square or verdured square, best known from its English examples. As he discusses it, he touches upon the types which we now call, variously, 'garden square,' 'residential square,' and 'public garden.' What he is talking about is the first definition that Webster gives of the word square, 'An open area enclosed by residential buildings and commonly laid out with trees, grass, walks, and gardens.' The French edition translated the word in each case as 'public garden'; we have tried to select the proper word for each context as we did with *Allee*.

On this type of civic improvement, see S. Giedion, Bibl. 181, Part VII.

page 182

316. SITTE'S OWN PLANNING: Sitte did not illustrate any of these plans. Olmütz is to be found in Hegemann & Peets, *Civic Art*, Fig. 150. See also Note 17.

page 185

317. CONSTANTINOPLE: Sitte was acquainted with Constantinople through his Mediterranean travels and the fact that he did a parcelling plan there for the Mechitarists. See Note 17.

It is amusing to note that Le Corbusier, who denounced Sitte so bitterly for his ideas about planning, made almost identical comments about Constantinople in the same book (Bibl. 187, pp. 71–72).

318. MUNICH FOUNTAIN: The fountain of Wittelsbach by A. von Hildebrand (1895), with groups of figures and allegorical masks, served as an ornamental terminus to the city aqueduct.

319. UNIFIED NATIONAL WORK OF ART: It is characteristic that this essay should end on the note of *Gesamtkunstwerk*, war-cry of the artistic reformers of the turn of the century. On this and Sitte's nationalism, which ties him to younger German Jugendstil contemporaries like Obrist, see above, pp. 14–15.

The concluding paragraph of the French translation is feeble by comparison:

> 'The art of arranging public gardens and *allées*, like that of building cities, is not a mechanical office job. It is truly a work of art—a great and popular art that could bring forth masterpieces if it could surmount the narrow bounds that limit it in our day.'

Notes on Appendix II

TO OUR READERS

page 189

320. HEADPIECE: Designed by Hanns Anker (1873–), a German painter, engraver, and writer on aesthetics.

page 190

321. CITY-PLANNING PERIODICALS: For a discussion of early city-planning journals see Note 107.

page 191

322. MAX JOSEPH VON PETTENKOFER (1818–1901), German chemist and hygienist, best known for his work in epidemiology and other aspects of public health. Founder and editor of the *Zeitschrift für Biologie* from 1865–82 and of the *Archiv für Hygiene* from 1883–94, he established the first hygienic institute (Munich, 1879). He was an exponent of fresh air, pure water, proper clothing and housing, and adequate sewage disposal, having been drawn to these problems by the disease-ridden conditions of Munich, a city which he transformed into one of the most healthy of Europe.

He experimented, lectured, and published on most of the questions of atmosphere and plants that we have discussed in Note 308: for instance, the possible relationship between ozone and cholera epidemics (in *Untersuchungen und Beobachtungen über die Verbreitungsart der Cholera*, Munich, Cotta, 1855, pp. 288–289, 364–365). For an interesting evaluation of his activities, which ranged from classic quantitative-chemistry tests to the restoration of oil paintings in the Munich gallery, and from the manufacturing of illuminating gas out of wood to improving Portland cement, see E. E. Hume, *Max von Pettenkofer*, New York: Hoeber, 1927. See also p. 19 above and Note 30.

323. CITY DUST: Compare Note 197 where we have already gone into this matter. The point made here about the hygienic value of narrow streets was not original with Sitte and Goecke in 1904. Stübben had already emphasized this in his *Handbuch* (p. 70), and he made the point with

almost the same words that they use in his Bibl. 405 (p. 28). It is interesting that his latter statement was quoted in full by Horsfall when he reported in 1904 to the English people on the state of city planning in Germany (Bibl. 467, p. 155).

The matter of the interval between buildings or 'yield' (*Bauwich*) had been a basic tenet of German building ordinances and was discussed at great length by Stübben in his *Handbuch*.

page 194

324. INTERIOR BUILDING FRONTAGE LINE: Compare *Sitte*, p. 182. Sitte and Goecke are actually concerned here with the advantages and disadvantages of what were later to become known as the 'neighborhood' and 'superblock' theories of urban planning.

AUTHOR'S NOTE

We have been grieved to learn, while this book is in the press, that Josef Schwarzl of Vienna, who assisted us in so many ways with our work, passed away on 15 December 1964 and will never see the results of his generosity in our behalf.

BIBLIOGRAPHY

The bibliography is divided into a number of sections in order to make clear the relevance of the items listed. Wherever practical a few words have been added to the citation in order to explain its importance or a reference has been inserted indicating the place in this book where the publication is described. A gap has been left in the code numbers between the sections of the bibliography.

Key to abbreviations

AA: American Architect and Building News
ABZ: Allgemeine Bauzeitung (Vienna)
AF: Architectural Forum
ARec: Architectural Record
ARev: Architectural Review (London)
Arch.Congr.London: Transactions of the VII International Congress of Architects in London, 1906. See Bibl. 487
Arch.Congr.Vienna: Berichte über den VIII Internationalen Architekten-Kongress in Vienna, 1908. See Bibl. 451
BB: Brickbuilder
CBB: Centralblatt der Bauverwaltung (Berlin)
DB: Deutsche Bauzeitung (Berlin)
GCTP: Garden Cities and Town Planning (London)
Ghent Congr. 1913: Premier Congrès International et Exposition Comparée des Villes, Ghent, 1913. See Bibl. 474.
HZ: 'Hannoverische Zeitschrift,' Zeitschrift für Architektur und Ingenieurwesen (Hannover)
JAIA: Journal of the American Institute of Architects
JAIP: Journal of the American Institute of Planners
JRIBA: Journal of the Royal Institute of British Architects
JSAH: Journal of the American Society of Architectural Historians
JTPI: Journal of the Town Planning Institute (London)
KC: Kunstchronik (Leipzig)
NIZ: Neue Illustrierte Zeitung (Vienna)
NWT: Neues Wiener Tagblatt
SGB: Salzburger Gewerbeblatt
StB: Der Städtebau. See Bibl. 484
Stb. Berlin 1910: Allgemeine Städtebauaustellung, Berlin, 1910. See Bibl. 323
StBK: Stadtbaukunst. See Bibl. 483
StBV: Städtebauliche Vorträge. See Bibl. 485
SZ: Salzburger Zeitung
TG: Technisches Gemeindeblatt (Berlin)
TPR: Town Planning Review (Liverpool)
TRIBA: Transactions of the Royal Institute of British Architects
Trans.London 1910: Transactions of the Town Planning Conference, London, 1910. See Bibl. 486.
WBZ: Wiener Bauindustrie Zeitung

WOV: Wochenschrift des Österreichischen Ingenieur- und Architekten-Vereins (Vienna)
ZB: Zeitschrift für Bauwesen (Berlin)
ZOV: Zeitschrift des Österreichischen Ingenieur- und Architekten-Vereins

A

EDITIONS AND TRANSLATIONS OF SITTE'S BOOK

These are discussed at length in our Chapter 7.

1. *Der Städte-Bau nach seinen künstlerischen Grundsätzen.* Ein Beitrag zur Lösung moderner Fragen der Architektur und monumentalen Plastik unter besonderer Beziehung auf Wien von Architekt Camillo Sitte, Regierungsrath und Director der K.K. Staatsgewerbeschule in Wien. Mit 4 Heliogravüren und 109 Illustrationen und Detailplänen. Wien, Verlag von Carl Graeser, [May], 1889.
Reviews:
2. *CBB*, IX, 1889, p. 234 (Hd.).
3. *DB*, XXIII, 1889, pp. 408–409 (D.).
4. *HZ*, XXXV, 1889, pp. 617–619 (Stübben). See p. 57.
5. *KC*, n.s. I, 1890, pp. 425–431 (Necker). See p. 76.
6. *Idem*, 2nd edit., Vienna, Graeser, [June], 1889.
7. *Idem*, 3rd edit., Vienna, Graeser; Leipzig, B. G. Teubner, 1901.
Review:
8. *Blätter für Architektur und Kunsthandwerk*, XVI, 1903, No. 2, p. 12 (P. Graef).
9. *L'art de Bâtir les Villes.* Notes et Réflexions d'un Architecte traduites et complétées par Camille Martin. Avec 17 dessins à la plume de F. Puetzer, H. Bernouilli et H. Hindermann: 106 plans de villes et 4 planche hors texte. Genève, Ch. Eggiman & Cie. Paris, Librairie Renouard, H. Laurens, éditor, 1902.
Reviews: See pp. 71–72.
10. *Journal des Débats*, CXIV, Dec. 19, 1902, pp. 1–2 (A. Hallays).
11. '*L'art de Bâtir les Villes*, d'après un livre récent.' Conférence faite le 15 février 1903 par Michel Clerc. Marseille, Barlatier, 1903.
12. *L'Architecture*, XVI, 1903, pp. 85–87 (P. Wallon).
13. Same as Bibl. 1. 4th edit., with the addition of 'Grossstadtgrün.' 1 heliogravure, 114 illustrations and detailed plans. Vienna, Graeser; Leipzig, B. G. Teubner, 1909.
Review:
14. *StB*, VI, 1909, p. 68 (T. Goecke). See p. 58.
—.N.B. There was no French edition in 1912 as is sometimes reported. See p. 68.
15. Same as Bibl. 9. 2nd edit., with 106 plans and 1 plate. Publishers as previously; 1918. There is also an imprint: Genève, Editions Atar.
Review:
16. *Revista municipal y de intereses económicos* (Havana), XVI, 1921, pp. 127–129.

17. Same as Bibl. 13. 5th edit. Vienna, Graeser and A. Schroll & Co., 1922.

Review:

18. *Der Baumeister*, XX, 1922, Heft 12, p. 68, (H. Jansen). See p. 58.

19. *Gorodskoe stroitel'stvo s tochki zreniia ego khudozhestvennykh printsipov. S prilozheniem, Zelenye nasazhdeniia v bol'shikh gorodkh.* Translated by I. I. Vul'fert from the 5th German edition under the editorship of P. A. Mamatov. Moscow, Printing Office of the Moscow District Engineer, 1925.

20. *Construcción de Ciudades según principios artísticos* por Camilo Sitte, Arquitecto Director de las 'Höheren baugewerblichen Lehranstalten' de Viena. Traducción de la quinta edición alemana por Emilio Canosa, arquitecto. Barcelona, Editorial Canosa, 1926.

21. *The Art of Building Cities.* City building according to its artistic fundamentals by Camillo Sitte. Translated by Charles T. Stewart, former Director, the Urban Land Institute. New York, N.Y., Reinhold Publishing Corp., 1945.

Reviews: See pp. 74–75.

22. *TPR*, XIX, 1946–47, pp. 164–169 (R. Wittkower).

23. *Pencil Points*, XXVII, Apr. 1946, pp. 126, 128 (T. H. Creighton).

24. *ARec*, XCIX, Apr. 1946, p. 132.

25. *AF*, LXXXV, July 1946, p. 158 (H.P.O.).

26. *Annals of the Amer. Acad. of Political and Social Science*, CCXLV, May 1946, p. 216 (C. S. Ascher).

27. *The Nation*, CLXII, June 1946, p. 697 (A. Guerard).

28. *JAIP*, XII, July–Sept. 1946, pp. 30–32 (H. Stevens).

29. *Journal of Aesthetics and Art Criticism*, V, Sept. 1946, pp. 69–70 (P. Zucker).

30. *N.Y. Times Book Review*, Sept. 22, 1946, p. 26 (L.E.C.).

31. *JTPI*, XXXIII, Nov.–Dec. 1946, p. 23 (T.H.H.).

32. *ARev*, C, Dec. 1946, p. 186 (N. Pevsner).

33. *Social Forces*, XXV, Dec. 1946, p. 224 (N. J. Demerath).

34. *JRIBA*, LIV, Apr. 1947, p. 338 (R. Townsend).

35. *L'arte di costruire la città*, a cura di Luigi Dodi. Versione del testo originale: *Der Städtebau nach seinen künstlerischen Grundsätzen.* Milan, Antonio Vallardi Editore, 1953.

B

OTHER WRITINGS BY SITTE ON CITY PLANNING

For periodicals that Sitte edited see Bibl. 481 and 484. Unpublished manuscripts listed here are in the estate of Josef Schwarzl of Vienna or the Technische Hochschule in Vienna.

51. 'Die Kohlenbergpläne,' *NWT*, Aug. 21, 1872.

52. 'Die Konkurrenz-Projekte für den Justizpalast,' *NWT*, June 1, 1874.

53. (With V. K. Schembera), 'Gottfried Sempers Ideen über Städteanlagen,' *NWT*, Jan. 22, 1885, pp. 1–2. See above p. 11 and Note 15.

54. 'Über alte und neue Städteanlagen mit Bezug auf die Plätze und Monument-Aufstellung in Wien,' *WOV*, XIV, 1889, pp. 261–263, 269–271. A lecture on the subject of his book while it was still in press. See Note 266.

55. 'Über die Wahl eines Platzes für das Wiener Goethe-Denkmal,' *Chronik des Wiener Goethe-Vereins*, IV, 1889, pp. 18–20. A lecture. See Note 294.

56. 'Über moderne Städtebauten,' *Mährisches Tagblatt*, Nov. 5 & 6, 1889.

57. *'Das Wien der Zukunft,' Monatsblätter des Wissenschaftlichen Club in Wien*, XII, Spec. suppl. to No. 4, 1891, pp. 25–31. A lecture. See our p. 43.

58. 'Wiener Stadtbaufragen,' a series of articles in *NWT* for 1891, including:
   59. 'Die Kunst des Städtebaues,' Mar. 5.
   60. 'So geht's nicht!' Mar. 21.
   61. 'Die Neue Stadterweiterung,' Sept. 27.
   62. 'Das Radetzky Denkmal,' Oct. 4. See Note 266.
   63. 'Stadterweiterung und Fremdenverkehr,' Oct. 11.
   64. 'Station Wien,' Oct. 25.
   65. 'Die Ausweisung Wiens,' Dec. 6.
   66. 'Neu-Wien—Ein Willkomm,' Dec. 20.

67. 'Gutachten über den neuen Baulinienplan von Teschen,' Jan. 22, 1892. Manuscript, apparently unpublished.

68. 'Auf gleicher Höhe,' *NWT*, Feb. 15, 1892.

69. 'Die Regulierung des Stubenviertels,' *NWT*, Mar. 5, 1893. A part of the 1893 competition won by Karl Mayreder; see *ABZ*, LVIII, 1893, pp. 41–42 and plates.

70. 'Der Wille des Stadtbauamtes,' *NWT*, Mar. 12, 1893.

71. 'Wiener Villenzone,' *NWT*, Sept. 3, 1893.

72. 'Das Waldviertel einst und jetzt,' *NWT*, Sept. 25, 1893.

73. 'Das Wien der Zukunft,' *NWT*, Mar. 6, 8, 14, 31, 1894. See p. 44.

74. 'Die Parcellierung und die Monumentalbauten von Přivoz,' *Der Architect*, I, 1895, pp. 33–35, plates 50–52. See Notes 17, 19.

75. 'Zur Errichtung eines Kaiser Franz Joseph-Denkmals in Olmütz,' *Mährisches Tagblatt*, May 2, 1895 (1896?).

76. 'Bebauung des Wasserthurmplatzes in Mannheim,' *Neue Badische Landes-Zeitung*, June 27, 1895, and *Süddeutsche Bauzeitung* (Munich), Aug. 8, 1895.

77. 'Discussion über den General-Regulierungs-Plan von Wien,' *ZOV*, XLVIII, Nos. 27–31. Sitte's contribution on p. 410 of No. 27. See our p. 44 and Note 70.

78. 'Thurm: Freiheit,' *NWT*, Mar. 1, 1896.

79. 'Grossstadt-Grün,' *Der Lotse, Hamburgische Wochenschrift für deutsche Kultur*, I, 1900, pp. 139–146, 225–232. Added as Appendix to the 4th edition of this book; see Bible. 13 and *Sitte*, pp. 167–185.

80. 'Gutachten über die Platzwahl für den Theaterbau von Biehlefeld,' Dec. 8, 1900. Manuscript, apparently unpublished.

81. 'Der Städtebau nach seinen künstlerischen Grundsätzen,' *Biehlefelder Zeitung*, Mar. 6, 1901.

82. 'Eine Kunstfrage (die Concurrenz zum Stadt Wien-Museum)' *NWT*, Nov. 22, 1901.

83. 'Die Ergebnisse der Vorconcurrenz zu dem Baue des Kaiser Franz Josef-Museums der Stadt Wien,' *ABZ*, LXVII, 1902, pp. 61–66, plates 28–30. Also published separately: Vienna, Waldheim, 1902.

84. 'Am Karlplatz des Kaiser Franz Josef-Museum der Stadt Wien,' *NWT*, June 12, 1902.

85. 'Enteignungsgesetz und Lageplan,' in *ZOV*, LV, 1903, pp. 245–246, and in *Zeitschrift für Transportwesen und Strassenbau*, XX, 1903, pp. 279–280, 288. Extract from a lecture by Sitte, which was published in full after his death (Bibl. 88) with comments by others. See Note 41.

86. 'Erklärung zu dem Lageplan für Reichenberg,' June, 1903. Place of publication unknown; in Schwarzl files. See Note 17.

87. (with T. Goecke), 'An unsere Leser,' Forword to *StB*, I, 1904, pp. 1–4. Translated in *Sitte* pp. 189–196.

88. 'Enteignungsgesetz und Lageplan,' *StB*, 1904, pp. 5–8, 17–19, 35–39, plates 1, 2. Posthumous. See our p. 23 and Bibl. 85.

89. 'Die Sammlung von deutschen Stadtplänen auf der Dresdner Städteausstellung,' *StB*, I, 1904, pp. 137–139. Posthumous.

90. 'Erläuterungen zu dem Bebauungsplane von Marienberg,' *StB*, I, 1904, pp. 141–145, plates 73–76. See Notes 17, 19.

91. *Der Städtebau nach seinen wirtschaftlichen Grundsätzen*, intended as vol. II of his book. Never published; see pp. 12, 14.

C

SELECTED WRITINGS BY SITTE ON OTHER SUBJECTS

For his writings on the following subjects see elsewhere, as indicated: on perspective, drawing, anatomy, etc., Note 8; on arts and crafts, Notes 11, 12; on the preservation of buildings and monuments, Note 13; about his friends Eitelberger and Ilg, Note 7; about Gottfried Semper, Note 15.

Not included here are about two dozen critical writings by Sitte on art, art exhibits, books, music, opera, theater, etc., that appeared, for the most part, in *NWT* from 1869–1895. The majority of these are listed by title in Bibl. 161; clippings of them are in the files of Josef Schwarzl of Vienna, who also possessed unpublished manuscripts cited in this section, or in the Sitte archive of the Technische Hochschule in Vienna.

101. 'Richard Wagner und die deutsche Kunst,' 2. *Jahresbericht des Wiener Akademischen Wagner-Vereins*, 1875. Also published separately, Vienna, Guttmann, 1877. See p. 10 and Note 14.

102. 'Führich und Dombaumeister Schmidt,' *NWT*,1875.

103. *Über Zweck und Nutzen des Gewerbeschulwesens: Ein Vortrag gehalten im Arbeiter-Bildungsverein von Salzburg*, Apr. 4, 1875, Salzburg, Dieter, 1875. See Note 12.

104. 'Lohengrin,' *SZ*, Mar. 12, 1877.

105. 'Die Perspektivlehre des Pietro degli Franceschi,' May 1879.

106. 'Über den praktischen Wert der Lehre vom goldenen Schnitt,' (manuscript of c. 1880, later published in *Wiener Bauhütte*, Hefte 6–8, 1930).

107. 'Der neue Wiener Styl,' *NWT*, July 8, 1881.

108. (with Josef Salb), *Die Initialen der Renaissance. Nach den Constructionen von Albrecht Dürer*. Vienna, K. K. Hof- und Staatsdruckerei, 1882.

109. 'Über Akustik in Theatern und Concertsälen,' 1883.

110. 'Über die Stellung der Architektur unter den übrigen Künsten,' 1884. Lecture, apparently unpublished, in the Ingenieur- und Architektenverein.

111. 'Die neuere kirchliche Architektur in Oesterreich und Ungarn,' *Oesterreichisch-ungarische Revue, Monatsschrift für die gesamten Culturinteressen Oesterreich-Ungarns*, n.s. III, 1887, pp. 65–87.

112. 'Die Ornamentik des Islam,' *Oesterreichische Monatsschrift für den Orient*, XV, 1889, pp. 39–41.

113. 'Ferstel, Hansen, Schmidt,' *NWT*, Jan. 30, 1892.

114. 'Die Schönheit des Armes,' *Allgemeine Zeitung* (Munich), Beilage No. 214, Sept. 15, 1893, pp. 4–6. Review of a book by one of his teachers, the physiologist and anatomist Ernst W. von Brücke: *Schönheit und Fehler der menschlichen Gestalt*, Vienna, Braunmüller, 1891 & 1893.

115. 'Eine Doppelvilla,' *Der Architekt*, I, 1895, pp. 3–4, plate 1. See our p. 13.

116. 'Erklärung einiger bautechnischer Ausdrücke,' *op. cit.*, pp. 37–38.

117. 'Ein stiller Mann der Wissenschaft (Ludwig Blume),' *NWT*, May 12, 1897. See our p. 9.

118. 'Der neue Kurs am Österreichischen Museum,' *NWT*, Nov. 25, 1897.

119. 'Über die Bemalung figuraler Plastik im griechischen Alterthum,' in *Festschrift für Otto Benndorf zu seinem 60. Geburtstag*, Vienna, Hölder, 1898.

120. 'Die Moderne in der Architektur und im Kunstgewerbe,' *ZOV*, LI, 1899, pp. 145–151, 161–168, 183–189. A lecture by F. R. von Neumann. Sitte's contribution to the ensuing discussion appears on p. 166.

121. 'Josef Hoffmann,' *NWT*, Jan. 18, 1900.

122. 'Über Farbenharmonie,' *Centralblatt für das Gewerbliche Unterrichtswesen in Österreich*, XVIII, 1900, pp. 196–227. A thorough discussion of color theory from ancient to modern times.

123. 'Secession und Monumentalkunst,' *NWT*, May 5 & 6, 1903.

124. A seven-volume history of art, left unfinished at his death. See our p. 14. The essay, 'Weltanschauungsperioden' of 1902, in the possession of Josef Schwarzl, may have been part of this.

D

IMPORTANT DISCUSSIONS OF SITTE AND HIS BOOK

This section includes items devoted exclusively or principally to discussing Sitte. A number of other writings of this type will be found in Bibliography F, especially Nos. 297, 344, 345, 363, 406.

For further biographical articles see Note 1. For other reviews of the various editions of his book see Bibliography A, especially Nos. 4, 5, 14, 18, 22, 32.

151. Andrés Angulo, 'Los grandes maestros del urbanismo: Camillo Sitte,' *Revista municipal y de intereses económicos* (Havana), XXX, 1935, pp. 27–28.

152. S. D. Adshead, 'Sitte and Le Corbusier,' *TPR*, XIV, 1930, pp. 85–94.

153. Leopold Bauer, 'Zum 80. Geburtstag Kamillo Sittes am 17. April, 1923,' *Neue Freie Presse* (Vienna), April 15, 1923, p. 25; April 17, 1923, p. 13.

154. Alvin Simon Boyarsky, *Camillo Sitte: City Builder*, thesis presented to the Faculty of the Graduate School of Cornell University for the Degree of Master of Regional Planning, Sept. 1959. Unpublished. See our p. 102.

155. F. von Feldegg, 'Kamillo Sitte: Gedenkrede zum 80. Geburtstage,' *ZOV*, LXXV, 1923, pp. 125–127.

156. George E. Hooker, 'Camillo Sitte, City Builder,' *Chicago Record-Herald*, Jan. 15, 1904, p. 6.

157. Erwin Ilz, *Festrede zu Camillo Sittes 100. Geburtstag*, Vienna, Stolzenberg & Benda, 1943.

158. Josef Schwarzl, *Franz, Camillo und Siegfried Sitte: 100 Arbeitsjahre einer Wiener Architektenfamilie*, Vienna, Manzsche, 1949.

159. John W. Simpson, 'The Planning of Cities and Public Spaces, *JRIBA*, s. 3, XII, 1905, pp. 341–371. Reprinted in *House and Garden*, IX, 1906, pp. 281–289. A summary of Sitte's book.

160. Heinrich Sitte, 'Camillo Sitte,' *Neue Österreichische Biographie*, Part I, vol. VI, 1929, pp. 132–149. The most complete biography, by his son.

161. C. von Wurzbach, *Biographisches Lexikon des Kaisertums Österreich*, Vienna, K.K. Hof- und Staatsdruckerei, XXXV, 1877, pp. 34–38. Biographies of the Sittes, father and son, during their lifetimes.

162. Branko Maksimovič, 'Esthétique d'urbanisme de Camillo Sitte,' *Recueil des travaux de la Faculté d'Architecture de l'Université de Belgrade*, VII, 1961/62. (32 pp.) The article is written in Serbian but has this subtitle and a brief summary in French.

E

GENERAL PUBLICATIONS ON ARCHITECTURE AND CITY PLANNING THAT DISCUSS SITTE OR HIS BOOK

Sitte is commented upon in most writings that deal with the development of modern city planning and architecture. Included here are a few such general works and a number of specialized studies which touch upon Sitte. Others are to be found in Bibliography F, especially Nos. 298, 326, 378.

171. Patrick Abercrombie, *Town and Country Planning*, London and New York, 1933. 2nd edit., 1943.

172. ———, 'Vienna,' *TPR*, I, 1910–11, pp. 220–234, 279–293. One of our best summaries of its growth and planning.

173. Thomas Adams, *Recent Advances in Town Planning*, New York, Macmillan, 1932.

174. ———, *Outline of Town and City Planning*, New York, Russell Sage, 1935. Both these books discuss the influence of Germany on British planning.

175. Gaston Bardet, *Urbanisme*, Paris, Presses-Universitaires, 1947. Contains a brief summary of the beginnings of modern city planning. Most of Bardet's books mention Sitte.

176. Sylvester Baxter, 'The German Way of Making Better Cities,' *Atlantic Monthly*, CIV, 1909, pp. 72–85. A concise summary of the German contribution as of 1909. Regarding Baxter see Note 100.

177. Joseph Brix, 'Aus der Geschichte des Städtebaues in den letzten 100 Jahren,' *StBV*, IV, 1911, No. 2. Basic survey of German planning.

178. W. A. Eden, 'Studies in Urban Theory: the *De Re Aedificatoria* of Leon Battista Alberti,' *TPR*, XIX, 1943, pp. 10–28.

179. Ferdinand von Feldegg, 'Wiens zweite Renaissance,' *Der Architekt* (Vienna), I, 1895, pp. 1–2. Editorial by a close friend of Sitte.

180. Alice Fischer, *An Analysis of the Writings of Alfred Lichtwark as they apply to the City and Civic Improvement*, Master's essay in the Faculty of Philosophy, Columbia University, 1961. Unpublished thesis to which we have referred at several points, esp. Notes 310, 24.

181. Sigfried, Giedion, *Space, Time and Architecture, the Growth of a new Tradition*, Cambridge, Harvard University Press, 1941 and later.

182. Percival and Paul Goodman, *Communitas, Means of Livelihood and Ways of Life*, Chicago, Chicago University Press, 1947. 2nd edit., New York, Vintage Books, 1960. Especially good on Sitte's aesthetic position and the Le Corbusier controversy.

183. Brian Hackett, *Man, Society and Environment*, London, Percival and Marshall, 1950. See also *Landscape Architecture*, XL, 1950, pp. 114–118.

184. Talbot Hamlin (editor), *Forms and Functions of Twentieth-Century Architecture*, New York, Columbia University Press, 1953. Especially vols. II and IV.

185. Rudolf Hartog, *Stadterweiterungen im 19. Jahrhundert* (*Schriftenreihe des Vereins zur Pflege Kommunalwissenschaftlicher Aufgaben e. V. Berlin*, VI), Stuttgart, Kohlhammer, 1962. This study is devoted to some of the same subjects as our book but from a more political and economic standpoint.

186. Eugène Hénard, *Études sur les transformations de Paris*, Paris, Librairies-imprimeries réunies, 1903–09.

187. Charles Edouard Jeanneret-Gris (Le Corbusier), *Urbanisme*, Paris, Crès, 1925.

188. ———, *Quand les Cathédrals étaient blanches*, Paris, Plon, 1937. For both of these, see p. 101 and Note 126.

189. Frank Koester, *Modern City Planning and Maintenance*, New York, McBride & Nast, 1914.

190. H. V. Lanchester, *The Art of Town Planning*, New York, Scribner, 1925.

191. Pierre Lavedan, *Histoire de l'urbanisme*, Paris, Laurens, 3 vols., 1926–52. Especially vol. III.

192. O. March, 'Stand und Ziele der Städtebaukunst," *StB*, X, 1913, pp. 29–31, 38–41. See Note 104.

193. Thomas H. Mawson, *Civic Art*, London, Batsford, 1911.

194. Robert Mielke, 'Die Entwicklung der dörflichen Siedlungen und ihre Beziehungen zum Städtebau alter und neuer Zeit,' *StB*, VI, 1913, No. 5.

195. Lewis Mumford, *The Brown Decades, A Study of the Arts in America*, New York, Harcourt Brace, 1931.

196. ———, *The Culture of Cities*, New York, Harcourt Brace, 1938.

197. ———, *The City in History*, New York, Harcourt Brace, 1961.

198. Hermann Muthesius, 'Städtebau,' *Kunst und Künstler*, VIII, 1910, pp. 531–535. Enthusiasm over Sitte.

199. Thomas Paulson, *Den Glömda Staden*, Stockholm, 1959. Good general survey, with English summary. See also his *Ny Stad*, Stockholm, 1958.

200. Nikolaus Pevsner, *Pioneers of the Modern Movement*, Harmondsworth, Penguin, 1960. Revised edition.

201. O. Pflugschmid, '"Endlose" Strassen, unübersehbare und spitzwinklige Plätze,' *Deutsche Bauhütte*, V, 1901, pp. 279–280.

202. C. B. Purdom, *The Building of Satellite Towns*, London, Dent, 1949. On the German influence in England.

203. Robert Riedel, 'Vom Städtebau,' *Reclam's Universum: Moderne*

illustrierte Wochenschrift, XXV, 1909, pp. 1214–1218. An engineer and Sitte follower in Leipzig.

204. Eliel Saarinen, *The City, its Growth, its Decay, its Future*, New York, Reinhold, 1943. See also his introduction to the 1945 American edition of Sitte.

205. Fritz Schumacher, *Strömungen in deutscher Baukunst seit 1800*, Leipzig, Seemann, 1935. 2nd edit., 1955. Basic.

206. ———, *Stufen des Lebens, Erinnerungen eines Baumeisters*, Stuttgart, Deutsche Verlags Anstalt, 1935.

207. ———, *Lesebuch für Baumeister*, Berlin, Heusel, 1941. 2nd edit., 1943. Anthology. See Note 127.

208. G. E. Kidder Smith, *Italy Builds*, New York, Reinhold, 1955.

209. Cecil Stewart, *A Prospect of Cities*, London, Longmans, Green, 1952. German influence in England.

210. Hans Tietze, *Wien, Kultur-Kunst-Geschichte*, Vienna and Leipzig, 1931. Vienna and the Sittes figure in several of his publications.

211. H. Inigo Triggs, *Town Planning, Past, Present and Possible*, London, Methuen, 1909. The portion on Sitte and squares is also in *JRIBA*, s. 3, XVII, 1909, pp. 41–69. See Note 103.

212. Christopher Tunnard, *The City of Man*, New York & London, Scribner, 1953.

213. Raymond Unwin, 'The Planning of the Residential Districts of Towns,' *Arch. Congr. London*, pp. 417–425.

214. ———, 'Buttstedt,' *JRIBA*, s. 3, XVII, 1909, pp. 70–73. (Transl. from *StB*, V, 1908, Heft 12.)

215. ———, *Town Planning in Practice, an Introduction to the Art of Designing Cities and Suburbs*, London, Unwin, 1909. This book, by which German theory, and especially Sitte's, entered British planning, has appeared in numerous editions. See Note 103.

216. Dora Wiebenson, *Tony Garnier's Cité industrielle and its relation to its nineteenth and early twentieth-century background*. Master's thesis, Institute of Fine Arts, New York University, June 1958. Unpublished. See Note 123.

217. Paul Wolf, *Städtebau, das Formproblem der Stadt in Vergangenheit und Zukunft*, Leipzig, Klinkhardt & Biermann, 1919.

218. Bruno Zevi, *Architectura in Nuce*, Venice & Rome, Istituto per la collaborazione culturale, 1960.

219. Paul Zucker, *Entwicklung der Stadtbilder: die Stadt als Form*, Munich, Drei Masken, 1929.

220. Mario Morini, *Atlante di Storia dell' Urbanistica*, Milan, Hoepli, 1963. This large and comprehensive volume (1432 illustrations), a successor to *Civic Art* of Hegemann & Peets (Bibl. 326), appeared while our book was in press. It discusses Vienna, Sitte, O. Wagner, Stübben, Unwin, etc.

221. Emanuel Grushka, *Rasvitie Gradostroitel'stva* (The Development of Town Planning), translated from Czech into Russian by Ladislav

Gornisk and wife; Bratislava, Academy of sciences, 1963. Smaller format than No. 220, but about 1750 plans and other illustrations. A remarkable compendium of historical material, especially on Russia and Eastern Europe.

222. Patrick Geddes, *Cities in Evolution: an Introduction to the Town Planning Movement and to the Study of Civics*, London, Williams and Norgate, 1915. Geddes' remarks about Sitte and his most interesting comments about the German scene in 1909 are cut out of the 1949 revised edition of this book.

F

PUBLICATIONS BY OTHER IMPORTANT INDIVIDUALS

This list includes writings of interest on city planning by a number of people, mainly planners, who figure in this book. Their publications about Sitte and about the problems he raised are also cited.

For Gottfried Semper see Notes 15, 62, 63, 288. For Siegfried Sitte see Note 21.

REINHARD BAUMEISTER

See also the bibliographies in the three editions of Stübben's *Handbuch*.

251. 'Grundzüge für Stadterweiterungen,' *DB*, VIII, 1874, pp. 337–346. The Berlin *Verein* resolutions. See Note 42.

252. *Stadt-Erweiterungen in technischer, baupolizeilicher und wirtschaftlicher Beziehung*, Berlin, Ernst & Korn, 1876. His basic book.
Review:
253. *HZ*, XXIII, 1877, pp. 157–161 (Albrecht).

254. *Normale Bauordnung nebst Erläuterungen*, Wiesbaden, Kriedel, 1880. This served as a basis for several German projects-for-law.

255. *Moderne Stadterweiterungen: Vortrag* (*Deutsche Zeit- und Streitfragen*, Heft 7), Hamburg, Richter, 1887. A summary of No. 252.

256. (with Miquel) 'Massregeln zur Erreichung gesunden Wohnens,' *Deutsche Vierteljahrsschrift für öffentliche Gesundheitspflege*, XXI, 1889, pp. 9ff. See Note 31.

257. *Städtisches Strassenwesen und Städtereinigung* (*Baukunde des Ingenieurs*, Abt. III, Heft 3), Berlin, 1890.

258. Translation of 2nd half by J. Goodell as *The Cleaning and Sewage of Cities*, N.Y.C., Engineering News Publishing Co., 1891; 1895.

259. (with J. Classen and J. Stübben) *Die Umlegung städtischer Grundstücke und die Zonenenteignung* (*Denkschriften des Verbandes Deutscher Architekten- und Ingenieur-Vereine*, XII), Berlin, 1897. See Note 41.

260. *Stadtbaupläne in alter und neuer Zeit* (*Zeitfragen des christlichen Volkslebens*, XXVII, Heft 6), Stuttgart, 1902. Useful historical survey.

261. 'Die Zuwachssteuer, Vorträge und Aussprache auf dem 14. Bundestag der deutschen Bodenreform zu Darmstadt,' *Soziale Streitfragen* (Berlin), XVIII, 1904, pp. 1–18.

262. 'Grundsätze des Städtebaues (1906)' in Stübben, *Handbuch*, 1924, pp. 700–702. Berlin *Verein* resolutions. See Note 43.

263. 'Bauordnung und Wohnungsfrage,' *StBV*, IV, No. 3, 1911.

264. 'Städtebau,' in *Deutschland unter Kaiser Wilhelm II*, Berlin, Hobbing, 1914, III, pp. 1519–1532. Excellent summary.

265. 'Gemeinwohl und Sondernutzen im Städtebau,' *StBV*, VIII, No. 4, 1918.

ALBERT E. BRINCKMANN

266. 'Zur Ästhetik des bepflanzten Platzes,' *StB*, III, 1906, pp. 80-81.

267. *Platz und Monument*, Berlin, Wasmuth, 1908. 2nd edit., 1912. 3rd edit. 1923.
Reviews:
268. *StB*, V, 1908, pp. 161–162 (Goecke).
269. *DB*, XLIII, 1909, pp. 102–106 (Stübben).

270. 'Französische Idealstädte um 1600 und 1800,' *StB*, VI, 1909, pp. 148–150.

271. 'Entwicklung des Städtebau-Ideals seit der Renaissance,' *Trans. London 1910*, pp. 146–160. Eng. transl. pp. 161–166.

272. 'The Foundation of French and English Gothic Towns in the South of France,' *Trans. London 1910*, pp. 166–176.

273. *Deutsche Stadtbaukunst in der Vergangenheit*, Frankfurt, Keller, 1911. 2nd edit., Frankfurt, Verlags Anstalt A.G., 1921.
Review:
274. *StB*, VIII, 1911, pp. 105–106 (Hegemann).

275. 'Stadtbaukunst des 18. Jahrhunderts,' *StBV*, VII, No. 1, 1914.

276. *Stadtbaukunst, Geschichtliche Querschnitte und neuzeitliche Ziele*, Berlin-Neubabelsberg, Athenaion, 1920. 2nd edit., 1922.

CHARLES BULS

277. *Vienne en 1873*, Brussels, Muquardt, 1873.

278. *Esthétique des villes*, Brussels, Bruylant-Christophe, 1893; 2nd edit., 1894.
Review:
279. 'Die Schönheit der Städte,' *Kölnische Zeitung*, No. 361, April, 1894 (J. Stübben).
Translations:
280. *Ästhetik der Städte* (trans. from 2nd edit. by Ph. Schäfer), Giessen, Roth, 1898.
281. 'City Aesthetics,' in *Municipal Affairs* (NYC), III, 1899, pp. 732–741.
282. *Estetica della città* (trans. by M. Pasolini), Rome, Associazione Artistica, 1903.

283. *La Construction des villes*, Brussels, Lyon-Claesc, 1895. A trans-

lation by Buls of Stübben's 1893 paper with a special introduction about Buls and Stübben. See Bibl. 390.

284. *La Restauration des monuments anciens*, Brussels, Weissenbruch, 1903.

285. 'De la Disposition et du development des rues et des espaces libres dans les villes,' *Trans. London, 1906*, pp. 369–382.

286. *Esthétique des villes: l'isolement des vielles églises*, Brussels, Van Oest, 1910. His paper at the 1908 *Denkmalpflege* meeting in Lübeck.
Translation:
287. 'Über das Freilegen von alten Kirchen,' *StB*, VI, 1909, pp. 29–33.

288. 'La conservation de la coeur de la cité de Bruxelles,' and Gurlitt, 'Conservation du coeur des anciennes villes,' (a lecture at Strasbourg trans. by Buls), Brussels, 1912. (This is from the Belgian magazine *Tekhne*, Nos. 64–66.)

289. 'Faut-il préconiser l'isolement complete ou le dégagement partiel des grandes edifices?', *Ghent Congr. 1913*, pp. 21–22.

RUDOLF EITELBERGER VON EDELBERG

290. *Über Städteanlagen und Stadtbauten. Ein Vortrag gehalten am 10. März 1858 . . . zu Wien*, Vienna, Gerolds Sohn, 1858.

291. *Die preisgekrönten Entwürfe zur Erweiterung der inneren Stadt Wien*, Vienna, 1859. The official publication of the results of the 1857 competition.

292. *Kunst und Künstler Wiens der Neueren Zeit,* vol. I of his *Gesammelte Kunsthistorische Schriften*, Vienna, Braumüller, 1879.

EUGEN FASSBENDER

293. *Ein Volksring für Wien: Ein Vorschlag seiner Vaterstadt*, Vienna, Lechner, 1898.

294. 'Der Städtebau und seine gesetzliche Regelung,' *Arch. Congr. Vienna*, 1908, pp. 576–590. A lecture and discussion that were reprinted in part in No. 295.

295. *Grundzüge der modernen Städtebaukunde*, Leipzig & Vienna, Deuticke, 1912.

THEODOR FISCHER

296. *Stadterweiterungsfragen, mit besonderer Berücksichtigung auf Stuttgart*, Stuttgart, Deutsche Verlags Anstalt, 1903.

297. 'Camillo Sitte,' *DB*, XXXVIII, 1904, pp. 33–34. Obituary.

298. 'City Building' (transl. by Sylvester Baxter), Boston, the Metropolitan Improvements Commission, c. 1908. This mimeographed translation of a lecture by Fischer in Munich exists in the Harvard University Libraries in several copies.

299. *Sechs Vorträge über Stadtbaukunst*, Munich, Oldenbourg, 1919. 2nd edit., 1922.

300. *Zwei Vorträge über Proportionen*, Munich & Berlin, Oldenbourg, 1934.

FELIX GENZMER

301. 'Die Entwicklung des Städtebaues und seine Ziele in künstlerischer Beziehung,' *TG*, III, 1900, pp. 49–53.

302. 'Kunst im Städtebau,' *StBV*, I, No. 1, 1908.

303. 'Die Gestaltung des Strassen- und Platzraumes,' *StBV*, II, No. 1, 1909.

304. 'Die Ausstattung von Strassen und Plätzen,' *StBV*, III, No. 2, 1910.

(Also see other lectures in the *StBV* series.)

THEODOR GOECKE

For further articles by Goecke, consult *Der Städtebau*, vols. I–XVI. He also edited *Die Kunstdenkmäler der Provinz Brandenburg*, vols. II, 1, 3; V, 1; VI, 1, 2, 3.

305. 'Verkehrsstrasse und Wohnstrasse,' *Preussische Jahrbücher*, LXXIII, 1893, pp. 85–104.

306. 'Soziale Aufgaben der Architektur . . .', in *Fortschritte auf dem Gebiete der Architektur*, No. 6, 1895. (These are supplementary fascicules to Durm's *Handbuch der Architektur*.)

307. 'Städtebaufragen mit besonderer Beziehung auf Berlin,' *DB*, XXXV, 1901, pp. 226, 233, 251, 272 (Baumeister), 307, 398 (Stübben), 438 (Haller). Although a local matter, the discussion is of interest because of the intervention of Baumeister and Stübben.

308. Review of Brinckmann's *Platz und Monument* in *StB*, 1908. See Bibl. 268.

309. Review of Sitte's 4th edition in *StB*, 1909. See Bibl. 14.

310. 'Krumme und gerade Strassen,' *StB*, VI, 1909, pp. 164–165. Reply to an attack by Brinckmann on Sitte. See Note 36.

311. 'Allgemeine Städtebauausstellung, Berlin, 1910,' *StB*, VII, 1910, pp. 61–62, 73–92. One of our most complete reportages of this event. See our p. 93.

312. 'Von den Beziehungen öffentlicher Gebäude zum modernen Stadtbild,' *StB*, X, 1913, pp. 2–3, 21–23. Cf. Note 98.

CORNELIUS GURLITT

Not included here are Gurlitt's publications in behalf of the preservation of monuments. See Bibl. 288 and Note 37.

313. *Historische Stadtbilder*, Berlin, Wasmuth, 1901–12. Twelve large volumes of street views in old European towns.

314. 'Der deutsche Städtebau,' in Wuttke, Bibl. 489.

315. Translated as 'German City Planning,' by Sylvester Baxter in *ARec.*, XXIV, 1908, pp. 135–148, 350–363.

316. *Über Baukunst*, Berlin, Bard, 1904. (See our p. 80.)

317. *Handbuch des Städtebaues*, Berlin, Der Zirkel, 1920. See p. 80.

318. Editor of *Stadtbaukunst*, 1920–31. See Bibl. 483.

319. 'German Town Planning,' *GCTP*, XIII, 1923, pp. 66–71.

WERNER HEGEMANN

(For *Civic Art* see No. 326 below.)

Writings on strictly economic and political problems are not included here. We have not cited his reports on his own city plans, or his many articles in *Wasmuths Monatshefte* which he edited.

320. *Der neue Bebauungsplan für Chicago*, Berlin, Wasmuth, 1910.

321. Review of Brinckmann's *Deutsche Stadtbaukunst* in *StB*, 1911. (See Bibl. 274).

322. *Amerikanische Parkanlagen . . .*, Berlin, Wasmuth, 1911.

323. (editor), *Der Städtebau nach den Ergebenissen der allgemeinen Städtebau-Ausstellung in Berlin*, 1910, 2 vols., Berlin, Wasmuth, 1911–13, Catalog of the Berlin and Düsseldorf exhibitions of 1910 with supplementary material on the Düsseldorf exhibition of 1912.

324. 'Die Entwicklung des städtebaulichen Gedankens in Gross-Berlin seit 1848,' *Schriften der Gesellschaft für soziale Reform*. Ortsgruppe Berlin, 1912, pp. 97–124.

325. 'European city plans and their value to the American city planner,' *Landscape Architecture*, IV, 1913–14, pp. 89–103.

326. (with Peets), *The American Vitruvius: an Architects' Handbook of Civic Art*, NYC, Archit. Book Publ. Co., 1922. See our pp. 89–91

Reviews:
327. *Landscape Architecture*, XIII, 1922, pp. 76–78.
328. *GCTP*, XII, 1922, p. 178.
329, *JTPI*, VI, 1922–23, p. 15 (Adshead).
330. *JAIA*, XI, 1923, pp. 65–67 (Bigger).

331. (editor) Intl. Federation for Housing and Town Planning, 7th Congress (Gothenburg), 1923, *International Cities and Town Planning Exhibition*, Gothenburg, Zachrissons, 1923.

332. *Amerikanische Architektur und Stadtbaukunst . . .*, Berlin, Wasmuth, 1925. 2nd edit., 1927. Derived from 326 and 331.

333. *Das steinerne Berlin . . .*, Berlin, Kiepenheuer, 1930. An extension of vol. I of No. 323. Reprinted by Ullstein, 1963.

334. *City planning, housing*, 3 vols., NYC, Archit. Book Publ. Co., 1936–38. A sequel to *Civic Art*, completed after his death by William W. Forster, Robert S. Weinberg, and others. See pp. 90–91.

KARL HENRICI

See also the bibliographies in the three editions of Stübben's *Handbuch*. Henrici wrote a number of articles for *Der Städtebau* in its early years.

335. *Konkurrenz-Entwurf zu der NW Stadterweiterung von Dessau*, Aachen, Mayer, 1890. His own winning plan. See Note 295.

336. 'Gedanken über das moderne Städte-Bausystem,' *DB*, XXV, 1891, pp. 81–83, 86–91. Review of Stübben's *Handbuch*.

337. 'Der Individualismus im Städtebau,' *DB*, XXV, 1891, pp. 295–298, 301–302, 320–322. Reply to Stübben, Bibl. 385. Henrici's prize-winning Hanover plan illustrated on pp. 320–322.

338. *Preisgekrönter Konkurrenz-Entwurf zu der Stadterweiterung Münchens*, Munich, Werner, 1893. His own winning plan. See also Bibl. 387.

339. 'Langweilige und kurzweilige Strassen,' *DB*, XXVII, 1893, pp. 271–274.

340. 'Zur schönheitlichen Gestaltung städtischer Strassen,' *DB*, XXVII, 1893, p. 326. Reply to Stübben, Bibl. 388.

341. 'Einiges zur Beachtung bei Anlage von Strassen, Plätzen, und Gebäuden auf unebenem Gelände,' *DB*, XXVIII, 1894, pp. 501–502, 506–509, 524. (Also p. 628, which is a reply to Stübben Bibl. 394).

342. *Von welchen Gedanken sollen wir uns beim Ausbau unserer deutschen Städte leiten lassen?* Trier, Lintz, 1894.

343. 'Grossstadtgrün,' *Deutsche Bauhütte*, V, 1901, pp. 161–164, 169–170. A summary of Sitte's Bibl. 79.

344. 'Camillo Sitte,' *StB*, I, 1904, pp. 33–34. Obituary.

345. 'Camillo Sitte als Begründer einer neuen Richtung im Städtebau,' *ZOV*, LVI, 1904, pp. 157–158. Obituary.

346. *Beiträge zur praktischen Ästhetik im Städtebau: Eine Sammlung von Vorträgen und Aufsätzen*, Munich, Callwey, 1904.

347. 'Die Künstlerischen Aufgaben im Städtebau,' *Deutsche Stadtzeitung*, 1905, p. 271ff.

ALFRED LICHTWARK

(See Bibl. 180.)

348. *Blumenkultus: Wilde Blumen*, Dresden, Küthmann, 1897; 2nd edit., 1902 (included in *Auswahl*, II, 73–117).

349. *Park- und Garten-Studien*, (*Die Probleme des Hamburger Parks, Heidegarten*), Berlin, Cassirer, 1909.

350. 'Die drei Entwicklungsphasen des deutschen Städtebaues,' 1911 (included in *Auswahl*, I, 153–163).

351. *Eine Auswahl seiner Schriften* (edit. Wolf Mannhardt), 2 vols., Berlin, Cassirer, 1917.

352. *Reisebriefe* (edit. Gustav Pauli), 2 vols., Hamburg, Westermann, 1923.

HERMANN MAERTENS

353. *Der optische Maassstab oder die Theorie und Praxis des ästhetischen Sehens in der bildenden Kunst*, Bonn, Cohen, 1877. 2nd rev. edit., Berlin, Wasmuth, 1884. His basic work on art in general.

354. *Zwei Elementarpunkte der Kunstbetrachtung und Kunstübung*, Bonn, Cohen, 1881; an elementary pamphlet on the above for laymen and craftsmen.

355. *Über Deutlichkeit und Harmonie der Druckschriften mit ihren pflanzlichen und figürlichen Ornamenten*, Bonn, Cohen, 1881. Similar to No. 354.

356. *Skizze zu einer praktischen Ästhetik der Baukunst und der ihr dienenden Schwesterkünste in einem neuen System zusammengestellt*, Berlin, Wasmuth, 1885. 2nd edit. called *Praktische Ästhetik der Baukunst und der gewerblichen Künste*, Bonn, Cohen, 1887. Another general manual.

357. *Über die Grössenmaase und über den Stil des in Berlin am Lustgarten zu erbauenden Domes*, privately printed, n.d. A preliminary for No. 358.

358. *Optisches Maas für den Städtebau*, Bonn, Cohen, 1890. His most specifically city-planning study.

359. *Die deutschen Bildsäulen-Denkmäler des XIX Jahrhunderts: nebst einer Abhandlung über Grössenverhältnisse, die Materialienwahl, die Gruppierung, die Aufstellungsweise, und die Kosten derartiger Monumente*, Stuttgart, Hoffmann, 1892. His summation.

ELBERT PEETS

Included here are only those publications directly related to our study. Peets has written frequently on the plan for Washington, D.C.

360. (with Hegemann) *Civic Art*, 1922. See Bibl. 326.

361. 'Central Park,' *American Mercury*, IV, 1925, pp. 339–341.

362. 'The Landscape Priesthood,' *American Mercury*, X, 1927, pp. 94–100.

363. 'Famous Town Planners,' *TPR*, XII, 1926–27, pp. 181–190 (Haussmann); pp. 249–259 (Sitte); XIII, 1928–29, pp. 30–49 (L'Enfant); XIV, 1930–31, pp. 13–30 (London, 1666).

364. 'Washington, Williamsburg, the Century of Progress, and Greendale,' the final (27th) chapter of *City Planning, housing* of 1936–38. See Bibl. 334, vol. II.

365. 'Camillo Sitte," unpublished typescript manuscript, 10 pp. c. 1945. Copies are deposited in Library of the Public Housing Adminstration (Washington, D.C.) and Avery Architectural Library (Columbia University).

CARL FRIEDRICH REICHARDT

366. *Einige Worte über die Wahl des Plans zum Wiederaufbau Hamburgs*, Hamburg, Nestler & Melle, 1842.

367. *Freie Phantasieen über Hamburgs bauliche Ausdehnung und äussere Verschönerung, Hamburg*, Herold, 1854.

368. *Über den neuen Rathaus-Bau*, Hamburg, Basset, 1855.

369. *Hamburgs Staats-Bauwesen in seinen gegenwärtigen Zuständen*, Hamburg, Meissner, 1857.

370. *Ideen zur Organisation des Staats-Bauwesens*, Hamburg, Meissner, 1861.

371. *Zur Begründung einer allgemeinen Bauordnung in sanitäts-, sicherheits-, verkehres-, und ästhetischer Beziehung*, Hamburg, Meissner, 1863.

JOSEPH STÜBBEN

(For '*Handbuch*' see No. 377 below.)

See also the bibliographies in the three editions of his *Handbuch*. This list includes only his major publications and such minor items as are referred to in our book. He also wrote many reports on the planning of specific towns for the German professional periodicals from the 1870's on, as well as brief reports to many congresses which we have not mentioned.

372. 'Gerade oder krumme Strassen,' *DB*, XI, 1877, pp. 132–134. This early statement of the problem was incorporated into his *Handbuch*.

373. 'Über die Anlage öffentlicher Plätze,' *DB*, XI, 1877, pp. 393–395, 403–406. Supersedes Baumeister's 1876 book on this question.

374. 'Mittheilungen über Strassenbauten in den belgischen Städten . . . ,' *HZ*, XXIV, 1878, pp. 170–186.

375. 'Paris in Bezug auf Strassenbau und Stadterweiterung,' *ZB*, XXIX, 1879, pp. 377–412, pls. 52–54. Another classic reportage.

376. Review of Sitte's *Städtebau* in *HZ*, 1889. See Bibl. 4.

377. *Der Städtebau*, being the 9th half-volume of 'Entwerfen, Anlage und Einrichtung der Gebäude,' which is in turn Part IV of the *Handbuch der Architektur*, published from 1883–1933 under the editorship of Josef Durm and others. We refer to this as '*Handbuch*'; all citations are to the 1890 edition unless otherwise noted.

Editions:

377. 1st: Darmstadt, Bergsträsser, December, 1890.
378. 2nd: Stuttgart, Kröner, 1907, completely revised.
379. 3rd: Leipzig, Gebhardt, 1924, completely revised.

Translations:

380. Typescript translation by A. Albrecht of all but Part V of the 1907 edition, Cambridge, Mass., 1911. No illustrations. Available in Harvard University Library in several copies.

381. Summarized translation of Chap. VII-a of Part V (pp. 500–506), printed as 'Municipal Memorials: Forms and Sites of Monuments,' in *Municipal Affairs* (NYC), III, 1899, pp. 724–731. From the 1890 edition, of course, but supplements the above somewhat. No illustrations.

382. Summarized translation of the various sections of Part II (1890 edition) dealing with plazas: T. M. Newton, 'Public Squares,' *American Architect* (Boston), XLIII, 1894, pp. 52–54, 64–67, 101–104, 137–138. This is a bad translation, and its illustrations, copied from Stübben, are frequently inaccurate and wrongly labelled. Stübben is nowhere acknowledged as author. The editors explained that this was 'A Graduating thesis of the Architectural Department of Columbia College, N.Y.' Mr. Newton, A.I.A., 1868–1924, was graduated in June 1893, but his College transcript lists no project such as this.

Reviews:

383. 1st edit.: *DB*, XXV, 1891, pp. 81–83, 86–91 (Henrici). See our p. 83.

384. 3rd edit.: *StB*, XX, 1925, pp. 26–27 (Jansen). See Note 48.

385. 'Über Fragen der Städtebaukunst,' *DB*, XXV, 1891, pp. 122–128, 150–155. Retort to Henrici's review (No. 336).

386. 'Der Individualismus im Städtebau,' *DB*, XXV, 1891, pp. 368–370. Reply to Henrici, Bibl. 337.

387. 'Die Preisbewerbung für Entwürfe zur Münchener Stadterweiterung,' *DB*, 1893, XXVII, pp. 193–194. Report and critique of Henrici's winning Munich plan.

388. 'Zur Schönheitlichen Gestaltung städtischer Strassen,' *DB*, XXVII, 1893, pp. 294–296. Comment on Henrici, Bibl. 339.

389. 'Einseitigkeit im Städtebau und ihre Folgen,' *DB*, XXVII, 1893, pp. 349–350, 373–374, 415–418. Reply to Henrici's rejoinder, Bibl. 340.

390. 'Practical and Aesthetic Principles for the Laying Out of Cities,' (prepared for the International Engineering Congress of the Columbian Exposition of 1893), *Transactions of the American Society of Civil Engineers*, XXIX, 1893, pp. 718–736. Transl. by W. H. Searles.
391. Discussion by James Owen in *op. cit.*, XXX, 1893, pp. 591–593.
392. German text printed in *ZOV*, XLV, 1893, pp. 441–447.
393. French translation by Charles Buls: *La Construction des villes*, Brussels, Lyon-Claesc, 1895. Sec pp. 32–33.

394. Review of Fritz' *Deutsche Stadtanlagen* (Bibl. 461) in *DB*, XXVIII, 1894, pp. 608–610. Also contains comment on Henrici, Bibl. 341.

395. 'Der General-Regulierungsplan für Gross-Wien,' *DB*, XXVIII, 1894, pp. 123–125, 133–135. Report on the Vienna competition which he won himself. See our p. 43.

396. Review of Buls' *Esthétique des Villes,* in *Kölnische Zeitung,* 1894. See Bibl. 279.

397. 'Der Bau der Städte in Geschichte und Gegenwart,' *CBB*, XV, 1895, pp. 105–107, 119–121, 126–129. A lecture at the Schinkel celebration of the Berlin *Verein.*

398. 'Hygiene des Städtebaues,' in IV, part 2 of Th. Weyl, *Handbuch der Hygiene*, Jena, Fischer, 1896 (2nd edit. with J. Brix, 1914).

399. 'Der Baulinien-Plan für die Altstadt Wien,' *DB,* XXX, 1896, pp. 501–503. 509–510. His report on the Sitte debate. See Bibl. 77 and p. 44.

400. (with Baumeister and J. Classen) '*Die Umlegung . . .*' 1897. See Bible. 259.

401. 'Irrungen und Bestrebungen im Städtebau,' *Von Fels zum Meer,* XVIII, 1897–98, pp. 64–70, 111–113.

402. Report on Streets, Plazas, and Monuments at Premier Congrès de l'Art Public, Brussels, 1898: in *L'Art Public,* III, 1899, pp. 89ff.

403. 'Der Stadterweiterungsplan und seine Durchführung,' *Neue Untersuchungen des Vereins für Sozialpolitik über die Wohnungspflege in Deutschland und im Auslande*, I, Leipzig, 1901.

404. 'Die Grossstadt der Zukunft,' *Die Umschau,* 1902, No. 12.

405. *Die Bedeutung der Bauordnungen und Bebauungspläne für das Wohnungswesen,* Göttingen, Vandenhoeck & Ruprecht, 1902.

406. Obituary of Camillo Sitte, *ZB*, XXIII, 1903, p. 600.

407. 'Stadtbauplan, Enteignung und Umlegung,' *StB*, I, 1904, pp. 127–130. Answer to Sitte Bibl. 88. See our p. 23.

408. 'Entwerfen und Anlegen von Strassen und freien Plätzen im Städtebau,' *Trans. London, 1906*, pp. 409–411. A very brief summary of his principles.

409. 'Die Durchführung von Stadterweiterung mit besonderer Berücksichtigung der Eigenthumsverhältnisse,' *StBV*, I, No. 6, 1908.

410. 'Städtebau in der Kunstgeschichte,' *DB*, XLIII, 1909, pp. 102–106. Review of Brinckmann's *Platz und Monument*, see Bibl. 267.

411. 'Über den Zusammenhang zwischen Bebauungsplan und Bauordnung,' *StBV*, II, No. 4, 1909.

412. 'Recent Progress in German Town Planning,' *Trans. London 1910*, pp. 309–312. See our p. 94.

413. 'Städtebau in England,' *StBV*, IV, No. 8, 1911.

414. 'De la necessité et de la méthode de differencier le règlement des bâtisses.' *Ghent Congr. 1913*, pp. 99–104.

415. 'Vom französischen Städtebau,' *StBV*, Nos. 2 & 3, 1915.

416. 'Die Entwicklung des deutschen Städtebaues und ihr Einfluss auf das Ausland,' *StBK*, I, 1920, pp. 113–116, 129–133, 151–154. This lecture at the Prussian Akademie des Bauwesens was incorporated into the 1924 edition of his *Handbuch*.

417. 'Die Anordung der Grünflächen in und bei den Städten,' *Proceedings of the National Conference on City Planning*, 1925, pp. 367–377, 420–422.

BRUNO TAUT

Only his publications that deal with matters of planning are included here.

418. *Alpine Architektur*, Hagen, Folkwang, 1919.

419. (with Paul Scheerbart, Erich Baron, Adolf Behne) *Die Stadtkrone*, Jena, Diedrichs, 1919.
Review:
420. In *1919, Neue Blätter für Kunst und Dichtung*, II, 1919, p. 57 (Schapiro).

421. (with others) the supplement 'Frühlicht,' in *StBK*, I, Nos. 1–14, 1920. Excerpts have been reprinted in a paperback *Frühlicht* edited by U. Conrads, Verlag Ullstein, 1963.

422. (with others) 'Utopischer Briefwechsel,' 1919–20. Extracts are published in Bibl. 456 and in *Die gläserne Kette*, Berlin, Akademie der Künste, 1963.

423. *Die Auflösung der Städte*, Hagen, Folkwang, 1920.

424. 'Characteristics of German Town Planning,' Garden City Press, n.d.

OTTO WAGNER

425. *Erläuterungs-Bericht zum Entwurf für den General-Regulierungsplan über das gesamte Gemeindegebiet von Wien mit dem Kenn-*

wort: 'Artis sola domina necessitas,' Vienna, Jasper, 1893. 2nd edit., 1894.

426. *Moderne Architektur. Seinen Schülern ein Führer auf diesem Kunstgebiete*, Vienna, Schroll, 1896, 2nd edit., 1899, 3rd, 1902, 4th, 'Die Baukunst unserer Zeit,' 1914. His manifesto on architecture and planning.
Translation:
427. (abridged) (by N. C. Ricker) in *BB*, X, 1901, pp. 124–128, 143–147, 165–171.

428. *Die Grossstadt: eine Studie*, Vienna, Schroll, 1911.
Translation:
429. as 'The Development of a Great City,' *A Rec*, XXXI, 1912, pp. 485–500. With biographical essay by A. D. F. Hamlin.

G

MISCELLANEOUS PUBLICATIONS

This section includes background materials for the study of the period that do not fit into any of the previous categories. Most works of a specialized nature are listed in the appropriate Notes and have not been repeated here. For instance, publications dealing with the Transformation of Vienna will be found in Notes 53, 57, 62, 67, 68, 70.

451. *Berichte über den VIII Internationalen Architekten-Kongress in Wien*, Vienna, Schroll, 1908.

452. Wolfgang Braunfels, *Mittelalterliche Stadtbaukunst in der Toskana*, Berlin, Gebr. Mann, 1953.

453. George R. Collins, 'The Ciudad Lineal of Madrid,' and 'Linear Planning throughout the World,' *JSAH*, XVIII, 1959, pp. 38–53, 74–93.
454. Summary in *AR*, CXXVII, 1960, pp. 341–345, and updated in *Architects' Year Book*, No. 11, 1965.

455. Congrès international de l'Art Public, 1st, Brussels, 1898. *Oeuvre de l'art public*, Liège, Bénard, 1899.

456. U. Conrads and H. G. Sperlich, *The Architecture of Fantasy: Utopian Building and Planning in Modern Times* (transl. and expanded by C. C. & G. R. Collins), New York, Praeger, 1963.

457. 'Denkschrift über die künftige bauliche Entwicklung Wiens,' *WOV*, II, 1877, pp. 65–75. Considerations by the Austrian *Verein* of the matter of Vienna's general plan.

458. Max Eisler, *Historischer Atlas der Wiener Stadtansichten: Das bürgerliche Wien, 1770–1860*, Vienna, Staatsdruckerei, 1929.

459. Jakob von Falke, *Hellas und Rom*, Stuttgart, Spemann, 1878–80. Sitte's source for Pls. I–a and II.

460. Frederick R. Farrow, 'The Recent Development of Vienna,' *TRIBA*, n.s., IV, 1888, pp. 27–42.

461. Joh. Fritz, *Deutsche Stadtanlage: Beilage zum Programm des*

Lyceums in Strassburg im Elsass, Strassburg, Hertz, 1894. See Note 95.

462. *Führer durch die Allgemeine Städtebau-Ausstellung in Berlin*, 1910, Berlin, Wasmuth, 1910.

463. *Führer durch die Internationale Städtebau-Ausstellung in Düsseldorf*, 1910, Düsseldorf, Bagel, 1910. These two guidebooks contain brief descriptions of all exhibits, including the plans of the Sitte school. See also Bibl. 323.

464. Frederick Gibberd, *Town Design*, London, Architectural Press, 1953. See Note 98.

465. Henry-Russell Hitchcock, *Architecture, Nineteenth and Twentieth Centuries*, Harmondsworth, Penguin, 1958.

466. George E. Hooker, 'The German Municipal Movement,' *Chicago Record-Herald*, Jan. 30, 1904, p. 8. See Note 100.

467. Thomas C. Horsfall, *The Improvement of the Dwellings and Surroundings of the People: the Example of Germany*, Manchester, University Press, 1904.

468. Jane Jacobs, *The Death and Life of Great American Cities*, New York, Random House, 1961.

469. Waldemar Kaden, et al., *Italien: eine Wanderung von den Alpen bis zum Aetna* (woodcuts by A. Closs), Stuttgart, Engelhorn, 1876 (English translation, New York, 1882). Sitte's source for Pls. III, IV, VI, XI, and ours for Pl. V–a.

470. Gordon Logie, *The Urban Scene*, London, Faber & Faber, 1954. See Note 98.

471. *Municipal Affairs, a Quarterly Magazine devoted to the Consideration of City Problems from the Standpoint of the Taxpayer and Citizen*, New York, Reform Club, I–VI, 1897–1902. See pp. 86–87.

472. Österreichischer Ingenieur- und Architekten- Verein, *Wien am Anfang des XX Jahrhunderts: ein Führer in technischer und künstlerischer Richtung*, 2 vols., Vienna, Gerlach & Wiedlin, 1905–06.

473. Mark L. Peisch, *The Chicago School of Architecture: Early Followers of Sullivan and Wright*, New York & London, Random House & Phaidon, 1964–65.

474. *Premier Congrès International et exposition comparée des Villes . . . , Ghent, 1913*, Brussels, Union internationale des villes, 1914.

475. Wolfgang Rauda, *Raumprobleme im europäischen Städtebau*, Munich, Callwey, 1956. See Note 180.

476. ———, *Lebendige Städtebauliche Raumbildung*, Stuttgart, Hoffmann, 1957.

477. ———, 'Urban space and how to see it,' *Landscape*, IX, 1960, pp. 3–6.

478. Josephine P. Reynolds, 'Thomas Coglan Horsfall and the Town Planning Movement in England,' *TPR*, XXIII, 1952, pp. 52–60.

479. Georges Rohault de Fleury, *Les monuments de Pise au moyen âge*, Paris, Morel, 1866.

480. ———, *La Toscane au moyen âge: architecture civile et militaire*, Paris, Lacroix & Morel, 1870–73. These two publications were the source of a number of the plans used in the French editions of Sitte.

481. *Salzburger Gewerbeblatt*. Founded by Sitte in 1877. See Note 12.

482. Albert Shaw, *Municipal Government in Continental Europe*, New York, Century, 1895.

483. *Stadtbaukunst alter und neuer Zeit*, I–XII, 1920–1931, Berlin, Verlag Stadtbaukunst. Editors: Cornelius Gurlitt, Bruno Möhring, and (Nos. 1–14 only) Bruno Taut. See pp. 79–80 and Note 94.

484. *Der Städtebau; Monatsschrift für die künstlerische Ausgestaltung der Städte nach ihren wirtschaftlichen, gesundheitlichen, und socialen Grundsätzen*, Berlin and Vienna, Wasmuth. Founded by Camillo Sitte and Theodor Goecke, I–XXIV, 1904–1929. See Note 107.

485. *Städtebauliche Vorträge aus dem Seminar für Städtebau an der königlichen Technischen Hochschule zu Berlin*, Berlin, Ernst, I–X, 1908–20, editors Joseph Brix and Felix Genzmer.

486. Town Planning Conference, London, 1910, *Transactions*, London, R.I.B.A., 1911.

487, *Transactions of the VII International Congress of Architects, London 1906*, London, R.I.A.B.A., 1908.

488. *Wasmuths Monatshefte für Baukunst und Städtebau* (title varies), Berlin, Wasmuth. I–XXVI, 1914–1942. Absorbed *Der Städtebau* in 1930. See Note 107.

489. Robert Wuttke, *Die deutschen Städte*, Leipzig, Brandstetter, 1904. Catalog of the Dresden cities exposition of 1903.

490. Paul Zucker, *Town and Square from the Agora to the Village Green*, New York, Columbia University Press, 1959.

INDEX

INDEX

The companion volume is separately indexed.

COLUMBIA UNIVERSITY STUDIES IN ART HISTORY AND ARCHAEOLOGY

Other titles will be announced as ready

ARCHITECTURAL PRINCIPLES IN THE AGE OF HUMANISM

by Rudolf Wittkower

CITY PLANNING ACCORDING TO ARTISTIC PRINCIPLES

by Camillo Sitte

Translated by George R. Collins
and Christiane Crasemann Collins

CAMILLO SITTE AND THE BIRTH OF MODERN CITY PLANNING

by George R. Collins
and Christiane Crasemann Collins

THE RADIANCE OF CHARTRES

by James Rosser Johnson

THE CHICAGO SCHOOL OF ARCHITECTURE

by Mark L. Peisch